WHOLE PEOPLE IN A BROKEN WORLD

WHOLE PEOPLE IN A BROKEN WORLD

The Ethics of Mercy and the Pastoral Mission of the Church

JEREMIAH J. McCARTHY

Paulist Press
New York / Mahwah, NJ

Cover image of the icon "Descent into Hell" by Rev. Rausch, OMI, is reproduced with permission.
Cover and book design by Lynn Else

Library of Congress Cataloging-in-Publication Data.
Names: McCarthy, Jeremiah J., author.
Title: Whole people in a broken world: the ethics of mercy and the pastoral mission of the church / Jeremiah J. McCarthy.
Description: Paperback. | New York: Paulist Press, [2025] | Includes index. | Summary: "This book draws upon moral theology to promote a deeper understanding of the criteria for evaluating moral action and the formation of the moral agent"—Provided by publisher.
Identifiers: LCCN 2024040063 (print) | LCCN 2024040064 (ebook) | ISBN 9780809157242 (paperback) | ISBN 9780809188925 (ebook)
Subjects: LCSH: Francis, Pope, 1936– —Ethics. | Christian ethics—Catholic authors. | Francis, Pope, 1936– Amoris laetitia.
Classification: LCC BX1378.7 .M397 2025 (print) | LCC BX1378.7 (ebook) | DDC 241—dc23/eng/20250409
LC record available at https://lccn.loc.gov/2024040063
LC ebook record available at https://lccn.loc.gov/2024040064

ISBN 978-0-8091-5724-2 (paperback)
ISBN 978-0-8091-8892-5 (ebook)

Published by Paulist Press
997 Macarthur Boulevard
Mahwah, NJ 07430
www.paulistpress.com

Printed and bound in the
United States of America

Contents

Preface

"LET ME READ YOU A STORY," says a mother to her rambunctious brood of children, perhaps with the aid of a well-worn copy of *The Wind in the Willows*—in hand. Having secured their rapt attention, she proceeds to engage their imaginations with the twists and turns of this clever and charming narrative. It may seem odd to begin an introduction to a book of moral theology with a children's story, but, as linguistic creatures, human beings are instinctively drawn to storytelling. Stories are not to be dismissed as idle fiction.

Rather, the form and shape of a story enables us to display the complexities and contours of our lived experience of the world, of God, and of one another. Interpreting our experience of life, exploring its historical lineage and development over time, the ramifications and resonances of life's multifaceted textures and nuance among our many companions on our sojourn in this world, are crucial to the formation of a narrative that helps us to make sense of ourselves, our cultures, and the communities that we establish. The story of faith that informs and shapes our identity, specifically, for the purposes of this book, as Catholic Christians, partakes of the same wonder and engagement that characterizes children wrestling with the adventures and foibles of the animal inhabitants of a quaint countryside setting.

Since we dwell in time and space, the shared experience of life as Catholic Christians is captured by way of a story or narrative that displays patterns and connections amid the variegated experiences of prayer, liturgy, theological reflection, and service that have formed the community of believers over time. The development of moral theology as an ongoing conversation about the response to the divine initiative in one's life is woven into the narrative arc of the story of God that constitutes "theology" more precisely.

The story of moral theology, especially historical developments throughout the course of the twentieth century, is a key theme in this book. The contributions to the tradition of the discipline are recounted not just out of historical or intellectual interest. Rather, my purpose is to connect these trajectories to the profound pastoral vision of our current pontiff, Pope Francis. The pope's well-known outreach to the divorced and remarried members of the Church, who are often denied access to the Eucharist, or his welcoming advocacy for those on the margins of society, especially the poor, immigrants, sexual minorities, and victims of racism and oppression, have earned him accolades from many. Yet, there are others who fear that his message of mercy and compassion, while well-intended, risks undermining the clarity and force of Church teaching in moral matters. My argument is quite simply that Pope Francis stands in continuity with the moral tradition of the Church and that his pastoral vision reflects an authentic appropriation of contemporary scholarship in moral theology.

I will unfold this argument in five chapters.

Chapter 1 addresses two interrelated themes. First, I offer an overview of the intellectual architecture of the pope's theological and pastoral vision, which is influenced by two prominent scholars: Erich Przywara, SJ, and Romano Guardini. Second, I begin a discussion of an important paradigm shift in the discipline of moral theology, elegantly captured by James Keenan, SJ, as a move from "confessing sins to liberating consciences."

Chapter 2 explores the implications of this paradigm shift by comparing and contrasting a typology consisting of four models of the moral life: consequentialism (which prizes desirable outcomes to guide one's ethical deliberations); deontology (obligation theories, which affirm the centrality of rules/principles to guide reflection); the natural law tradition (the classic locus of the Catholic moral tradition, which affirms the role of critical reason); and the model of character and virtue (which highlights the importance of moral agency and formation of a wise, discerning moral actor). I argue that an integrated model of natural law and character/virtue provides a grounding for an ethics of discernment that emerges in the thinking of Pope Francis.

In chapter 3, I focus on the intellectual odyssey of Josef Fuchs, SJ, as an exemplar of the paradigm shift in moral theology, especially the shift from a virtually exclusive focus on the nature of the moral act to a more balanced, coequal emphasis on the formation of the wise, moral agent. I further argue that the critical retrieval of the natural law tradition finds a valuable ally in the important work of virtue theorists, including one of its premier exponents, Stanley Hauerwas, emeritus professor of theology at Duke University. Invoking the signature theme of the Catholic theological imagination, its "both/and" sensibility, I argue that an integrated model of natural law thinking, and character/virtue scholarship provides a solid foundation for an ethics of discernment.

In chapter 4, I explore the contours of an ethics of discernment, including the interface between the long spiritual tradition of the Church on the discernment of spirits and moral life. A central figure in this exposition is the important work of William Spohn. A critically important implication of a recovery of moral agency and discernment is a re-examination of the moral anthropology it presupposes. As Walker Percy insightfully observes, "everyone has an anthropology, even if it is only an implicit anthropology." Essentially, Percy is arguing that everyone has a basic understanding or set of convictions about what it means to be a human being who can think and act in the world. An important subtheme that I address is the significant difference between the legacy of Descartes, with its emphasis on the rational "thinking subject" (*res cogitans*), and the holistic Catholic anthropology that affirms the inextricable nexus of body and soul. The Cartesian vision lies at the root of modern rugged individualism and autonomy, while a more cohesive understanding of an embodied moral self (drawing from the work of philosophers Charles Taylor, Alasdair MacIntyre, Robert Bellah, and O. Carter Snead), provides a richer portrait of the moral life as relational and connected to communities of shared meaning and purpose. With this ethics of discernment outlined, I turn in the concluding chapter to explore its implications in the work of Pope Francis.

Chapter 5 is an extensive review of the encyclical *Amoris Laetitia* (The Joy of Love), Pope Francis's meditation on married life. Pope Francis deftly weaves together in his vision of pastoral care two critically important insights of a sound Catholic moral anthropology foreshadowed in the previous chapter: the shared, universal dimensions of human moral striving (the legacy of the natural law or "common ground" morality), and the distinctive, irreducibly personal, or existential dimensions inherent in one's unique moral personality. To tease out the implications of his holistic anthropology, I draw upon the work of the Redemptorist moral theologian Brian Johnstone, CSSR, and the French Catholic philosopher Jean-Luc Marion. Marion's invocation of the language of gift and disclosure to unveil the mystery of reality, human and divine, is the source for Johnstone's reimagining of human moral action, not as a relationship between "subject" and "object," but, more deeply, as a relationship of "giving" and "receiving." Johnstone's recovery of the doctrine of the resurrection of Christ, long neglected as a resource for moral theology, provides further grounding for seeing our moral agency in terms of gift and receptivity. Key to the doctrine of the resurrection is the divine intention that "nothing will be lost," that God desires not annihilation but transformation of creation.

The clear pastoral implication of this divine intention and outreach is captured by the notion of mercy. Mercy is not cheap grace, but the fullest expression of grace as love which heals, restores, and reconciles. Pope Francis, who challenges the Church to "go out to the peripheries," to seek the lost, and to heal our broken world, including the environment that has been entrusted to us, builds his pastoral vision on the solid ground of the Church's moral tradition. The image that best summarizes the purpose of this book is the icon of the risen Christ, the *Anastasis,* beloved in the Eastern Church. As portrayed by artist Clyde Rausch, OMI (flyleaf/cover of book), the risen Jesus is not alone, but stands over the now empty tomb, with the chains of death around his feet unshackled, lifting us all, symbolized in the figures of Adam and Eve. So, with this introduction, let me tell you a story.

Acknowledgements

AS I WRITE THIS INTRODUCTION to the book that is before you, it is the Octave of Easter, and the words of Gerard Manley Hopkins in "The Wreck of the Deutschland" come to mind: "Let him easter in us, be a dayspring to the dimness of us." The publication of a new book is an occasion of gratitude, indeed Easter joy, for an author. It is an occasion to acknowledge the invaluable gifts and contributions of many that have enabled the crafting of this work. Authors and artists of all stripes know that they stand on the shoulders of mentors, guides, and friends who have "midwifed" their efforts. Flannery O' Connor, the self-proclaimed "hillbilly Thomist," echoing Aquinas, reminds us that an artistic creation, a "work well made," is itself a tribute to the Creator and Sustainer of all gifts. So, a few words are in order.

First and foremost, my beloved parents, Michael and Margaret McCarthy, who brought eleven of us into the world, who enjoy the peace of the risen Savior, and my ten siblings are inestimable gifts of goodness without whose love and care, my vocation and ministry would be forever impoverished.

I am most grateful to the great priests and teachers who have graced my life—the Sisters of Charity of Greenburg, Pennsylvania, the priests and bishops of the Diocese of Tucson, my seminary formators at St. John's Seminary, Camarillo, California, and the splendid professors who shepherded my graduate studies at the Graduate Theological Union, Berkeley, California. Jim McClendon Jr., my first advisor, sharpened my appreciation and love for the work of Wittgenstein and Stanley Hauerwas; William Spohn guided my dissertation with Christlike wisdom and holiness. Stan Hauerwas's work on the notions of character and virtue has deeply shaped my own thinking. Those of us privileged to teach moral theology and to help form the next generation of pastoral leaders are indebted to his profound scholarship and fierce devotion to the integrity of the Church's witness to the world.

The insights of wise mentors over the years (Michael Buckley, SJ, Drew Christiansen, SJ, John Coleman, SJ, Karen Lebacqz, Charles McCoy, John Noonan [UC Berkeley School of Law, Boalt Hall], Dick Benson, CM, Gerald Coleman, PSS, Charley Bouchard, OP, Kevin O'Neil, CSSR, Frank Colborn [who introduced me to the work of Stanley Hauerwas when I was a seminarian], Pete McGloin, Sr. Cecilia Canales, OP, Sr. Katarina Schuth, OSF, Jim O'Reilly, Archbishops George Niederauer and William Levada) have deeply shaped my thinking, and more importantly, have helped me to be a better disciple of Christ.

This book has been gestating for a long time. It is nurtured by an ecumenical sensitivity that drew me to the Graduate Theological Union, Berkeley—a spiritual and intellectual treasure for the Church that strengthened and stretched my Catholic imagination. The theme of mercy weaves its way throughout the text, and I have been blessed by the merciful and gracious gifts of those who made writing and research a pleasure and a joy. The magnificent library staff at the Oblate School of Theology in San Antonio never failed to be of assistance as I pursued the wonderful collection of the O'Shaughnessy Library and countless interlibrary loan requests. *Muchisimas gracias* to Maria Garcia, library director, and her splendid staff, Fran Gonzalez, Anne Richards, Mary Jane Burke, Bea Tovar, Carmen Rodriguez.

Special thanks to my dear sister, Dr. Jeanne Hornback McCarthy, impeccable Shakespeare scholar, who did her best to redeem and refine my prose. John Markey, OP, director of the doctoral program at the Oblate School of Theology in San Antonio, was a constant source of support and encouragement. His mastery of classical and modern approaches to philosophy and theology was an invaluable gift of wisdom and insight. I am profoundly grateful to Ron Rolheiser, OMI, and the Oblate School of Theology president, Scott Woodward, for extending to me the opportunity to teach and to be part of their marvelous theological faculty. Fr. Al Laubenthal, Sr. Anne Anderson, and Fr. John Arnold were generous critics who sharpened my arguments.

A special word of thanks to the bishops and priests of the Diocese of Tucson who have never let me forget I am their brother and friend. Bishop Francis Green granted me permission to pursue advanced studies, and his successors, Manuel Moreno, Gerald Kicanas, and Edward Weisenburger, provided constant support and affirmation for a life of ministry devoted to priestly formation, theological education, including the opportunity to serve the Association of Theological Schools in the United States and Canada as a member of its splendid accreditation staff. Prior to ATS service, my wonderful years at St. John's Seminary, Camarillo, California, as a faculty colleague, combined with service in the Archdiocese of Los Angeles, shaped my pastoral vision in powerful ways. For those years of blessed grace, thanks.

I would be remiss indeed not to extend special thanks to the support of ATS colleagues and friends—Dan Aleshire, Bill Myers, Bill Miller, Tisa Lewis, Marsha Foster Boyd, Charles Willard, Nancy Merrill, Chris Meinzer, Chris Olsztyn, Mary McMillan, Eliza Smith-Brown, Sue Beckerdite, Karen Kuder. My service at ATS also led to another blessing—service on the board of the In Trust Center for Theological Education—special kudos to Amy Kardash and her superb staff. Colleagues on the board drew me to the work of the great African American preacher Dr. Howard Thurman, whose insights profoundly influenced my assessment of the role of conscience in the moral life.

The ideas for this book began during my tenure as executive director of the Seminary Department of the National Catholic Educational Association. Karen Ristau, Kathy Schmitt, Cedric Bernescut, Sr. Dale McDonald, and Regina Haney enabled me to see the gift of mercy in action in their tireless labors on behalf of Catholic education. Pope Francis could not have better ambassadors for the signature theme of his pontificate.

My special thanks to the marvelous editing staff at Paulist Press, Paul McMahon, Donna Crilly, and Travis Ables for their gracious professionalism and expertise in shepherding the publication process.

Finally, my thanks to the wonderful parishioners and students who have kept me on my toes with their keen questions and desire to serve the Church. They are, to invoke that fine insight from the old *Baltimore Catechism*, "occasions of grace." I hope that the theme of this book, moral theology viewed through the lens of mercy, may contribute to the advancement of the Church's mission in the world.

1

Moral Theology in the Key of Mercy

THE TITLE OF THIS BOOK, *Whole People in a Broken World*, comes from a pastoral experience early in my priestly life. Shortly after ordination in 1972, Bishop Green asked me to assume the office of diocesan vocation director. My office was located at the diocesan pastoral center, Regina Cleri, on the east side of the city of Tucson, Arizona.[1] Brother Francis Rees, who directed the program for children and adults with special needs, was down the corridor and we frequently engaged with one another. One morning Francis asked if I would be willing to preside at a liturgy for the children and adults who occupied the Arizona home for the developmentally disabled in Coolidge, midway between Tucson and Phoenix.

I happily agreed and we set off for Coolidge. When we arrived, Francis said, "Jerry, I'd like you to meet my favorite residents." He opened the door to a long ward and my breath was taken away. Approximately forty beds, each of them containing a child or adult with hydrocephalus, greeted us. A tragic affliction, untreated hydrocephalus can cause its victims to have disproportionately large heads. At worst, they are unable to lift their heads, remain bedridden, and need constant care. Francis, undaunted with a big smile on his face, visited each person with a kind word and an affectionate embrace. Gregory, whom I remember fondly, grinned from ear to ear. I thought to myself, "Francis is visiting his flock."

The Mass went as I expected. A lot of off-key singing, with younger children wandering around the altar curious about this stranger in their midst—overall, a wonderful liturgy, a true occasion of grace. Francis knew that I was the eldest of eleven children, and I suspect that was my main qualification for the job—my ability to be liturgically flexible and roll with the punches. We had a pleasant lunch with the medical staff and social workers and off we went.

On the return home, I posed a question to Francis: "Francis, what gives you such energy and enthusiasm for this very difficult ministry, attending to the needs of these residents, many of whom are effectively wards of the state since their birth families are unable to care for them? Do you ever get discouraged or overwhelmed by the magnitude of the challenge?" Francis smiled and said, "Jerry, you know most people think that we are broken people in a whole world, that it is somehow up to us to fit in and make things work to 'get our act together' in the so-called real world out there. I think Jesus sees things very differently. I believe that the Lord sees each of us as 'whole people in a broken world,' seeing the goodness within each of us. Jesus sees us with the eyes of love and mercy." Brother Francis in effect was telling me, "Yes, there is brokenness within each of us, but the deeper reality, the most profound truth about us is not our weakness or failure, but our dignity and beauty as God's own beloved."

The vision of Brother Francis is the leitmotiv for this essay on moral theology. I intentionally describe this book as an essay in moral theology because an essay, by definition, is an "effort, an attempt," *une essayer*, to present an argument that is not the definitive, last word but a selective interpretation that I hope will contribute to a vast, robust, and ongoing conversation. It is impossible to recapitulate, much less to acknowledge, the enormous scholarship that represents the field of moral theology today. I will do my best to recognize and honor the sources of my thinking, but I ask the kindness of the reader to forgive or at least forbear the inevitable shortcomings, lacunae, and missteps along the way. Fortunately, human knowledge is a process of trial and error, a communal enterprise, that demands critique, correction, and amendment in the pursuit of the true, the good, and the beautiful, and wise critics will ensure that my errors do not perdure. I hope that the foregoing disclaimer from an all-too-fallible Irishman is sufficient for the reader to persevere with this effort. I will do my best to make the journey a worthwhile encounter.

What does it mean for us to conceive of the work of moral

formation and development, not as exclusive adherence to a set of commands or rules (without discounting in any way the importance of commandments and rules, as we will see), but as a response to a God who sees us as lovable, as friends called to eternal intimacy and communion with Godself? What does it mean for us to conceive moral theology in a different paradigm, a paradigm that I will call the moral imaginary of mercy? Mercy is the signature idea and practice that characterizes the ministry of Pope Francis, formerly Cardinal Bergoglio from Buenos Aires, Argentina. In powerful encyclicals, Pope Francis highlights the centrality of the Church's mission to accompany the faithful in their journey of discipleship. This model of accompaniment, of solidarity and pastoral care, invites us to reexamine the remarkable shift and focus called for in the renewal of moral theology by the Second Vatican Council.

Brother Francis's vision of "whole people in a broken world" is an apt metaphor to help us engage with the work of Pope Francis. The pope's dramatic outreach to those who are broken by personal tragedies and social discord, indeed, his clarion cry to heal the brokenness that afflicts our "common home," the planet, provides both the rationale and opportunity for this book, namely, to display the solid theological and pastoral roots of the papal vision. As I hope to demonstrate, Pope Francis is building upon the hard work and insights of moral theologians who have endeavored to bring forth new treasures from the Church's rich, moral tradition. Pope Francis, far from undermining the clarity and stability of the moral teaching of the Church, as critics have alleged, is, in my view, standing in continuity with the authentic trajectory of that teaching.

Envisioning Moral Theology through the Lens of an Imaginary of Mercy

This moral imaginary of mercy, which I will unfold in more detail later in this discussion, is a construal or approach to moral formation and action that "imagines" or "sees" the world through the central notions of mercy or compassion, building on the notion of a social imaginary, a key concept in the thought of

Canadian philosopher Charles Taylor and a notion that provides the framework for this discussion. An imaginary of mercy, as I conceive it, serves as a robust framework that weaves together, in a more holistic fashion, elements of moral theology that often appear to be in conflict, for example, the relationship between the discernment of what counts as a morally good action and the formation of individual conscience. This "subject-object divide" (that is, moral agency on the one hand, and objective morality on the other hand), contributes to a bifurcation if not alienation between the importance of establishing clear, binding, moral teaching, and the pastoral care of individuals who struggle to interpret and apply moral teaching to their personal situations and circumstances.

I wish to explore here what I call Pope Francis's "imaginary of mercy." By this claim I mean, in one sense, his moral vision. At the same time, I always want to convey here the set of profoundly Christlike values and principles at the core of longstanding tradition in Catholic teaching and theology emphasizing mercy, forgiveness, reconciliation, inclusion, love, a charitable spirit, and pastoral care, rather than dogmatic judgment, condemnation, and exclusion. Through such an imaginary of mercy, a view deeply rooted in the history of Catholic theology, Pope Francis offers a moral vision grounded in Christlike mercy. This vision recovers and clarifies the way Catholics have long imagined their collective moral, ethical, and social lives and thereby models and shapes how we ought to act, mercifully, whether as priests—and pastors—or as a Catholic community, now and in the future.

We live in complex times. Important tools to navigate this complexity involve, of course, an overview of central themes and concepts in the Church's moral tradition. In due course, attention will be given to various models or approaches to ethical decision-making, to the formation of personal conscience and character, and to the various sources that contribute to Catholic ethical deliberation (Church teaching, scripture, human experience, philosophical traditions, particularly the tradition of the natural moral law). The conversation in moral theology has grown to include the voices of women and the witness of a truly global Catholicism—voices from Africa, Asia, Latin America, the marginalized, and the poor. These stories, too, enrich and further shape the contours of the "moral imaginary" that I am sketching.

While clarity is always needed in the effort to resolve complex moral matters, conflict and ambiguity are also part of our lived experience. Mercy, I will suggest, provides a way for us to wrestle with the tension between the claims of well-formed principles and the inescapable particularity of concrete situations and circumstances. The recognition of similarity amid difference, the capacity to hold together in a dialogical tension moral rules and individual discernment is constitutive of the moral vision I am proposing.

A theme that I am also pursuing in this book is the importance of the dialectical imagination that, as we shall see, informs what I describe as Pope Francis's "moral imaginary of mercy." Dialectics, at the risk of oversimplification, is the intellectual skill of holding opposing viewpoints in a critical conversation, whereby each viewpoint retains its own significance and integrity without being collapsed either into the opposing perspective or transformed into a higher synthesis. An example of this dialectical or dialogical, tensive unity is the relationship between unity and diversity, or the relationship between the whole and the part.

A "tensive unity" made possible through a dialectical imagination is essential to the central argument of the book, which is that the relationship between generalizable or universal moral principles and the concrete contingent reality of human beings in which these principles are instantiated is one of tensive unity. This "tensive unity" provides a pathway between two extremes in moral analysis: on the one hand, an abstract moral theology that divorces itself from the contingencies of history and lived experience, and on the other, a subjective, situational morality that is immunized from critical encounter with the accrued wisdom of a moral community. Relying on the work of those who have reclaimed the importance of virtues and the narratives/stories of faith communities to shape and form the character of moral agents, notably Stanley Hauerwas, I propose that the tensive unity between communal wisdom and moral action is supported by a particular narrative, the imaginary of mercy.

Hans Urs von Balthasar provides an eloquent insight into this tensive unity:

> When it comes to shaping one's personal behavior, all the rules of morality, as precise as they may be, remain

> abstract in the face of the infinite complexity of the concrete. Even when these rules of morality are applied to "cases of conscience" where they are limited in scope and complement one another reciprocally, the fact that they are combined with one another means that they cannot provide an exact coincidence with a human "situation," which is always susceptible to an infinite analysis. If one goes right to the limits of the thing, from rules of conduct to a conduct that is regulated, there always subsists a gap that can only be surmounted by the decision to love that is free. The same is true of theology. As precise as one may suppose it to be, the history of dogma will never yield more than fragmentary formulas that will never provide a decisive, "ready-made" solution to the difficulties of our contemporary situation, a situation that is entirely unique![2]

Von Balthasar accentuates an important notion, which is that, in application, any moral principle or rule is subject to qualification. Moral principles, despite their philosophical acuity and level of precision, retain a degree of imprecision in the encounter with the concrete human situation. As Aquinas notes in his discussion of law in the *Summa Theologiae*, "the law applies in most instances" and cannot envision every conceivable circumstance warranting its application. In other words, law requires interpretation as it confronts novel and challenging contexts. For example, a rule requiring a driver to stay on the right side of the road must be adapted if a driver suddenly encounters children playing by the right side of the road. This emergency requires a deviation from the path to avoid harm or injury. In this situation, the principle of *epikeia* or "fairness/equity" is invoked. Given the novel situation, the driver interprets the meaning of the rule intelligently, interpreting the "mind" or sense of the lawgiver, namely, to ensure public safety, and makes the necessary course correction. Slavish adherence to the letter of the law would result in a greater injustice, namely catastrophic injury or loss of life.

A related insight from Aquinas, which I will highlight in further reflections on the tradition of natural law, is his observation based on Aristotle's *Nichomachean Ethics* that the more concrete and specific a moral principle becomes in its application to the presenting issue or matter for deliberation, the less universal is its reach.[3] Just as Aquinas notes that law requires the balance of equity or *epikeia* if it is to approach a more comprehensive realization of justice, he also observes that moral principles not only dynamically engage the object for action and choice, but also are appropriately qualified and modulated by the concrete, contingent reality to which they are directed by the moral agent.

The action theory of Aquinas is holistic and synchronous and provides an alternative to models of moral choice that fragment or separate the interrelated components of a moral act (the intention of the agent, the purpose or goal of the action, and the contemplated action, or object, for choice).[4] This dialogical interplay between rules and contexts will be considered as an ongoing feature of moral discernment and not as an anomaly that can be eliminated from ethical deliberations.

For Pope Francis, the image of a circle portrays a symmetry, a harmony whereby any tensions are resolved, or perhaps better stated, dissolved in a unified vision. By contrast, Francis prefers the image of a polyhedron, whereby all the opposing sides of the figure are connected, each retaining its own independent reality or structure while contributing to the tensive strength of the whole figure.

In his embrace of a dialectical imagination, Pope Francis, as his intellectual biographer Massimo Borghesi demonstrates, is profoundly influenced by the insights of his Jesuit confreres, Erich Przywara and Henri de Lubac, and the diocesan priest Romano Guardini.[5] Each of these seminal thinkers addresses the power of "unity in difference" with characteristic emphases. From Przywara, Francis takes the notion of the analogy of being, which enables the Catholic theologian to acknowledge the similarity between the creature and Creator while maintaining the ever-greater dissimilarity between them. De Lubac is the master of paradox, who holds in tension the nature of the Church as the instrument of divine grace and the sinful, pilgrim community ever in need of renewal, *semper reformanda.* Guardini provides for Francis the key notion of *polarity,* which is his term for holding opposing viewpoints together, the famous *coincidentia oppositorum* (coincidence of opposites), proposed by the fifteenth-century philosopher, Nicholas of Cusa.

Regarding the moral and pastoral vision of Pope Francis, at this juncture, permit me to cite the brief and brilliant appeal to analogy reflected in the proceedings of the Fourth Lateran Council of the Church in 1215: "Inter creaturam et creatorem, tanta similitudo non possit notari, quin tamen inter eos tanta maior dissimilitudo notanda" (Between the creature and the Creator, no similarity, however great, can be noted, without observing an even greater dissimilarity between them). Przywara, as he explores the topic of analogy in the mid-twentieth century, comments extensively on this passage as the key to understanding the character of the relationship between God and the creation that owes its existence to the free and sovereign action of God.[6] Created reality, whether it be tigers, trees, human beings, or subatomic particles, because its existence is finite and time conditioned, is not an independent source of its reality. Its ability to act, to exist, bears a resemblance to the existence of God upon whom it depends, but the similarity gives way to the greater dissimilarity with divine existence that is eternal and all-powerful. This "likeness in difference" maintains a real bond that holds creature and Creator in a unified but differential relationship. It is a "unity in tension" that Przywara captures by his German neologism *Spannungseinheit* (a unity, *einheit*, within the tension, *spannung*; in this case, the tension/difference between creature and Creator).

The importance of analogy in moral matters is that amid the welter of diverse, distinctive experiences available for human deliberation and action-driving to work—cooking a meal or welcoming a child, for example—we can recognize patterns or similarities among them that help us to discern what is most apt or fitting for us to choose in each situation or circumstance.

Karl Barth, the great Protestant theologian of the Reformed tradition, who famously described the Catholic sensibility for the analogy of being as the "work of the anti-Christ," grudgingly acknowledged that the "great Catholic word is 'and.'" The analogy of being is the signature theme in the melody of the Catholic theological imagination. It accentuates the essential quality of "relationality," or the "unity in difference" that characterizes every theological construct, whether it is the relationship between nature and grace, or the relationship between the moral claims of scripture and the ethical wisdom that is accessible to human reason, also known as the natural law tradition. This distinctive sensibility is a Catholic strength that enables us, in moral matters, to seek clarity wherever possible, but also to "hold things in tension" when issues are not so easily resolvable. Some matters, I suggest, require of us the virtue of patience as we live the challenge of the question while the clarity of an answer may presently escape our grasp.

The analogy of being is more than simply a recognition of a similarity in difference; for example, as human beings, our continued persistence in existence is real and genuine, but also, as we know, finite and mortal—each of us will die. Our existence is similar in kind to the most perfect realization of existence, namely God, whose very being is simply to "be," to exist; there is no difference between God's nature, essence, or actuality, that is, God's never-ending act of existing. God is not "the highest being" or *summum bonum*, but as Aquinas claims, *ipsum esse subsistens*, existence itself. Now, this point I am raising may appear to be an arcane philosophical distinction that has no bearing on the topic of this book, namely moral theology, but it is not an authorial affectation or digression.

Significantly, analogy as the core notion that underwrites the great Catholic *and* noted by Barth holds similarity and difference in a dynamic tension. Barth nonetheless feared that the analogy of being, by acknowledging the finite, existential claims of lowly human creatures, no matter how appropriately qualified that acknowledgement must be, undermined God's absolute sovereignty and grace. Przywara engaged in a powerful dialogue with Barth over the latter's disparagement of analogy. As John Betz, Przywara's excellent interpreter and translator of his works, notes, both thinkers were committed to preserving the transcendent sovereignty of God, but Barth purchases this transcendence at the expense of the immanence of created being, whereas Przywara invokes analogy to hold transcendence and immanence in a dynamic but qualified unity. As we have noted, Przywara coins a beautiful word in German, *Spannungseinheit*, which means "unity in tension," to describe the power of analogical language to "span" the difference between the infinite and the finite, holding together in relationship the realm of the transcendent God and the immanent realm in which we humans "live and move and have our being" (Acts 17:28).

Przywara's thought forms one of the anchors for the theological and pastoral vision of Pope Francis. Pope Francis incorporates the influence of Przywara with the insights of another great theologian, the German-Italian scholar Romano Guardini, as the second anchor of his vision. Briefly, Guardini, who was the subject of Pope Francis's unfinished doctoral dissertation, develops the notion of polarity.[7]

Polarity means the coordination of items that are opposed to one another, but paradoxically are held together in a "dynamic tension" (akin to Przywara's notion of analogy) rather than in a situation of mutual contradiction. For example, unity and multiplicity, while in a sense "opposite," are not necessarily in contradiction to one another. Pope Francis builds on these theological insights to express his powerful pastoral and moral vision that "holds together" in dynamic tension both a firm adherence to well-founded moral principles and values and their application to challenging, and frequently, complex situations of individual human suffering and need. The architecture of what I describe as the "imaginary of mercy" in the pastoral moral theology of Pope Francis is shaped by the coordinates of these allied notions, analogy, and polarity.

To explore the significance of these developments, I think it is helpful to express my understanding of moral theology. Moral theology is a sustained reflection on the implications for choice and action that flow from one's baptismal commitment as a disciple of Christ. It is "theological" because the intellectual effort to understand the mystery of God (the classic definition of theology by St. Anselm, *fides quaerens intellectum* [faith seeking understanding]) also addresses the concrete choices and actions of baptized Christians (the moral or ethical dimensions of daily life) as they live out their identity in Christ.

The resources available to guide these deliberations include the witness of the sacred scriptures, the commandments and virtues that are rooted in the long tradition of the Church, the lived experience of faithful Christians over time yielding a wisdom conveyed by the gift of the teaching authority or magisterium of the Church, and, of course, the formation of one's own inviolable and sacred conscience. We will explore these resources in due course.

Different visions of the task of moral theology have developed over the course of the Church's long history. These visions provide an overarching perspective that influences how the various resources outlined above are ordered and shaped to guide the process of moral discernment. Let me propose two contrasting visions, or models, for consideration.

The first model is the approach of Bernard Häring, CSSR. Häring is widely regarded as one of the most influential moral theologians of the twentieth century.[8] His classic books, *The Law of Christ* and *Free and Faithful in Christ,* have greatly informed my own approach. The following quotation is taken from *Free and Faithful in Christ*:

> The title of this book, *Free and Faithful in Christ,* reveals its identity and main program. It is not an abridged or revised edition of *The Law of Christ,* but I hope the reader will find in it a continuity of the thought and message of the earlier book, centering on the love of Christ. With the Apostle of the Gentiles, I see in Christ's love the greatest manifestation of God's creative love and liberty. His saving justice reveals God's creative fidelity to his own name as Father. Christ, who comes from the Father and leads us to the Father, remains always the focal point of our reflection.
>
> A Christocentric moral theology tries to synthesize theocentrism and Christian anthropocentrism. The very origin, countenance and goal of freedom is love; and we cannot understand the fulness of love revealed in Jesus Christ unless we see it as given in total freedom, total fidelity, and with its specific quality of creativity.
>
> ...Moral theology, as I understand it, is not concerned first with decision-making or with discrete acts. Its basic task and purpose is to gain the right vision, to assess the main perspectives, and to present those truths and values which should bear upon decisions to be made before God.[9]

Häring's description of the task of moral theology comports with the call of the Second Vatican Council for the renewal of moral theology in its decree on the training of priests, *Optatam Totius* (Decree on Priestly Training) 16:

> Special attention needs to be given to the perfecting of moral theology. Its scientific exposition, nourished

> more on the teaching of the Bible, should shed light on the loftiness of the calling of the faithful in Christ and the obligation that is theirs of bearing fruit in charity for the life of the world.[10]

If you will, please keep this quotation in mind. The reason for its importance will quickly become clear. James Keenan, SJ, in his fine and brilliantly titled book, *A History of Catholic Moral Theology in the Twentieth Century: From Confessing Sins to Liberating Consciences*, observes that the classic manuals of moral theology, handbooks developed after the Council of Trent (1545–1565) to guide priests in administering the sacrament of reconciliation, operated with quite a different conception of the moral life. As an example, Keenan cites the following passage from a prominent English manualist, Thomas Slater:

> They [books on moral theology] are the product of centuries of labor bestowed by able and holy men on the practical problems of Christian ethics. Here, however, we must ask the reader to bear in mind that the manuals of moral theology are technical works intended to help the confessor and the parish priest in the discharge of their duties. They are as technical as the textbooks of the lawyer and the doctor. They are not intended for edification, nor do they hold up high ideals of Christian perfection for the imitation of the faithful. They deal with what is of obligation under the pain of sin, they are books of moral pathology.[11]

The journey from diagnosing and healing "moral pathology," to forming mature and discerning disciples who "bring forth fruit in charity for the life of the world," is part of the narrative arc of the Catholic moral tradition. The contrast between Häring and Slater could not be clearer. Significant questions emerge from even a cursory appraisal of these perspectives. Avoiding sin and the forces of darkness that are always with us is certainly an enduring imperative for us, but is "avoiding moral pathology" enough? Missing from Slater's view is the correlative need to grow and deepen our discipleship. What else must we do to cultivate, nurture, and strengthen our relationship with Christ? As we will see,

Pope Francis reminds us that the task before the Church is "to form consciences, not to replace them."[12] This duty is one of merciful accompaniment.

Häring's distinction between "discrete acts" and "the right vision of the moral life" is an important insight that I will develop. Identifying criteria to evaluate whether a particular choice or action is permissible or not involves us, invariably and necessarily, with the place of rules and principles to guide our deliberations. Determining whether medical care should be continued aggressively when hope of cure is unlikely, or whether it should be modified in favor of palliative, or comfort, measures, involves a prudential appraisal of whether the venerable distinction between ordinary and extraordinary (heroic) means of care is applicable. Valuable as such rules and principles are, they do not tell the whole story.

Equally, and arguably more importantly, are considerations that focus not solely on the criteria for determining a good moral action, but upon the character and virtues of the good moral agent. In other words, one's moral horizon must be enlarged to attend to the vision, the framework, in which moral rules and principles apply. What are the skills, the attitudes, the dispositions, or virtues that inform the understanding and context for the application of rules and principles? Do I see the person before me who is suffering and in transition from one level of care to another as one who summons compassionate accompaniment, or as a nondescript nobody whom I view with cold, clinical detachment? Principles and rules are certainly important for helping us discern the demands of the gospel. But are they sufficient? Does the call of grace invite us to a deeper understanding of our moral lives, not only to discern the demands of the gospel, but to fulfill them?

The model of moral theology that I am proposing is, I hope, an inclusive and holistic one. The deployment of the ideas of analogy and polarity is an effort to hold together good moral actions and the good moral agent, from whom these actions flow. The recovery of the tradition of the moral virtues in recent ethical scholarship is an essential component of this vision of the imaginary of mercy.[13] Virtues, namely good habits or skills, require commitment and practice so that their acquisition facilitates and enables good actions. Classically, virtues are either acquired or infused.

Acquired virtues are precisely as described, that is achieved and developed through the decisive choices of the moral agent.

The habit of perseverance—as a persistent disposition to "keep trying" despite difficulties, for example solving a difficult algebra problem or learning through trial and error to master a recipe for dinner—requires effort and commitment. Infused virtues (those bestowed upon us by divine initiative), according to St. Thomas Aquinas, are gifts of grace, specifically the virtues of faith, hope, and charity. They give us the capacity to embrace the offer of graced relationship with God. Faith strengthens us by enabling us to keep our minds open to the good news that is beyond our finite grasp and to trust in divine providence. As the wonderful Catholic writer Flannery O'Connor observed, "Don't expect faith to clear things up for you. It's trust, not certainty."[14] The virtue of hope is the confident assurance that God will be faithful to the divine promise of mercy and eternal life. It is not naïve optimism, but a tenacious trust, captured by G. K. Chesterton in his *bon mot*, "Hope means hoping when things are hopeless, or it is no virtue at all."[15] The virtue of charity disposes us to active love on behalf of others. Whether acquired or infused, virtues are anchored in the commitments that flow from a community of faith. The moral and spiritual claims of a community, its central narrative or story, profoundly influence the meaning and shape of virtue.

Virtues are not to be understood as isolated, singular skills or abilities, lacking a historical basis or anchor. They are shaped and contextualized by the communities of meaning and purpose in and from which they arise. Virtues encode a portrayal of the human good that has been developed over the course of time and form the capacities that are essential for the enactment of this communally shaped notion of the good life. For example, the virtue of courage, as portrayed in the Greek epic *The Iliad*, is understood as a quest for glory and honor on the battlefield. The rage of Achilles erupts as he seeks to avenge the death of his friend Patroclus, a rage that reaches its climax in the killing of the Trojan warrior and hero Hector. Simone Weil insightfully analyzes *The Iliad* as the "poem of force."[16] Writing during the fall of France in 1940 to Nazi terror, she excavates from within Homer's gorgeous metaphors a subtle critique of the folly and seductions of violence and war.

The poem's vision of courage as the pursuit of personal

glory, exalting the triumph of power and strength, is dramatically different from the Christian portrayal of the virtue of fortitude, which is rooted in a radically different conception of the meaning of life—not as the pursuit of personal glory, but as the work of charity, of self-sacrificial love. For Christian disciples, fortitude is the virtue that strikes a mean or balance between two antitheses: on the one hand, reckless abandon in the face of mortal danger; on the other, cowardly flight when confronted with trial and tribulation in the pursuit of the good.

The point of this short excursus into the tradition of virtue (which we will elaborate further in our text), is to call attention to an important implication of Vatican II's call for a more biblically rooted moral theology. Sacred Scripture is more than a rule book. While it contains narratives of the commandments (Exodus and Deuteronomy), it is a library of diverse literary genres (parables, psalms, proverbs, songs, historical narratives, for example), all of which are profitable for our growth in Christ. As William Spohn noted in his fine book *Go and Do Likewise*, the cultivation of root attitudes, dispositions, and virtues has been much overlooked as a source for moral and spiritual development.[17] Scripture is indeed a source of action, but crucial to wise action is the formation of the wise actor. The "doing" side of moral theology requires the nourishment of the "being" side of moral theology: the moral agent who is schooled, trained, in the ability to see what is required and empowered to realize it in concrete action and service.[18]

The moral life of a committed Catholic disciple takes its moorings from the controlling narrative of scripture and the formational practices of a faith community that embodies its deeply held convictions in liturgy, prayer, and service. Immersed *in* the world but not *of* it, in the words of the Johannine Jesus, Christian disciples navigate a world of conflicting visions and understandings of the good life. The intellectual resources of this community can find common ground with others, most especially in the natural law tradition that constitutes a site for dialogue with the *saeculum* or secular, where St. Augustine's "City of God" (the realm of grace and divine initiative) confronts and engages the "City of Man" (the realm of sinful humankind alienated from grace and in need of redemptive pardon). The dialectic between the two cities indeed runs through each one of us, not just a defined group or political entity.

The central insight from this preliminary excursus into the nature of moral theology is that the horizon or perspective that informs our approach to moral and spiritual questions shapes and orients the more specific challenges before us. Because moral theology was carved out from its connections with scripture and dogmatic or systematic questions in theology, that is, confined to the rigorous strictures of canon law to order the life of the faithful and to equip ordained clergy with handbooks to adjudicate sins and to provide appropriate penances for healing, moral theology became, in the telling phrase of Slater, a strategy to ameliorate "moral pathology."

Sin is real, and it is important that we confront it. As theologian Michael Buckley, SJ, observes, "sin is the chosen absence of God, an absence chosen by human beings."[19] One of my priestly brothers cheekily describes our ministerial raiment as a "sin-fighter suit." However, as Häring noted, anticipating the vision of the Vatican Council, moral theology is about more than reparative therapy for a humanity seduced by the depredations of evil. It must nurture the growth of spiritually adept disciples with mature, adult consciences, who are empowered to act as free and strong agents of God's grace in this world, so that the kingdom may advance, albeit ever so slowly.

It is in this vein that I offer a distinctive horizon or vision of the moral/spiritual life. As an important first step in describing this model, the reader will note that I connect "moral" and "spiritual." Norbert Rigali, SJ, long ago observed that the division between moral theology—understood as the scientific analysis of moral action and the mysterious nexus of grace and sin—and the pastoral practice of the Church must be overcome.[20] Otherwise, these two essential components of an integrated moral and spiritual life pass one another like ships in the night.

On the one hand, we benefit from technical, philosophical distinctions, and fine-tuned appraisals of the merits of proposed courses of action (e.g., can barrier methods of birth control be permitted to save the life of a spouse whose partner is HIV-positive? Can restrictions be imposed that limit liberty in a public health emergency such as COVID-19?); and, on the other hand, we apply these principles to the practice of pastoral care that attends to the concrete, contingent, and complex circumstances facing a specific, human person. According to Rigali, moral theology and pastoral theology are two wings of the spiritual life. We need both. One without the other leads to an impoverished moral theology as well as an impoverished pastoral theology.

Each of these various strands converge in a new moral vision consistent with Francis's embrace of dialectical approaches and prepare us for a discussion now of the imaginary of mercy.

Key Elements of the "Imaginary of Mercy"

What I am calling a "moral imaginary of mercy" draws upon the influential work of Canadian philosopher Charles Taylor and his notion of a social imaginary. An astute interpreter of the philosopher Georg Hegel, whose dialectical methodology analyzes competing philosophical ideas by argument or "dialectics" with a view toward a higher synthesis or integration of ideas, Taylor adapts Hegel's methodology to address the interplay of social, political, and philosophical ideas that shape moral and cultural values, values that are, in turn, instantiated or realized in distinctive historical epochs. Like shifting tectonic plates that constantly, slowly, and sometimes convulsively alter our physical landscape, moral and spiritual ideas are dynamic forces that take root for a time, yet develop, mutate, and almost imperceptibly transform the felt sensibilities that define the life world of an age. These sensibilities form the context, the taken-for-granted understandings that inform the practices and attitudes, the behaviors, and actions of a given culture.

For Taylor, a "social imaginary" is his term to describe a worldview or perspective that is not so much a theory of how various elements within the landscape of a culture are organized as it is a set of governing assumptions, attitudes, and values that are implicitly rather than explicitly articulated. For example, in the stratified, hierarchical social structure of the late Middle Ages, the idea of widespread disbelief in the existence of God was virtually unthinkable. In our setting of late modernity, with the widespread acceptance of human technical skills and mastery of many aspects of the natural world, it is possible to construe reality exclusively in an immanent frame of meaning, effectively exiling the divine or the transcendent from our conceptual ordering of the world. As Taylor states in *Modern Social Imaginaries*, "The social imaginary is not a set of ideas; rather, it is what enables, through making sense of, the practices of a society."[21] This working definition informs Taylor's brilliant exegesis of the emergence of the assumptions of modernity, especially the understanding of "secularity," that occupies his magisterial tome, *A Secular Age*.

Taylor, according to his astute interpreter James K. A. Smith, describes three portraits of secularity.[22] Portrait (1) views the secular as a remainder concept once religion and the "stuff" of religious trappings are subtracted from the rhythms, the comings, and goings, of daily life. Portrait (2) views the secular realm, once the transcendent referent is effectively exiled, as areligious, that is effectively immunized from theologically informed interpretations. However, Taylor develops a more optimistic portrait (3) in which the transcendent, far from being absent, is accessible and discoverable, albeit with effort, from the immanent confines of a closed universe. In this frame, morally and spiritually charged experiences are "underdetermined" by the closed zeitgeist of modernity. Peter Berger's "rumors of angels" or "holy longings" (in the fine phrase of Ron Rolheiser, OMI) continue to escape from the seemingly hardened carapace of an areligious secularity.[23] The "buffered self," in Taylor's phrase, deceptively locked into an immanent world of self-interest, hauntingly experiences hungers for authenticity, for community, for solidarity that create an opening for a retrieval of theological themes and ideas.

Taylor's conceptualization of an interpretive matrix, conveyed by the noun *imaginary* that he coined, is suggestive for envisioning a different conceptual framework for the moral enterprise. I propose a "moral imaginary of mercy" as a theological device to resituate and to reorient the task of moral theology. This imaginary lies at the heart of the interpretation or hermeneutic of the moral life by Pope Francis. Such an orientation or construal deeply influences the approach to the practices of faith, especially the sacramental practices of the Church, including Eucharist and reconciliation.

A moral theology informed by an imaginary of mercy, of grace-filled compassion and accompaniment, differs from a moral theology informed exclusively by an imaginary of law and order. Each of these perspectives has obvious strengths and limitations. The former equips the Church with the skills of pastoral patience, a certain "tolerance for turbulence," as the many conversions required to achieve mature discipleship develop in the moral agent. The latter model equips the Church with clarity and precision, finding useful analogies and patterns in the analysis of concrete "case studies" (hence the venerable term *casuistry*) to guide moral deliberation. My constructive proposal is that an imaginary of mercy incorporates and integrates compassion and conceptual clarity, so that we can recover the moral tradition of casuistry and overcome the separation between pastoral care and moral theology that Rigali has so insightfully noted.

As an example, Häring, in his book on the sacrament of reconciliation, *Shalom*, contrasts two models or approaches to the role of the confessor.[24] Given the authority of the confessor to absolve the penitent for sins committed, the task of discriminating among sins and adjudicating an appropriate penalty or penance accentuates the role of the confessor as a judge. This forensic metaphor understandably achieves prominence due to the historical linkage of the sacrament to the discipline of canon law to guide and order the life of the faithful. The forensic model requires precise delineation of the character of moral fault in terms of its gravity and frequency of occurrence.

Alternatively, Häring attends to a deeper theme within the tradition of sacramental practice, namely a medicinal model that stresses healing, mercy, and forgiveness. In this model, the confessor serves not so much as a judge, but as a physician ministering to the spiritual health and well-being of the penitent. The Church's Code of Canon Law testifies to this model in its portrayal of the role of the ordained minister as one charged with the "care of souls."

Each of these models has distinctive strengths that require their integration into a more comprehensive pastoral vision. In the forensic model, attention to specificity, to concrete details in the naming of moral fault, is essential to the formation of virtues and habits needed to sustain a healthier and holier spiritual life. However, such an approach can devolve into a highly individualized "act" orientation to the moral life, neglecting the formation of a wise, discerning, moral agent with the insight to see the connections between discrete, individual actions and the holistic character of the moral life. For example, to focus narrowly upon individual moments of irritation or anger with a spouse, may lead one to overlook the need to incorporate into one's character active listening and conflict resolution skills. Individual indiscretions are revelatory of a deeper issue that is essential to resolving the pattern of marital discord. Unless the root cause, lack of communication skills, is addressed, the symptoms will continue to fester and disrupt the relationship.

However, the confessor acting as spiritual physician, or "doctor of the soul," helps the penitent to identify not just the symptoms of moral failure manifested in discrete sinful acts, but the underlying source of these manifold expressions of moral distress. Like a good doctor, a good confessor moves beyond a diagnosis of symptoms to the root cause of moral and spiritual dysfunction. This model retrieves the biblical metaphor of the "heart" as the source of all moral praise and blame. From a disordered heart, a broken center, come forth all forms of licentiousness, lust, and the myriad manifestations of "disordered love" that wound the human heart (Mark 7:1–24).[25]

An imaginary of mercy integrates these forensic and medicinal dimensions into a cohesive pastoral vision. Mercy is a profoundly rich biblical notion that provides a framework to address the moral complexities of our time. Pope Francis calls the Church not to be a museum dwelling in a comfortable cocoon of privilege and complacency but animated by the tenderness of love to go out to the peripheries, to seek the lost, and to extend the healing "balm of Gilead" to a troubled, anxious, and wounded world.

Cardinal Walter Kasper's book *Mercy: The Essence of the Gospel and the Key to Christian Life* is a masterful treatise.[26] Two insights provide a working definition of mercy for my purposes. Citing Aquinas and Augustine, Kasper notes the attention given to the meaning of *misericordia,* to have one's heart (*cor*) aligned with the unfortunate (*miseri*), those who are poor and in distress. This sensitivity to the suffering of another gives rise to compassion, beautifully described as *miserum cor habens super miseria alterius* (having an unhappy heart because of the unhappiness of another).

Kasper amplifies this insight by citing Yves Congar, OP, the famed Dominican ecclesiologist, ecumenist, and theologian of the Holy Spirit. According to Congar, mercy is a "sovereign attribute of God." That is, in Kasper's summary of Congar,

> God is the sovereign Lord, who is not subject to the law of another, but rather is the Lord who imparts his gifts

> in a sovereign way. In this process, he does not proceed in an arbitrary fashion; rather, he acts according to his own loving kindness. Therefore, mercy is not opposed to justice. Mercy does not suspend justice; rather, mercy transcends it; mercy is the fulfillment of justice.[27]

In the apt phrase of Aquinas, mercy is "the superabundance of justice."

Hallmarks of this framework or imaginary of mercy are accompaniment of those who suffer, extension of redemptive pardon, and patience with the process of caring for and healing those who find themselves caught in seemingly impossible moral and spiritual dilemmas. This modality of mercy to guide moral decision-making can rescue moral theology from the sterility of serving as an ecclesiastical scold from a bygone era.

A theological motif that undergirds this conception of mercy is a tradition revered in the Eastern Church and given expression in the article from the Apostle's Creed, namely, the "descent into hell." Australian scholar Cristina Ella Laufer has written an extensive analysis of this tradition (also known as the "*descensus* [descent] clause" in the Creed), titled *Hell's Destruction.* Laufer reclaims the theological power of this creedal affirmation to integrate the full meaning of the doctrines of the incarnation and resurrection from the dead.[28]

The Eastern Church, following the theological principle articulated by Gregory Nazianzus that "what has not been touched" or "taken up," "has not been redeemed" (*quod non assumitur, non redimitur*), has maintained the breadth and reach of divine mercy, allowing for the possibility that those condemned to eternal perdition may not be forever lost, leaving open the hope that the population of hell may be zero. Hans Urs von Balthasar is the Western theologian most associated with this theological hope expressed in his profound meditation on the need for the Church to develop its theology of Holy Saturday, contemplating the significance of the Savior, extending grace to the darkest and most forsaken realm of the dead, in anticipation of the glorious dawn of Easter Sunday.

Theologian Michael Downey, editor of the *Dictionary of Spirituality,* in his most recent book on the "*descensus* clause" (the descent among the dead) in the Apostle's Creed, argues, convincingly in my opinion, that the descent among the dead testifies to the infinite reach of the divine mercy—there is no limit to how far God will go to save wandering and errant humanity.[29] Downey notes that Pope Francis intentionally speaks of the necessity for the Church to address "existential peripheries," a notion that encompasses not only those suffering from physical deprivations, but also spiritual wounds: "the peripheries here do not refer to the location of those cast aside because of poverty. These are 'existential' peripheries: sin, misery, ignorance, indifference, injustice."[30]

The Eastern icon of the resurrection, the *Anastasis*, depicts the risen Christ, not alone, but standing over the broken shackles of the empty tomb, with his two arms outstretched, raising Adam and Eve and with them all the dead from their graves. Fr. Clyde Rausch, a skillful iconographer and teacher of the theology of the icon in Eastern thought, provides the portrait of the *Anastasis* that graces the cover of this book. The icon is a visual evocation of the divine tenderness toward all of creation. Pope John Paul II's beautiful meditation on the Lucan parable of the prodigal son (or, as I prefer, the prodigal father, since the parable is about the love of God that is lavish, extravagant, reckless, foolhardy—in a word, "prodigal"), *Dives et Misericordia,* testifies to mercy as "God's other name." In a daring footnote, the saintly Polish pontiff highlights the Hebrew word *rahamim,* literally the maternal womb, to describe God's tenderness, his "womb-like love" for human beings.[31] Building on this architecture of mercy, Pope Francis eloquently defends all human life from the cruel disparities of a soul-less technocratic and consumer oriented political and economic order, which creates a "throw-away" culture that discards the weak, the poor, and the vulnerable among us as of no account.

Analogy and Polarity in the Imaginary of Mercy and the Pastoral Vision of Pope Francis

An imaginary of mercy, as I have described it thus far, is a theological perspective that accentuates the linkage between the repertoire of sophisticated moral principles that characterizes the discipline of moral theology, and the pastoral application of these resources to the everyday challenges of human life as it unfolds in time and space. Pope Francis creatively applies this model of mercy to the dilemmas of the divorced and remarried Catholic in his encyclical *Amoris Laetitia* (The Joy of Love).[32] I will address this text in due course, but first a brief overview of the two pillars of the pope's moral/pastoral vision: analogy and polarity.

These two anchors emerge from the pope's careful scholarly work prior to his ordination as bishop, and especially from his study of the work, as discussed above, of Przywara and Guardini. Although these theologians worked in the areas of philosophy (Przywara) and systematic/liturgical theology (Guardini), their insights, respectively in analogy and polarity, have deeply influenced Pope Francis's theological vision as he addresses complex moral and pastoral challenges facing the Church. Having touched upon Przywara's analysis of analogy, I now turn to the even stronger influence of Guardini on the pope's thinking. In a different key, Guardini further develops the Przywara thesis of "unity in difference" of "similarity amid dissimilarity."

I am indebted to Massimo Borghesi for his magisterial treatment of the intellectual odyssey of Cardinal Bergoglio prior to his ascendency of the chair of Peter as Pope Francis.[33] Borghesi's summary of Guardini's notion of polarity is simply unmatched in its clarity and depth. As mentioned above, polarity emerges from Guardini's study of the work of the medieval thinker Nicholas of Cusa, famous for his discussion of the "the coincidence of opposites." It is crucial in understanding Guardini's thinking to observe the distinction he makes between something that is an opposite of another idea, for example, unity and diversity, and something that is a contradiction, for example, good and evil. According to Guardini, terms that are opposites relate to one another as distinctive "poles" on a spectrum. They can be held over against one another, or viewed in critical correlation, but ultimately, they cannot be dissolved, with one pole disappearing or being absorbed into the other, or with both poles being mutually eliminated by fusion into a higher synthesis, the outcome of the famous Hegelian dialectic (thesis-antithesis-synthesis).

Polarity, for Francis, is integral to his vision of dialogue. Each party to a dialogue, for example the Ukrainian and Russian disputants in a war raging in Europe, retains inviolable and ineliminable dignity. Polarity ensures ongoing dialogue and resists premature closure to difficult and problematic conversations. Pope Francis modifies and adapts Guardini's categories for the notion of polarity to address social questions and to frame his approach to the pastoral concerns of the Church.

A good example of how the pope incorporates polarity to integrate doctrinal and moral teaching is from the following comments at an International Theological Symposium in 2015:

> Not infrequently a kind of opposition is constructed between theology and pastoral care, as though they were two opposing, separate realities, which have nothing to do with one another. Not infrequently, we identify doctrine with the conservative, the retrograde; and, on the contrary, we think that pastoral care is an adaptation, a reduction, an accommodation, as if they had nothing to do with one another. Thus, we create a false opposition between the so-called "pastorally-minded" and the "academics," those on the side of the people and those on the side of doctrine. We create a false opposition between theology and pastoral care; between the believer's reflection and the believer's life; life, then, has no space for reflection and reflection finds no space in life. The great fathers of the church, Irenaeus, Augustine, Basil, Ambrose, to name a few, were great theologians because they were great pastors.[34]

Throughout the course of this book, I will return to these anchors of analogy and polarity for the merciful imaginary of Pope Francis to affirm the dialectical and dialogical interplay between the technical precisions that accompany the formation of rules and guidelines in moral theology, and their application to the concrete, pastoral, realities of the Catholic faithful.

The signature principles that flow from the concept of polarity that Francis has developed in his papal writings are the following: time is greater than space; unity prevails over conflict; realities are more important than ideas; and the whole is greater than the part. *Evangelii Gaudium* (The Joy of the Gospel), the first and architectonic encyclical of Francis, sets out these principles in the context of the social questions of our time. There is an extensive literature of theological critique and analysis of these "Bergoglian principles," and my purpose in citing them is to adapt them for my construal of the discipline of moral theology.[35]

Notably, these principles are especially germane to the pope's political writings, informed as they are by his Argentinian context, especially the context of violence and social upheaval in his native land. However, the notion of polarity also deeply informs the moral and pastoral concerns of Francis for the poor and for those caught in desperate and seemingly impossible moral dilemmas. His observations that the task of the Church is "not to replace consciences but to form them" and his persistent claim that "no one can be lost forever," remind us that the arc of moral deliberation and formation is an ongoing process requiring an equally ongoing commitment to lifelong conversion to the demands of the gospel.[36]

The first of Francis's principles, "time is greater than space," means that the concrete, immediate, historical facticity of reality in all its complexity is superior to the normative, settled agreements, achievements, and patterns of order, in other words, the structures, that characterize the social space that human communities have developed over time. This polarity avoids the erasure of the contingent "everydayness" of our daily lives by powerful narratives that privilege order and cohesion over against difference and the disruptions of history.

The second principle, "unity prevails over conflict," affirms communitarian solidarity as the first pole of this dyad, while insisting that conflict is an ineradicable component in a tensive relationship. Unity is not a product of cheap grace but is forged from the annealing effects of encounter with conflict and division. Unity provides the impetus for ongoing struggle to maximize the realization of the common good, the core notion in Catholic social teaching that emphasizes the coequal and interdependent claims that all persons have on the resources and conditions essential for human flourishing—individually, socially, politically, ethically, and economically.

The third principle, "reality is more important than ideas," stresses the importance of avoiding the temptation to privilege ideas, which ossify into ideologies or rigid intellectual constructs that divorce critical thought from concrete, historical reality and lived experience. With this principle, Francis accentuates the value of critical dialogue, of the practical thinking that requires engagement and robust argument. All persons are stakeholders in this ongoing social argument and the temptation of the powerful to assert untrammeled hegemony must be resisted.

The Argentinian model of liberation theology, known as *la teología del pueblo* (the theology of the people) that Francis developed in dialogue with Argentinian, Spanish, and Uruguayan scholars, departs from the political and economic emphases of classic liberation theology in favor of the social and cultural dynamics that inform the identity and ethos of the *pueblo*, the people.[37] In my own estimation, perhaps we can discern here the rudiments of an Argentinian form of participatory democracy that attends to the voices of all, poor and rich alike, and avoids the erasure of the many in favor of the ideologically privileged and powerful.

The fourth principle, "the whole is greater than the part," is a critical principle that challenges any absolutization or freezing into stasis any historically conditioned actualization of the political or social order. The holistic notion of the dignity of the human person, for example, provides a normative standard against which to measure, for example, legislation for the expansion of health care insurance or provision of unemployment benefits.

At this point, permit me to draw together the threads of the argument thus far. The main objective of this chapter is to sketch the importance of overcoming several fissures in the approach to the moral life. The split between the discipline of moral theology and pastoral practice, or the split between moral principles and their application to contingent events, invite us to consider a more holistic account, namely an imaginary of mercy. At the heart of these dichotomies is the understanding of what it means to be a human being.

A distinctive Catholic moral anthropology views the human person as a unified moral agent, who thinks, wills, loves, and acts. Moreover, human beings live in space and time and inhabit communities of meaning. These communities provide the stories that enable them to engage in the practices and actions that sustain these communities through time.

Alasdair MacIntyre's magisterial philosophical work makes clear that the story of ethics we inhabit today is a story of fragmentation.[38] We have inherited bits and pieces of moral wisdom that are scattered like the shards from a once-beautiful vase. Whether it is the exaltation of the power of reason, exemplified by the "thinking" subject, the famous *Cogito ergo sum* (I think, therefore I am) of René Descartes, or the exaltation of the dutiful citizen esteemed by Immanuel Kant, who operates with a sovereign will attuned to obligations and responsibilities, the famous "categorical imperative" (Always act in such a way that your act would equally be chosen by another in similar circumstances), the anthropology, or image of human nature, that emerges from these philosophical titans is the Enlightenment ideal of the "imperial self." This imperial self is sovereignly free, immunized from the corrosive forces of history, finitude, and limitation, culture, religion—indeed, the inconvenient fact of the human condition itself—surveying the world, as it were, from Mount Olympus with cool, detached rationalism. In MacIntyre's brilliant analysis, a cohesive theological and philosophical vision is essential to hold together the elements of reason, will, and moral community, and thereby overcome the fragmentation and cacophony that characterizes the present state of ethics.

This imperial self is a bifurcated self. Reason and the affective life of the emotions are regarded as dueling contestants rather than complementary aspects of a unified, embodied, human subject. Indeed, embodiment itself must be recovered if we are to make sense of the human condition. O. Carter Snead, director of the de Nicola Center for Ethics and Culture at the University of Notre Dame, in his brilliant book *What It Means to Be Human: The Case for the Body in Public Bioethics*, makes the case that unless we heal this Manichean split of mind and body by recovering our shared human condition of mortality, namely, vulnerability, fragility, and finitude, we lack a cohesive and compelling response to the challenges of abortion, reproductive technology, and euthanasia.[39]

The Catholic imagination is an inclusive imagination. As we have seen, its signature idea is a "both/and" sensibility. The great Catholic word, *pace* Barth, is *and*. The notion of analogy as well as the notion of polarity, as developed by Pope Francis, are constitutive of this dialogical, interdependent, mutually enriching construal of reality, that avoids subdivision or separation by "holding in tension" ideas and realities that may appear to be in contradiction to one another.

The unfortunate bifurcation of moral theology from the spiritual and dogmatic theology of the church has led to distortion in moral practice and spiritual integrity. To discuss or view sin apart from the theology of grace is to devolve into the predilection of the classic manuals of moral theology that understand moral theology as the treatment of "moral pathology." The healing of the great divorce of moral theology from pastoral and spiritual theology is part of the good news that I am attempting to unfold.

Before turning to the contributions of moral theology to guide the process of making wise, prudent decisions—the practical payoff for this book—there is a value, in my estimation, in taking a preliminary overview of the landscape of moral theology. I have previously noted an important shift identified by Keenan, namely the shift from a penitential to a formational model of moral theology, but a deeper dive into these developments will be useful. Rather than a dry and discursive account of this history, I will focus in the third chapter on the odyssey of one of the Church's premier moralists of the past century, Josef Fuchs, SJ. His intellectual journey is an illuminating narrative of a dedicated scholar and pastor whose encounter with shifting currents in the life of the Church deeply informs my approach of forming "whole people in a broken world." Mark Graham's elegant and truly excellent study of the life and work of Fuchs guides the discussion that follows, and I duly acknowledge my profound indebtedness to his fine scholarship.[40] The journey of Fuchs from classically trained moral theologian who had written his own manual of moral theology, to a theologian who critically appropriated the *ressourcement* or renewal of moral theology in the twentieth century by a "return to the sources," will, I hope, repay rich dividends.

This review affords me, in subsequent chapters, the opportunity to discuss some important practical matters, including the philosophical and theological approaches to moral decision-making and choice, the various factors that contribute to a wise moral action (the nature of the moral act), the relationship of grace and sin, personal conscience and its formation by various sources: scripture, the lived tradition of the Christian community, human experience, and the magisterium or teaching authority of the Church.

My suggestion, pursuing an insight from Charles Taylor, is that an imaginary of mercy, whose lineaments can be discerned in Pope Francis's pastoral vision, provides a pathway to a more holistic, unified portrait of the moral life. The developments in moral theology that support my argument are deeply informed by the historical studies of distinguished scholars, Servais Pinckaers, John Mahoney, and Charles Curran.[41] I suggest that the developments they identify should be viewed not as dramatic departures or reversals of the tradition, for example, the shift from a focus on moral acts to a greater focus on moral agency, but rather, as a rebalancing of the tradition in alignment with the notion of polarity as elements that must be held in a dynamic, tensive, unity. With the aid of the analytical tools of analogy and polarity, I will suggest that a more integrative approach to moral decision-making is possible. In chapter 2, I will provide a map that I have devised to describe the distinctive features of four regnant approaches to ethics in the philosophical and theological literature. I will suggest that a model of "character and virtue" is the most promising candidate for a more integrated approach. The story of Fuchs in chapter three provides an interesting case study of this particular approach. After mapping four contrasting portrayals of philosophical and theological approaches to moral theology, I will extract from the discussion a more holistic model, namely, an ethics of discernment, which is reflected in the work of Pope Francis.

2

Reviewing the Landscape of Moral Theology

WE TURN IN THIS CHAPTER to the landscape of moral theology. Here, I propose that various philosophical and theological approaches to moral decision-making and choice, that is, the various factors that contribute to a wise moral action (the nature of the moral act), can be integrated into a new model for pastoral care focused on the moral agent as discussed in the previous chapter. I suggest that several strands in the moral tradition's focus on consequences, obligations, moral agency, character, and a conception of moral realism must be held in tensive unity. The fourfold scheme of ethical models, with due allowance for the inherent limitations of any typology, exemplifies the notion of polar opposition Pope Francis has highlighted in his writings. That is, rather than collapsing these models into a unitary or more encompassing ethical scheme, each of the thematic components central to the respective models must be held in tension with its partners.

The Vatican II call for the perfecting of moral theology highlights, as we have seen, two important themes: a greater nourishment from scripture and an affirmation of the vocation of the faithful to "bear fruit in charity for the life of the world."[1] This vision of the Christian life aligns beautifully with the "universal call to holiness" proclaimed in the Conciliar Decree on the Church, *Lumen Gentium* (Light of the Nations). The conciliar documents are influenced by two important ideas. On the one hand, they bear the imprint of the Italian word *aggiornamento,* which means an "opening" to new and emerging challenges to the proclamation of the gospel, and, on the other hand, as a necessary correlate of such openness, the French term, *ressourcement,* the "recovery of the sources," retrieving from the treasury of the doctrinal tradition wisdom to shape contemporary conversations.

The work of *ressourcement* has been embraced by theologians such as Josef Fuchs, SJ, and Bernard Häring, CSSR, who turned to the sources of the Christian life—scripture, sacraments, the baptismal vocation—to establish a new framework for the conceptualization of the moral life. It is exemplified in the scholarly labors of Gerard Gilleman and Fritz Tillman, both of whom authored powerful monographs on recovering the importance of the virtues to the moral life with a special emphasis on the virtue of charity.[2] On a similar note, new historical and theological scholarship into the work of St. Thomas Aquinas, initiated by Pope Leo XIII in his encyclical *Aeterni Patris,* is reflected in the historical study of the natural law tradition (more on this topic to follow) by Benedictine scholar Dom Odon Lottin.[3] These historical, biblical, and theological developments mark a dramatic departure from the traditional manuals of moral theology, a genre steeped in formulaic and legalistic appraisals of actions judged from the standpoint of compliance with the strictures of the commandments, the moral precepts taught by the Church, or ethical norms deemed to be congruent with the anthropology of scholastic philosophy grounded in the classic natural law tradition.

It is useful, I think, to preface these remarks inviting moral theologians to reclaim the intimate linkage between the spiritual life and the moral life with an overview of different approaches to moral decision-making. This overview will provide a solid context and reference point for the chapter and will also, hopefully, provide for the nonspecialist an introduction to some of the distinctive vocabulary and terminology that form the intellectual apparatus of moral theology. Familiarity with the basic architecture of these different perspectives will be useful in appreciating the ethical significance of the notion of polarity in the work of Pope Francis as previewed in the previous chapter. Indeed, the intellectual odyssey of moral theologians like Josef Fuchs affords an opportunity to address several significant debates that have enriched the discipline of moral theology and have prepared the way for the pastoral vision of Pope Francis.[4]

Let me issue here a "spoiler alert" like the warnings film reviewers often propose to readers of the review, lest the reader's sense of surprise and discovery when viewing the film be spoiled ahead of time. The alert is the following: while these models are, hopefully, informative and heuristically useful, it is my contention that they are of limited, secondary value for the discerning moral agent. Far more important, as I will argue, is the *character* of the moral agent (my preferred model in the typology), that is, how she or he is already disposed to act by a lifetime of formation in the traditions of a moral community is the crucial factor in making wise choices. Ethical models are helpful, illustrative, and enlightening, but they are handmaids to the discernment process undertaken by the moral agent. The ensuing discussion of ethical models is a prelude to a discussion of the need for a deeper formation in the virtues and practices of the Catholic faith.

A model, or typology, is an imaginative construal of a concept or set of ideas. It is a notion commonly used in scientific literature and was also creatively used by Cardinal Avery Dulles to describe different dimensions of the ecclesiology or theology of the Church. For example, the behavior of atoms can be imagined or interpreted as a set of particles interacting like billiard balls or as waves of modulating energy fields. A model is not exhaustive but rather illustrative. It captures specific features of a phenomenon, so that it can be described, compared, and evaluated. The relationships among the four models are best understood not as dueling or contradictory impulses (e.g., consequences vs. rules; moral character and agency vs. actions or deeds) but as conversation partners or as "polar opposites," to use the terminology of Romano Guardini, that is, to be held in "tensive unity." The goal is not to establish a champion among them, but to maintain them in dialogue. The four ethical models that follow exemplify this pattern of analysis.[5]

A Typology: Four Ethical Models for Understanding Moral Action and Moral Agency

Types	**Consequential Theories**	**Deontological Theories**	**Virtue and Character**	**Natural Law**
Features	End-directed (*telos*) Value laden (axiology) Purposive Means oriented Utility	Duty-directed (*deon*) Principles vs. results Violations of principle are seen as moral "deal-breakers" Coherence Categorical imperative Authority	Agent directed Virtue = skill Accent on good rather than right Communal focus	Reason directed Reality is a source of moral insight Norms formulated according to right reason Communal focus (common good)
Image	The human person as maker (*homo faber)*	The human person as citizen (*homo civis*)	The human person as responder (*homo dialogicus*)	
Approach	What is my ideal goal or *telos*?	What is the law? What is the first law of my life?	What is going on? What is the fitting response?	
Assets	Maximize results Rational analysis Consistency All values are commensurable	Features other than results are important Rigor Consistency and purpose	Subjectivity valued Room for discretion Religious dimension can be central	Givenness of the real Prudence as guide to decision-making Nature vs. cultural relativism In principle, open to "all of good will"
Debits	Reasons become "technical" reason Are all goods the same? End always justifies means? Excessively particularistic–i.e., tends to focus on particular situations; often neglects long-term implications	Rules/principles are absolute–no room for exceptions Little room for discretion in situations where there may be a "conflict of duties"	Since virtues are skills shaped by lived experience in a particular community, there is a risk that virtue ethics can become narrowly sectarian. How does one negotiate the tension between a virtue tradition and the aspiration for universal, "common ground ethical consensus"?	A "timeless" version of natural law minimizes attention to changing, historical variables Natural law is often confused with physical laws of nature/empirical science–e.g., the gravitational constant "Nature" in "Natural law" refers to human nature and capacity for intelligent discernment Natural law thinking and its principles are not a rigid code, but an exercise in "right reason reflecting on reality"

Continued

Figures	J. S. Mill Bentham J. Fletcher Oliver W. Holmes	I. Kant William May Paul Ramsey G. Grisez	Aquinas Aristotle Jonathan Edwards John Wesley Ascetical/spiritual tradition	Aquinas Catholic moral theologians
Medical Ethical Applica-tion	Risks and benefits Allocating scarce resources	"No procreation from beyond the sphere of marriage" (Ramsey) The patient is a person of absolute value and may never be used as a "means" for the other ends or purposes *Primum non nocere* "First do no harm"	How do virtues such as compassion and courage enable caregivers to address the following issues: "What does medical care mean for the dying?" "How do I deal with suffering and the limits of medical power/technology?"	Reasonable appraisals of medical care Ordinary vs. extraordinary means

Figure 1. Four Different Ethical Models

Figure 1 displays the features of different ethical theories, their respective strengths and challenges, an imaginative descriptor for each approach (taken from the work of H. Richard Niebuhr), the particular focus or objective of the respective models, some representative figures of each model, and finally, by way of illustration, an application to a specific moral issue in medical ethics. The map bears the strengths and limitations of the descriptive tool known as a "typology," which, by definition, is a selective, not an exhaustive, representation of ideas to identify a distinctive pattern or matrix for comparative purposes. Since its focus is to be illustrative, I am using it as an interpretive or heuristic device, rather than as a comprehensive account of the respective approaches. The conclusion from the exploration of these various models is a proposal for an integrated understanding of moral action and moral agency.

Consequentialism

The primary feature of **Consequentialism**, as the term implies, is its focus on the intended outcomes or consequences of a proposed course of action to determine if it should be pursued. For example, the chief executive officer (CEO) of a hospital is confronted with a difficult decision concerning the prospective purchase of an expensive piece of technology, an MRI or Magnetic Resonance Imaging machine, a powerful diagnostic tool that enjoys widespread support by the medical staff. The CEO must weigh the costs and benefits of the purchase given a limited acquisitions budget. On the one hand, the MRI will provide much needed technical precision for the doctors, but, on the other hand, the hospital serves a low-income population with an increasing need for greater prenatal and maternal health care. Where to invest the dollars? Arguing the relative merits of the decision requires an assessment of various consequential trade-offs largely influenced by the mission of the hospital and balancing the needs of all stakeholders.

H. Richard Niebuhr's classic treatise *The Responsible Self* provides the metaphors or images for the moral agent that I use to characterize the respective models. The image of the human person as an artist or a "maker," *homo faber*, captures the goal-oriented dimension of human action that is characteristic of consequentialism. With a distinctive purpose in mind, the artist uses the tools of her craft to produce an artifact. Consequential ethical approaches emphasize appropriate measures or means to achieve the goal. The Greek word *telos* signifies the end, purpose, or goal of an intended action. Moral theories like consequentialism are "teleological" theories, that is, they are goal oriented. The critical question, of course, is whether the means are genuinely, authentically appropriate to the objective intended. If the objective in mind, for example, destroying the productive capacity of an enemy nation, is achieved by means of saturation bombing, are the means justifiable on the grounds that civilian casualties are to be regarded as collateral damage, however regrettable that outcome may be?

One temptation (and limitation) of a consequentialist approach is that it allows one to reduce moral reason to instrumental reason, that is, effectively to consider all elements or factors as equally commensurable in terms of a means-end calculus. To apply such an instrumentalist approach to the saturation bombing example, the consequences are hardly easily reconciled or embraced. Is indiscriminate destruction of human life commensurable with a desired reduction in industrial productive capacity? A related question is the nature of the good or outcome that is desired. Are there limits to the pursuit of finite goods? For example, does national security trump all reservations or possible constraints to the use of military force?

Some representative figures of consequentialism in the history of philosophy and law include the British philosopher John Stuart Mill, famous for the utilitarian principle of maximizing as much good as possible, and the jurist Oliver Wendell Holmes, whose infamous declaration in the case *Buck v. Bell* (1903) that "three generations of imbeciles are enough" provides a seriously questionable warrant for sterilization of those deemed unfit to contribute to the gene pool of society. More positively, and in fairness to an outcomes-oriented or consequentialist perspective, a variety of public policy and political experts regularly employ sophisticated, cost-benefit analyses to allocate public goods and services, as in our example of the CEO of a hospital discerning how to spend limited procurement dollars.

Deontology

The central feature of **Deontology** is derived from the Greek word *deon*, which means a duty or an obligation. The Niebuhrian *image* or metaphor for this moral strategy is *homo civis*, the human person as a good citizen, dutifully adhering to the obligations of good order reflected in the laws and social norms of a given polity. The notion of obligation is central to deontological ethics. It requires fidelity to values and ideals that cannot be compromised or sacrificed in the pursuit of desired goals or outcomes. For example, truth telling is a value essential to honest communication and trustworthiness in our dealings with one another. Frequently, in deontological approaches, these core values and ideals are expressed in the form of rules or principles such as "always tell the truth, under all circumstances." In such a formulation, there is no justification for exceptions. The philosopher Immanuel Kant is perhaps the most famous figure associated with ethical deontology. Kant's well-known axiom, the "categorical imperative" (an imperative or obligation that is always or "categorically" binding) is expressed as "Always act such that your action would serve as a norm or rule for anyone acting under similar circumstances," or "Always treat persons as ends, never as means to an end."

The strength of deontology is that it provides a check on pure consequentialism. That is, not everything is "commensurable," or subject to a means-end calculus. In such a model, a core value, such as the sanctity of human life, demands absolute respect and protection. Human life, accordingly, cannot be instrumentalized or reduced to a means to achieve desired outcomes. For example, the resistance to the destruction of embryos to cultivate their highly desirable and potent stem cells for medical research and treatment regimens constitutes a deontological veto on these interventions because the human embryo, as a genetically distinct human being, is inviolable.

A limitation or weakness of pure deontology is the other side of its strength. That is, it can devolve into rigidity or inflexibility when confronted with the contingencies and complexities of many moral dilemmas. To return to the example of truth telling, would the family providing sanctuary for the Jewish family of Anne Frank, protecting them from the Nazis in WWII, be obligated to respond affirmatively to an SS Commando officer inquiring whether they were harboring a Jewish family in their domicile? Arguably, strict adherence to a deontological version of truth telling would result in grave harm, loss of life.

Significant figures who represent the deontological emphasis in moral thinking include Kant, and a more contemporary, prominent theologian, the Methodist scholar Paul Ramsey. Ramsey famously described the terrain of Protestant ethics as "a vast wasteland of relativism," and admired the strong "principleism" he found in the Catholic moral tradition. For example, his monograph *Ethics at the Edges of Life* exemplifies his commitment to invariant moral principles such as the autonomy of the patient with respect to the authorization of medical treatment, or the fundamental right to life.[6] Ramsey appropriately modifies or qualifies his principled commitments when considering withdrawal of medical treatment when the patient can no longer benefit from aggressive interventions, or conflict situations that arise when the lives of both mother and child cannot be saved. Ramsey suggests a "medical indications policy" to ensure that decisions to withdraw aggressive medical treatments in favor of palliative measures are based on a standard of "equality" of life rather than assessments of "quality" of life that can, if not carefully framed, result in unfair or unjust discrimination—for example, restricting or denying medical care based upon a negative appraisal of persons with cognitive impairments.[7]

Ramsey here embodies a form of "mixed deontology" that considers contingencies that modify or qualify the rigidity inherent in pure deontology. Adopting a less stringent approach to the issue of responsible parenthood than the official Roman Catholic position (*Humanae Vitae*, 1968), Ramsey expresses his deontological reservation in the form of a principle: "no procreation from beyond the sphere of marriage." Ramsey leaves space for various forms of birth regulation while ruling out artificial reproductive technologies such as *in vitro* fertilization.[8]

A characteristic feature of consequentialism and deontology is a focus on the assessment of the moral vectors associated with a prospective action. As with consequentialism in its pure form, deontology, in its pure form, is insufficiently nuanced to address dilemmas. In other words, as we will see, distinctions are necessary, even with strict deontological imperatives, to avoid a distorted or maladroit moral theology.

Indeed, a more adequate approach would include consequential and deontological features. Charles Curran, for example, suggests "mixed teleology" as a model to blend these elements in critical correlation. The other two models in the map, character and virtue and the natural law tradition, provide a deeper, and in my view, more robust response to the complexities that bedevil every theoretical approach to ethics. They invite consideration, not just of the elements for a justifiable moral action, but of the qualities and skills required of the human person to exercise agency and responsibility for contemplated courses of action. This shift, from action to agency, is a substantial and significant development that enriches and expands the horizon of moral theology.[9]

There are overlapping features of these final two models, hence their congruency on the proposed map. Niebuhr's image or metaphor of *homo dialogicus*, the dialogical, human person as a skillful language user, enmeshed in webs of meaning that implicate human beings in historical communities of discourse that form their members into skillful practitioners of the values embodied in the narrative traditions of these communities, is key to my interpretation of both traditions. Within the ecology of these narrative communities, the natural law tradition, I contend, contributes an important philosophical vision for engagement with a secularized modernity.

Character and Virtue

The features of the next model, **Character and Virtue**, include the development of a notion of moral character that testifies to the stable dispositions and habits of action, cultivated over time, which define a person's identity and public demeanor. My sister Mary Anne's lifelong concern for children with special needs is an expression of her deep-seated compassionate nature and concern for the most vulnerable little ones. Character as a stable exercise of good habits is reflected in the Gospel of Luke, which says everything about St. Joseph with its cryptic observation that he was a "just man." The Hebrew word *sadiq* means "righteousness" and summarizes the attributes and qualities of a faithful Israelite.

The image or metaphor of *homo dialogicus* captures Niebuhr's insight that a moral agent should consider what is the most "fitting" response in a moral situation. For Aristotle, the person of character is the *phronimos, the wise person,* who acts with insight, discernment, and deliberative skill among the array of goods that present themselves for choice and action. Character directs our attention to the moral actor, to the moral agent, rather than to the specific action or object of choice. To speak of character is to distinguish a finely tuned sensibility, the possession of a quality of judgment, whereby the individual interprets and responds to reality and the possibilities on offer for choice. The Thomistic notion of character includes the idea of "connaturality," which refers to a coherent and congruent alignment of thoughts, feelings, attitudes, and perceptions that dispose the *phronimos*, the wise one, to act as though by "second nature" with an internal compass unerringly focused on what is authentically good. The noted Harvard psychiatrist Robert Coles describes character as "what you're like when no one else is looking."[10]

A good character is formed over time by performing good actions. This practice of good actions establishes habits, patterns of action, or virtues, which render the agent capable of acting with facility and skill as the occasion demands. In a nice turn of phrase, Albert Plé, OP, a French Dominican noted for pioneering critical dialogue between the moral psychology of Aquinas and the psychoanalytic tradition of Freud and his successors, describes a virtue as a "structured dynamism."[11] For example, Plé describes the virtue of chastity, the skill that orders the proper exercise of one's sexuality as a dynamic virtue. This virtue integrates the emotional, psychological, and physical energies of human sexuality into the distinctive human quality of affective maturity that is essential for human happiness.[12] While the virtue appropriately requires modesty and restraint in the exercise of sexuality according to one's state in life, the virtue also requires the disciplined integration of sexual energy and passion for a whole and healthy personality.[13]

Virtues are dynamic skills. They grow and develop as they are exercised in response to changing needs and the variegated experiences encountered in daily life. This model anticipates a Christian disciple animated by the virtue of fortitude who appropriately modulates her response to a challenging situation. For example, an employee confronted with an example of workplace injustice such as an unwelcome sexual advance by a colleague or supervisor, can choose, exclusively, to flee from the scene, or to take the brave and risky step of bringing the matter to the human resources department for resolution. Virtues, as Plé contends, are action oriented, mobilizing and empowering our passions, emotions, and thoughts for the realization of the good.[14]

The work of theologian Stanley Hauerwas has been most influential in the recovery of character and virtue in moral theology. Hauerwas's dissertation, *Character and the Christian Life: A Study in Theological Ethics,* written under the direction of James Gustafson, provides a useful and insightful description of character as "the qualification of a man's self-agency through his beliefs, intentions, and actions, by which a man acquires a moral history befitting his nature as a self-determining being."[15] Through one's action, the agent becomes a distinctive sort of person whose actions are embodied in and give expression to her character. The moral history that anchors this identity is intrinsic to the very being of the agent and cannot be jettisoned or discounted as the agent displays this character in concrete choices and actions. For Hauerwas,

> the question "what ought I to be?" precedes the question "what ought I to do?" If we begin our ethical reflection with the latter question we stand the risk of misunderstanding how practical reason should work as well as the moral life itself. For the question "what ought I to do?" tempts us to assume that moral situa-

> tions are abstracted from the kind of people and history we have come to be. But that is simply not the case.[16]

The strength of the model of character and virtue is twofold. On the one hand, it focuses on the centrality of moral agency and its formation to the assessment of moral action. The "being" or nature of the moral agent cannot be exempted or isolated from an appraisal of a good moral act. On the other hand, the model invites us to examine the details, the particularity, that characterize the finite, historical contexts, communities, and social locations in which we live our lives.

A limitation or challenge that arises from an emphasis on the particularity of the individual and the narratives and stories that form the communities in which we live, for example, my place within the Catholic story of my own tradition of faith, is the charge that virtue ethics (or communitarian ethics since formation in the requisite virtues involves a schooling or training in the practices of a particular tradition) is too narrowly circumscribed by a particular tradition of discourse to provide ethical warrants for broader, public policy concerns. However, as we will see, this "sectarian" objection from those advocating more neutral and arguably more "universal" philosophical language is not as problematic as it appears to be. If the classic question of Tertullian in the third century as the nascent Church achieved ascendency in the Greco-Roman empire, "What has Athens to do with Jerusalem?" conveys the tension between the vision of the Gospels and the secular culture of the ancient world, the more modern form of the tension takes the form of the question, "What has Catholic Christianity (or any other religious tradition) to do with the philosophy of neoliberalism that characterizes late modernity or postmodernity?"[17] Are we dealing with two incommensurable moral languages, with different and irreconcilable values? Or, more constructively, can the process of critical engagement and encounter establish patterns and analogies that both critique and enrich these diverse patterns of moral argument?

The fear is that traditions anchored in distinctive communities of faith that have developed a particular understanding of reality and its ultimate destiny that, in turn, shapes their correlative practices of moral action, cannot dialogue or engage with secular or nonreligious forms of moral discourse. The likely outcome, if this fear is borne out, is a cacophonous chorus of pluralistic perspectives. Can these communitarian traditions participate in the forum of public debate, or must the public square be a "naked public square," a notion roundly criticized by the late John Neuhaus?[18]

Neuhaus invites us to reexamine the presuppositions underlying the claim of hegemony and dominance of the intellectual space of the public square as defined by a secular form of rational objectivity. This version of public reason is seen as a neutral umpire, and, because it is immunized from the taint of the particularity endemic to religious thought forms, it is adjudged as the authentically objective arbiter of the public domain. Hauerwas names this claimant the "standard account of morality." The standard account is the Enlightenment ideal of universal reason, a reaction to the wars of religion that ravaged Europe and fueled sectarian violence and social chaos. Advocates of the standard account hunger for a form of reason that can ground a minimal level of consensus to ensure, if not peace and well-being, at least a modicum of civility to keep us from killing one another.

For Hauerwas, as I read him, this thin, minimalistic narrative of the standard account, privileging procedural rules that maximize autonomy and freedom of choice, often couched in the language of rights grounded in a libertarian anthropology that privileges human beings as exclusive sovereigns of their destiny, lacks the kind of substantial convictions, anchored in the narratives of a tradition, to keep the forces of violence at bay. A society of individual, contentious, imperious egos, adhering to an allegedly neutral form of moral reason, clings perilously, at best, to social order. More importantly, the standard account is insufficient to account for and to display the convictions and habits essential for the formative practices of a faith community, whose witness and presence in the public square is essential to confront the finitude, vulnerability, and dependency endemic to the human condition.[19] Hauerwas, as we will see, finds a useful ally to counter the standard account in the pioneering work of philosopher Alasdair MacIntyre.[20]

Granting the fragmentation and loss of a shared philosophical and political consensus about what the moral good is, MacIntyre suggests that, through critical argument, it is still possible for an encounter among rival disputants to take place with the possible outcome of clarification and modulation of moral notions, if not rapprochement or a more fulsome consensus about them. All is not lost. It is possible to escape the prison of sectarian confinement, imposed by secular enforcers of the standard account, while maintaining one's distinctive moral voice in the chorus of diverse ethical interlocutors, including our consequentialist and deontological friends.

Rather than a Kantian notion of universality, whereby the test of a valid moral norm or principle is whether it is applicable in *all* situations, irrespective of circumstances (e.g., always tell the truth), for virtue or communitarian theorists (for whom moral values are always embedded in a community with a distinctive narrative or story), attention to the particularity of moral notions does not exempt them from the test of critical reason to assess the internal logic of such notions and their congruence, or the lack thereof, with moral concepts based on philosophical or nonreligious warrants (e.g., the Enlightenment ideals of "liberty, fraternity, equality").

Instead of a universality that flattens the differences inherent in every contingently distinctive ethical issue in the interest of uncontested uniformity, communitarian universalism takes the form of discerning similarities or analogies with alternative ethical schemes. The boundaries, in other words, between divergent approaches are porous rather than impermeable or impassible. This porosity is a strength, for just as cross-border traffic is good for trading partners to exchange goods and services, I think intellectual cross-border traffic between competing moral traditions is also essential to maintain critical integrity in moral analysis. As the philosopher Stanley Cavell shrewdly observes, "reason is nobody's property." Critical thinking, for all moral traditions, is an equal opportunity employer.[21] The fear of moral sectarianism, and its inevitable corollary creeping relativism (so many traditions, so many stories, which among them is true?), is not the threat it appears to be. Viewing moral rationality as rooted in a tradition of discourse, as Hauerwas and MacIntyre claim, does not threaten the critical appraisal of moral reasoning but rather deepens it by attending to the historical contexts and questions that have shaped its development. In this model, after all, are such representative figures as Aquinas as well as the brilliant Congregational divine Jonathan Edwards, whose books *The Nature of True Virtue* and *The Religious Affections* are invaluable contributions to the literature of the virtues in moral philosophy.[22]

An illustrative example to apply the model of character and virtue to an issue in medical ethics is the moral response to intractable pain or an incurable disease. Does one resort to despair in the face of suffering, or does one cultivate the virtue of patience, a skill in which the patient has been formed and shaped by her regular participation in the eucharistic sacrifice memorializing the suffering, death, and resurrection of Jesus of Nazareth? Or, when a family must live with and accompany a difficult member who resists medical treatment for a substance addiction, the virtue of patient forbearance becomes an essential skill to sustain it through the long ordeal of recovery and restoration to health.

Given the communitarian, Hauerwasian-influenced defense of narrative ethics that affirms the inescapable particularity inherent in religious traditions, what is one to make of the classic natural law tradition, the *ancilla moralitatis*, the handmaid of morality, beloved by the Catholic community?

Natural Law

The *locus classicus* for the scholastic understanding of the ethical tradition of **Natural Law** is the section of Aquinas's *Summa Theologiae*, I–II, QQ. 90–110 (*The Summa of Theology*, the first part of the second part of the treatise, Questions 90–110). It is important to note that this model's defining feature, and the context for this section, is the treatise on the virtues. As Fergus Kerr, OP, in his astute analysis of St. Thomas, *After Aquinas*, observes, Thomas's overall concern and major theme is the ultimate destiny of the human person, namely beatitude, or eternal happiness, the encounter with the sublime, the beatific vision.[23] An operative definition of natural law that is useful in deflecting erroneous conceptualizations is the following: "the created participation of the human subject in the divine work of ordering the creation."

The "natural" in natural law refers not to the external world of nature—of trees, squirrels, roses—but to the core reality or nature of the human person. According to the narrative in the Book of Genesis, human beings are fashioned *ad imaginem Dei*, "into" or "toward" the image of God. The Latin preposition *ad* is not an insignificant grammatical flourish. The preposition entails a movement, that is, concerted action directed toward the realization of this human identity. It means that humans are engaged in a dynamic process, a journey, the medieval theologian St. Bonaventure's famous *itinerarium mentis ad Deum* (journey of the soul to God), to actualize the divine image in which they are fashioned.[24] The distinctive human attributes of intelligence and volition, mind and will, are created exemplars of God who possesses these attributes in their most perfect form.

Natural law is to be distinguished from the natural laws of physics such as the gravitational constant, the electromagnetic force, and the like. Its philosophical precursors are in the Greco-Roman tradition, the works of Cicero, Ulpian, Aristotle, which are creatively appropriated and interpreted by Aquinas. Within human nature, distinguished philosophically from either sentient or nonsentient beings through its essential attributes of reason and will (intelligence and volition), there are ordered dispositions toward the goods that are desired, goods that are the object of the will. Hence there is an analogy between the moral reasoning that underpins natural law and the notion of positive or legislative law, defined by Aquinas as "an ordinance of reason, promulgated by legitimate authority, to promote the common good."

The typology highlights as a strength of natural law its value as an anchor for what I call "common ground morality." Henry Veatch, one of the excellent defenders of the critical realism of Aristotle and Aquinas, argues that the capacity for moral discernment inherent in the natural law tradition is an attribute that every person possesses, and this capacity provides an anchor or ethical purchase on the good so that a sense of moral goodness and of right and wrong is available to all thinking human beings. Veatch concurs with the Aristotelian vision of a reality that confidently asserts that there is a real world, independent of the human subject and knowable by human intelligence.

The tradition, of course, is not without criticism on both philosophical and theological grounds. However, as the fine scholar Heinrich Rommen trenchantly observes, "natural law always buries its undertakers."[25] Philosophically, the major critique emerges from the famous concern posed by David Hume in his *Treatise on Human Nature*, that one cannot derive an ethical obligation or an "ought" statement from a factual or empirical statement. Logically, Hume finds, since the elements of obligation (what one should do) are not contained within the premises of the factual statement (what is facing one), it is, therefore, impermissible to infer an ethical obligation from the factual premises. Thus, from the empirical facts of human nature, one cannot derive a correlative ethical duty or responsibility. In his response, the British philosopher G. E. Moore succinctly describes this error in thinking as the "naturalistic fallacy." The theological critique of natural law stems from the Reformation suspicion that the Catholic confidence in the capacity of unaided human reason to discern the ethical implications of the natural law effectively immunizes human intelligence from the comprehensive reach of original sin, the rebellion against the order of grace recounted in the pages of Genesis. Let me address these critiques in more detail. In doing so, I ask the reader's forbearance with an excursus into these debates. The payoff will be a clearer sense of how I am connecting the natural law tradition with the tradition of virtue and character.

In his brilliant analysis of moral concepts, philosopher Julius Kovesi (*Moral Notions*) validates our human capacity for arriving at ethical obligations or "ought" statements as no less authentic and reliable than our ability to describe the empirical, factual, world around us. Kovesi shows that the capacity for making moral evaluations, of making choices and acting accordingly, is not reducible to mere emotions or feelings. Critical insistence upon the irrationality of emotional moral judgement stems from the erroneous perception that moral notions, because, *pace* Hume, Moore, and philosophers who analyze how we use language (analytic philosophers), are not, in their construal of reality, truly objective (meaning that they are not reducible to empirical terms that refer to concrete realities, that is, tigers, trees, flowers), and that they only make sense as expressions of personal, felt preferences. The term *emotivism* captures this strain of thought in the analytic tradition.[26] Kovesi, however, argues that moral notions are amenable to reason, to argument, just like anything else that is of importance to us as human beings. Moral notions do not "evaluate the world of description, they describe the world of evaluation."[27] The dreaded fact/value problem, according to Kovesi, that is, the impossibility of deriving conditions of obligation or "ought" from "is" statements that describe the world, is not the philosophical deal breaker that it appears to be.

Analytic philosopher Anthony Lisska, Aristotelian and Thomistic philosopher Henry Veatch, and Thomistic scholar Fergus Kerr, OP, have provided a cogent and compelling rebuttal to the charge that the scholastic tradition of natural law, because it relies on a realist, natural set of foundational premises, is irredeemably trapped into the "fact/value" problem and its modern cousin, the "naturalistic" fallacy articulated by G. E. Moore.[28]

In his critique of natural law, Moore endorses the story of the crevasse separating the empirically discernible world of facts (stars, earthworms, tea shops) from the world of values (ideals, preferences, *desiderata,* and all manner of noble aspirations) as told by David Hume. Moore amplifies Hume's claim that facts cannot yield values by contending that the notion of "good" is a noncognitive, that is, nonobjective notion. It is not an "analytic" notion, empirically discernible, that is based on a factual, natural foundation. Rather, judgements about what is "good" lack tangible density so that, for Moore, "good" functions as a term of approval and can accommodate an infinite range of "anythings" deemed good, that is, worthwhile.

Lisska skillfully dismantles these objections to the natural law raised by Moore and Hume. Key to his rebuttal is his reflection on the meaning of "essence" in the philosophy of St. Thomas. For Aquinas, an essence is not a static description of the "whatness" or quiddity or character of a thing or dimension of reality—for example, "treeness" as the essence of a tree, or "dogginess" as the essence of humanity's, arguably, "best friend." Rather, an essence is a "set of dispositional properties" that move toward fulfillment in action as the terminus of the judgment of practical reason.[29] An essence is not static "stuff" but rather a dynamic capacity for fulfillment. Lisska (and Veatch) judge that the notion "good" describes the end or *telos* of this dispositional journey of the essence toward its fulfillment or realization in a concrete action. Good is an inbuilt tendency or evaluative vector whereby the basic structure or form of these dispositions toward a particular "good" (e.g., a desire for food, safety, friendship) awaits the deliberative, concrete action of the moral agent who constitutes the final cause of the action.

It is important to remember that Aquinas, following Aristotle, distinguishes between the speculative intellect, whose object is the necessary truth that can be expressed in a proposition (e.g., 2 + 2 = 4), and the practical intellect whose goal is the achievement of an action, an external manifestation of choice and of interacting with reality (e.g., I am enjoying a strong cup of coffee). The outcomes for these twofold dimensions of human intelligence differ. For the speculative intellect, its truth, its *telos,* is logical necessity, a congruence of the mind with the external world—to use the formula of Aquinas, *adequatio mentis et rei* (the "adequation" or alignment of mind and world). For the practical intellect, whose outcome is an artifact, a choice or action with tangible density in the world, it is always the case that "things could be otherwise." In other words, with respect to the *telos* or goal of the practical intellect, there is an ineluctable dimension of contingency and choice in moral matters.

Aquinas builds his moral theory on the Aristotelian distinction between act and potency. The odyssey of a potential act or choice, something within the realm of possibility, awaits its resolution in a decisive act or choice by the agent. This journey is a developmental, dynamic process. Accordingly, a "fact" is not a static chunk of reality divorced from the realm of evaluation and choice. It too is dynamic. The aporias or puzzles of the fact/value problem and the naturalistic fallacy so common in philosophical debates rest on some misunderstandings, that is, in the assumption of a static conception of essence as well as a problematic theory of knowledge (epistemology) that traces its lineage to the sixteenth-century philosopher René Descartes. Allow me to untangle the mischief inherent in the Cartesian construal of knowledge.

Descartes famously endeavored to establish a secure and firm foundation for human knowledge. He contended that the human person, relying upon the indisputable fact of cognition, expressed in his well-known formula, "I think, therefore I am" (*Cogito ergo sum*), could confidently proceed to understand the external world. This "turn to the subject," also known as the "transcendental turn," forms the presupposition for later work in philosophy. Kant, famous for the ethical notion of the categorical imperative, as we have seen in our previous discussion of deontology, privileges the deployment of mental constructs or "categories" of the human mind to grasp the external world. This mental framework shapes and directs our perception of phenomena or external realities. The direction of "fit" is from mind to world.

Problems abound, of course, when the relationship between subjectivity (personal agency) and objective, or extrasubjective reality, is either severed or misconstrued. The genius of the Catholic imagination, exemplified in the doctrine of analogy (discussed in chapter 1), is its commitment to unity in difference, to a dynamic and dialectical relationship between subject and object. By contrast, Descartes and his heirs posit a one-sided emphasis on subjectivity that constitutes an inherently problematic epistemology. As we have seen, objections to natural law, including the fact/value problem and the naturalistic fallacy, can be successfully countered. Is there a similar response to the threat to natural law posed by an exclusive focus on the "turn to the subject"?

In his challenge to the philosophy of G. E. Moore and its contention that while there may be reasons for moral actions, they are not grounded in objective or external reality (the fact/value problem), Henry Veatch applies an interesting logical test that he calls the "Euthyphro" test, based on the Platonic dialogue *Euthyphro*. In this dialogue, Socrates asks his interlocutor Euthyphro, "Is something pious because it loved by the gods, or is it loved by the gods because it is pious?" A scholastic form of this question is, "Are all things forbidden because they are evil, or are they evil because they are forbidden?" (*Sunt omnia prohibita quia mala, seu mala quia prohibita?*) According to the first question of the Euthyphro test, any reasons to be proposed, according to Moore's naturalistic fallacy, rest in the individual subject. This focus on the individual subject reflects the "transcendental turn," or "turn to the subject" noted above. In other words, the "piety," that is, the meaning of moral reasons, is determined by the "love," not of the gods, but of the human subject. The second question of the test, contra Moore's formulation, highlights the claim of moral realism, namely that reasons, the "pious matters" (to stay with the metaphor), must be grounded in objective reality, that is, "loved by the gods" (i.e., loved by the moral agent) because they are real.

Anthony Lisska insightfully quotes Veatch's approval of the Euthyphro test to respond to Moore:

> How could moral principles, to say nothing of ethical norms and standards generally, be at once nonobjective and at the same time universal and necessary?[30]

Lisska, in his comment on this passage, adds,

> In other words, rationality demands an objective character to ethical judgments. The absence of an ontological foundation, Veatch argues, destroys the possibility for rational justification.[31]

At the risk of belaboring this point, crucial for my purposes because it supports the case for moral realism against purely subjective preferences, Veatch and his colleague Joseph Rautenberg note,

> There is no better way, we think, to point out the sort of ambiguity that attaches to the notion of "good" or "value" than simply to apply what we have been wont to refer to as the *Euthyphro* test—a test that is borrowed from Plato's dialogue by that name, and that poses the question: is a thing to be pronounced "good" simply because it is what people like or desire, or is it something that people like or desire because they see it is good-that is, truly, or objectively good?[32]

One cannot have a moral judgement without both a moral agent and a natural world.

I would be remiss, at this point, if I did not acknowledge an alternative interpretation of the natural law tradition proposed by Germain Grisez, John Finnis, and Joseph Boyle. Differing with Veatch, Lisska, and Kerr, the "new natural law" theory of the Grisez school maintains the validity of the Humean fact/value dichotomy, while, nonetheless, arguing for the moral realism of the natural law tradition. For this group, moral realism is rooted in the recognition of eight basic goods that claim allegiance and respect by the moral agent exercising creativity in responding to novel and emerging challenges. This school accentuates an important element of the first principle of practical reason elaborated by Grisez in the *Ur* text of the new natural lawyers, his 1965 essay in the journal *Natural Law Forum*.[33]

As formulated in the *Summa* of Aquinas, the first precept of the natural law is *bonum faciendum et prosequendum et malum vitandum* (good is to be done and pursued, and evil is to be avoided).

The element accentuated by Grisez is the term *prosequendum*, namely, the pursuit of good, which requires the active engagement of the practical intellect and the direction of human intelligence toward the enactment of moral good. Rather than restricting themselves to a static conception of reality, or to a factual world that cannot yield moral value according to Hume, the new natural lawyers emphasize the dynamic power of human agency to shape the world according to the ethical possibilities available to it, while maintaining allegiance to the constraints on choice by the claims of basic goods that are incommensurable and cannot, accordingly, be instrumentalized.

I do not intend to register a final verdict on this intramural debate among natural lawyers, but rather to identify a key point of convergence, namely that some form of moral realism is essential if ethical reflection is to escape the trap of moral relativism inherent in the Cartesian *cogito ergo sum.* If an anthropology is a description of what "makes us tick" as human beings, everyone, as Walker Percy observes, has one, even if it is only implicit.[34] A Cartesian anthropology exalts the individual ego, the capacity of the subject to shape reality. Without the check of a countervailing reality, namely a moral vision that *resists* the imperialism of the self, ethics is reduced to the power of self-interest.

It is here that I think the models of character/virtue and natural law overlap. The moral realism of a community of faith, of a narrative tradition, as well as the moral realism of a sober philosophy of a "world to value fit," namely that of the moral subject situated within a world of meaning and value, find a common home. Somewhat grudgingly, and not without merit, Hauerwas will concede that natural law grounds a qualified confidence in human reason, even if that natural law is a thin reed on which to ground a comprehensive Christian ethic. Natural law, as scholars Pamela Hall and Jean Porter have brilliantly observed, requires the "thick" description of what is worthy of human aspiration that can only come from communities (and not merely an isolated self) deeply anchored in rich, robust, narrative traditions.[35]

Whereas Hume's objections are epistemological, the second major critique of natural law is theological, rooted in the Reformation concern that human nature and the correlative doctrine of natural law are not fully exempt from the corrosive effects of original sin. Skepticism of human reason is a consequence of the fall since not only does humanity suffer from a wounded heart, but it also suffers from a darkened intellect. Henry Fairlie's essay on *The Seven Deadly Sins Today* identifies the thread that links humanity's spiritual and moral failures, namely that they are all species of "disordered love."[36] Theologically, suspicion of natural law also stems from concerns that it lacks a biblical mooring, which further underwrites a fear that human nature, armed with the false security of its intellectual power to grasp moral realities, is, at a profound level, exempt from the need for the comprehensive healing available through the redemptive suffering of Christ.

James Gustafson thus insightfully contrasts the classic Protestant understanding of sin as an expression of basic mistrust in the grace of God, sin with a capital *S*, with the Catholic conception of sins, plural, as concrete manifestations, in particular acts and choices, of "disordered love."[37]

Considering these critiques, substantive theological efforts, including longstanding acknowledgement of the sinfully wounded, if not totally depraved, status of the human being as the *imago Dei* in the work of Aquinas, as well as constructive efforts by Josef Fuchs, Bernard Häring, and others, including Evangelical scholars, to ground natural law ethics on a more biblical basis, have fostered critical receptivity to the tradition.[38]

Suffice it to say, that natural law is undergoing a bit of a revival in theological and philosophical circles. The recent statement of the Roman Catholic International Theological Commission, *In Search of a Universal Ethic* (2009), has occasioned a considerable debate and response from scholars across the philosophical and theological spectrum.[39] The subject of natural law is worth an entire study on its own, but a personal summary of its key features and implications for moral reasoning is worth a brief review to round out this final model in the typology before teasing out important aspects of its overlap with communitarian ethics.

Summary Remarks on the Natural Law

As noted above, the key text for Aquinas on natural law is to be found in his *Summa Theologiae*, I–II, Questions 90–110. Natural law is how human beings, possessing a rational nature of intellect and will, participate in divine providence—the ordering of creation. What is noteworthy about Aquinas's locating his discussion of this foundational concept within the larger *Treatise on the Virtues* of the Christian life is the connection he draws between the natural law and the formation of the virtues. That linkage is a significant point for communitarian, narrative ethical traditions. Particularly useful is that among the virtues, Aquinas accords considerable weight to the virtue of prudence, "right reason acting well" (*recta ratio agibile*), the skill that enables the wise moral actor to exercise judgment and discretion in living a good life.

How Do We Know the Natural Law?

Built into our human nature are basic drives or fundamental orientations to goodness that Aquinas calls *inclinationes,* inclinations—for example, to preserve one's life, to pursue the good of procreation, basic imperatives, in other words, to seek fulfillment or genuine beatitude consonant with our human nature. There is a fundamental purpose, goal, or *telos,* to our striving that we can recognize and grasp through our reason and propose to the will for enactment. Because our ultimate *telos* is union with God, in the fine phrase of Albert Plé, OP, this ultimate objective "magnetizes" and orders the many finite goods that are worthy of our pursuit into alignment with the ultimate end.[40]

The will, the capacity to put our basic inclinations into action, operates from an attraction to goodness, *ratio boni* (for the sake of the good and based on our ability to know and seek the good). The driving imperative of the natural law, as previously noted, is that "good is to be pursued and achieved, and evil is to be avoided." A term that Aquinas uses to describe this fundamental orientation to do what is right is *synderesis*—it is a notion that will reoccur in our discussion of the role of conscience in the moral life.

How Does Natural Law Work in Practice?

Because there are many goods that contribute to our human flourishing (beauty, art, justice, access to food, resources, education, to name but a few), we discover the range of goods by learning from our experience and discernment through the exercise of our intelligence. These diverse goods can be realized in a myriad of ways. As we discern the range of goods, we develop secondary precepts or more detailed formulations to ensure their successful accomplishment. It is at this more detailed level of description and insight that we begin to express in rules or principles, indicators, or criteria, to achieve the good more specifically.

How Do Moral Rules or Principles Work?

A useful way to think of moral rules or principles is to view them as "ethical shorthand." They summarize our collective wisdom and experience about what we desire and value. As such, a principle affirms a desirable, moral value and incorporates two features: on the one hand, positive elements that are essential for its validation and sustenance; and, on the other hand, negative implications to be resisted in the furtherance of the value. A principle is a distillation of moral wisdom accrued over time by individuals and human communities. An example is helpful. Consider a principle that I will call "the sanctity of human life" principle. In the field of bioethics, commitment to this fundamental value is central to many debates that arise in health care ethics—for example, decisions to modify aggressive medical interventions in favor of palliative measures as a patient's medical condition deteriorates, or how to protect the lives of mother and child in a complicated pregnancy. One way to formulate the principle is the following:

1. That human life is sacred by the very fact of its existence; its value does not depend upon a certain condition or perfection of that life.
2. That, therefore, all human lives are of equal value.

Such a principle provides a helpful starting point for interpreting complex questions that arise. For example, is the principle violated if one is compelled to use lethal force to repel an attacker threatening one's life? Or is the principle violated when parents refuse surgery to repair an occlusion of the bowel (a low risk, and effective intervention) for an infant diagnosed with Down Syndrome? These answers will require further discussion and, perhaps, more refined distinctions, but the principle facilitates and strengthens these conversations.

For Aquinas, the moral life is not a passive adherence to sterile *diktats* emanating from nature, but an active response to the possibilities for choice and action that befit the human person as a steward of the manifold gifts of creation. Exercising responsible agency, human persons discern and discover what is fitting for them to pursue in fulfillment of their being and destiny. The insightful volume by Pamela Hall, *Narrative and the Natural Law: An Interpretation of Thomistic Ethics,* accentuates the importance of learning from lived experience and the shared histories embedded in distinctive communities of faith and life.[41]

Recovering this historical dimension of the moral life deeply informs a more dynamic and creative role for the natural law. The natural law is refined by the crucible of experience. It develops rules, principles, and action guides appropriate to newly emerging ethical challenges. Natural law requires for its full display and depth the wisdom encoded in the stories or narratives of moral communities and religious traditions. For Aquinas, pursuing the good and achieving it is rooted in the work of the practical intellect.

The practical intellect directs our intelligence to the concrete particulars of everyday life—things that change and develop. It deals with contingent matters, with things that "could be otherwise," and not with the necessary truths that are the object of the speculative intellect, such as the logical principle of noncontradiction—a thing cannot be and not be at the same time. The next port of call for moral egoism is the relativism of situational morality, a topic to which I will turn in short order.

Natural Law and Moral Certitude: Limited or Universal in Scope?

According to St. Thomas, certitude about the universal application or range of moral principles can be foreshortened due to limitations, stemming not only from our finite minds, but also from the difficulty of applying a rule or a principle to contingent reality that is anchored in the dynamic ecology of time and history. Particularly instructive in this context is the following quote from St. Thomas, which is also a seminal text for Pope Francis in his pastoral approach to moral questions and is cited in his encyclical on marriage, *Amoris Laetitia* (The Joy of Love):

> But, as far as the proper conclusions of practical reason, neither is truth or rectitude the same for all, nor even when it is the same, is it equally known. Thus, it is right and true that all act according to reason, and from this principle it follows as a proper conclusion that deposits [or belongings] should be returned. Now, this is true in most cases, but it could happen that in some case it would be harmful, and consequently unreasonable, if deposits were returned: suppose that someone sought to attack one's own country [with the returned goods]. And this principle will be *found to fail the more it descends into particulars.*[42]

An important implication of this Thomistic insight is the inescapability of wise judgment and discretion in moral matters. Morality is not mathematics. Contingency is ineliminable from the process of applying shared, generalizable, moral notions to concrete situations. The outcome need not lead to rampant relativism. The venerable tradition of moral casuistry that identifies patterns and similarities that emerge from an analysis of paradigmatic moral events (e.g., battlefield encounters involving lethal force that threatens the lives of noncombatants) provides an interpretive tool to make a specific, discriminating judgment about "this" distinctive moral situation. Reclaiming and renewing this tradition will be an invaluable resource for the deployment of a moral theology rooted in mercy.

Concluding Thoughts on the Model of the Natural Law

In bringing to closure this more extensive review of natural law, the insight of Bernard Lonergan, SJ, serves as an apt summary. In response to a question about the "absolute in ethics," Lonergan replied, "The Natural Law is: Be Attentive, Be Intelligent, Be Reasonable, Be Responsible, and any precept you arrive at you arrive at by following these precepts."[43] The overarching objective of this chapter is to introduce reflections on the landscape of moral theology, and a prelude to this reflection is an overview of a typology I have proposed concerning ethical models. As a transition to this more extensive conversation, I will focus on the work of

Josef Fuchs, SJ, trained in the manual tradition of moral theology and its conception of the natural law. As we will see, the odyssey of Fuchs from this more traditional approach to moral theology to a more historically and biblically shaped perspective enables me to touch upon significant developments in contemporary moral theology that undergird my vision of the moral life as an exercise in merciful accompaniment, according to the mind of Pope Francis, to form whole people in a broken world.

The fourfold scheme of ethical models, with due allowance for the inherent limitations of any typology, exemplifies the notion of polar opposition Pope Francis has highlighted in his writings. That is, rather than collapsing these models into a unitary or more encompassing ethical scheme, each of the thematic components central to the respective models must be held in tension with its partners. Elements of consequences, obligations, moral agency, character, and a conception of moral realism must be held in tensive unity.

As noted previously, Pope Francis prefers not the singularity and symmetry of a circle that resolves tension, but rather, the pluriform symmetry of a polyhedron. In this moral imaginary, the four models provoke questions that foster critical conversation and debate. Moral arguments are to be expected and not to be feared. Distinctive communities of discourse generate traditions of argument over time, and in the process, develop criteria to compare similar kinds of cases and to assess the logical consistency of the tradition's moral arguments.

As I expand on the landscape of moral theology in the next chapter, my goal is to explore the deeper connections between the ethics of virtue and character and the natural law tradition. That connection lies, I think, in the formation of wise, moral agents. Healing the split between moral theology and pastoral practice invites moral theologians to reclaim the intimate linkage between the spiritual life and the moral life. A subsequent chapter will explore the implications of this renewed vision for the spirituality of discernment of spirits and the formation of conscience.

3

Tracing the Shift to Moral Formation in the Landscape of Moral Theology

AS I CONCLUDED IN the previous chapter, the interface between the tradition of natural law and the issues of character and virtue has important implications for the relationship between moral theology and pastoral practice. This organic and integral relationship between the two moral traditions deeply informs the pastoral vision of Pope Francis. Rather than threatening a potential departure from the clarity and objectivity that are prized virtues of the tradition of the moral manuals, the resurgence of virtue ethics is an opportunity to reclaim the holistic vision of Aquinas and the Catholic moral tradition concerning the relationship between the natural law and the formation of a virtuous character.[1] In this chapter, I wish to explore in more detail how a new model of moral agency, one that encapsulates the idea of discernment, moves beyond the traditional categories in moral theology to integrate more coherently moral agency and moral action.

My purpose here is to trace an important shift in moral theology from a preoccupation with the contours of the moral act, the matter or object of moral deliberation, the "what" we are called to address (such as adjudicating medical care for a dying patient, or the just ordering of the economy) to a coequal concern for the "who," the moral agent acting in accordance with her dispositions, inclinations, qualities, motives, and reasons. Formation in moral agency is a dynamic skill and requires the intentional integration of the mind and the heart.

The Role of Discernment in the Natural Law and Virtues

In my view, the convergence of the model of natural law and the model of character and virtue is a noteworthy development that merits further attention. In the spirit of *ressourcement* mentioned earlier, it is helpful to recover and reconcile the insights of Aquinas on the natural law within such a discussion. Aquinas's discussion of the natural law is within the *Treatise on the Virtues* in his *Summa Theologiae*, which provides a critical interpretive clue to his conception of the moral life. The prevailing tendency to treat the natural law as a separate outlier from the conversation on the virtues is problematic. It ignores the context in which the discussion is situated and has contributed to an unfortunate bifurcation in the manuals of moral theology resulting in a desiccated moral vision emphasizing rules and obligations over against virtues and the formation of character. To explore the importance of restoring Aquinas's use of the language of character and virtue to the natural law framework, I will examine the intellectual odyssey of Josef Fuchs, SJ. A review of the development of his approach to natural law ethics in tandem with a recovery of Aquinas's thought provides a springboard for discussing a more promising model of moral theology whereby the imaginary of mercy more cohesively melds these important traditions in the pastoral vision of Pope Francis.

I draw here upon the insightful analysis of the work of Fuchs by Mark Graham. Graham's careful exploration of the evolution of Fuchs's thought on the natural law is a masterful snapshot of the development of Catholic moral theology in the twentieth century. More significantly, his elegant intellectual biography provides readers with a useful synopsis of contemporary debates in both Catholic and Protestant circles and serves as a catalyst for my own reflections on these matters.[2]

A brief, prefatory note before embarking on this conversation is in order. The shift from a virtually exclusive focus on moral acts in the manuals of moral theology to a more inclusive consideration of the role of moral agency involving issues of character, virtue, and formation in discernment is reflected in the theological vision of Pope Francis, to which I turn in chapters 4 and 5. The pope's focus on mercy as the governing paradigm for addressing the challenge of faithful discipleship is central to his pastoral imagination. The intellectual journey of Josef Fuchs provides a helpful lens with which to view developments in the Catholic natural law tradition that influence recent papal teaching, including the personalist vision of Pope John Paul II and the pastoral ministry of mercy in the writings of Pope Francis.

Fuchs's Journey from Neo-Thomist Scholasticism to a More Nuanced Approach to Moral Theology

In his early work, Fuchs exemplifies the neo-Thomist revival of Scholasticism, a revival spawned by the encyclical of Pope Leo XIII, *Aeterni Patris*, which affirmed the insights of the "Angelic Doctor" as an adept, intellectual apparatus to address the complex philosophical and political currents such as Marxism, evolutionary biology, rapid industrialization, and social dislocation swirling in the late nineteenth century. Fuchs invoked the neo-Thomist approach to natural law reasoning captured in the Latin manuals of moral theology for the training of future priests of which his own manual, *Theologia Moralis Generalis* (General moral theology), written in 1963, is a prime example. This approach emphasized clear trajectories for moral action via deductive reasoning from invariant, universal inclinations or dispositions built into human nature, a human nature that is objectively discernible as a cohesive source of moral stability despite historical, cultural, or other external influences. Buttressing this model of universal reasoning with its confident grasp of the intelligibility of moral goodness was an equally confident trust in the role of the magisterium (the teaching authority of the Church) to provide unimpeachably clear and definitive interpretations of two aspects of natural law, its absolute and relative character.[3]

By "absolute natural law," Fuchs meant the discernment of universal imperatives for action appropriate to humankind in its state before the fall of Adam recorded in Genesis, that is, "prelapsarian" humanity. For example, ensuring equitable access to basic human goods would not require legal sanctions by the state.

"Relative natural law" refers to natural law under the conditions of a postfall ("postlapsarian") world, suffering the negative consequences of sin, including the diminishment, although not extinction, of the light of reason. Universal imperatives such as the necessity of the state can still be discerned by assiduous attention to nature and human nature, but in the now extant state of humanity, marred by the reality of sin, coercion by authority is an essential condition for the realization of the common good for all.

Fuchs found this classical approach extremely valuable as an antidote to the relativism or situational morality that emerged during the Second World War. The experience of the collapse of cultural norms and societal sanctions in the dire circumstances of warfare lead to actions such as the summary executions of traitors, without trial and due process, by the *maquis*, the underground guerrilla forces of the French resistance.

While World War II conditions of moral and social collapse provide a context for "situation specific" killing by the *maquis*, there are deeper currents supporting this form of ethical relativism. One of these currents that provides a warrant for situational morality can be found in Protestant ethical thought, which from the time of the Reformation has entertained a deep-seated suspicion of Catholic confidence in the natural law. Since natural law affirms the capacity of human reason to discern moral imperatives grounded in an objective appraisal or grasp of reality, the Protestant objection is that reason itself cannot be immunized from the corrosive acids of human sinfulness.

More importantly, as we saw in the previous chapter, Reformation suspicions of Catholic natural law reasoning also flowed from its concern that the tradition lacked sufficient scriptural grounding, despite the Pauline claims in Romans 2:15 that even the pagans are "without excuse" since they, too, are subject to the claims of conscience about the moral good. In response to this complaint, Fuchs wrote a detailed monograph attesting to the scriptural foundations for the natural law tradition.[4] Notwithstanding these important affirmations, there is a deeper rebuke to natural law stemming from elements of the Calvinist wing of the Reformation and its theological commitment to the sovereignty of God.[5] Karl Barth's *Church Dogmatics* highlights this theme to affirm the divine prerogative to order reality according to the divine will, a will that cannot be constrained by the vicissitudes and preferences of the created order, including the human being as the crown of creation.[6] Barth is the principal architect of the famous Barmen Declaration of the Evangelical German Churches (1934), which attacked Hitler's Nationalist Socialist Party.

Barth's ethics, as developed in his magisterial theological opus, is framed around the metaphor of "command and obedience." In this conceptualization, the Christian moral agent must be open to the immediate occasions of grace that flow from divine purposes, revealed as claims upon the conscience of the disciple. These moments of grace are moments of decision. They partake of a concept of time, understood not as *chronos* or the sequentially ordered events that characterize our daily comings and goings, but as *kairos,* a time for judgment and action that is, decisive, life-altering, and fraught with eternal significance.

The power of this ethical construal is that it invests every moment of choice with the offer of fresh grace and the potential for conversion to deeper discipleship. This situational receptivity, however, has a shadow side. Missing from this account is the connection and relationship of these *kairos* moments to the formational identity of the disciple, who is not a solitary actor but one who is socially located, a historical being, and whose identity is also shaped by the narratives of the many communities to which she belongs, most especially, the story of the community of disciples, the Church. Our individual choices and experiences contribute to the formation of our character, a source of continuity and stability as we enact a moral history, influenced, of course, by existential moments of grace and encounter, that weaves these threads into a larger fabric and pattern befitting a creature who dwells in space and time.

The ability to respond gracefully in the moment of decision requires a moral character, a center of unity, continuity, and stability that perdures amid changing, historically contingent events. By focusing, exclusively, on the moral demands of the concrete, existential situation, "situational ethics" minimizes or overlooks the larger patterns, the continuities, and similarities that are disclosed by our reflection on these individual encounters. The moral agent is not a prisoner of the present moment. Moral agents can discern patterns and themes that emerge from past experiences. Knowledge gleaned from previous experience informs the present reality and raises implications for the future. Will this choice ratify or alter my experience of the past, and what will it mean for me going forward? Is the immediate ethical challenge so distinct, so unique, that it bears no resemblance to past learning and insights gleaned? Absolutizing the immediate issue, freezing it in a time warp, immunizes it from the critical purchase available through consultation with the collective wisdom of one's fellow travelers on the journey of life and the life of faith.

Throughout the postwar period and into the early 1960s, situation ethics dominated Protestant ethical discourse, exemplified by Joseph Fletcher's text, *Situation Ethics* (1960).[7] Reviewing this landscape of Protestant ethical thought, the distinguished Methodist scholar Paul Ramsey declared it to be a "wasteland of relativism."[8] If ethical analysis is restricted to the contours of the presenting situation, one is reminded of the dictate of the pre-Socratic philosopher Heraclitus: "No man can ever step in the same river twice, for it's not the same river, and he's not the same man."

The perils of relativism and subjectivism are inescapable corollaries of ethical situationism. A "moment by moment" sensibility invariably privileges a shifting cascade of novel and emerging experiences, leaving the moral agent bereft of interpretive tools beyond his or her individual preferences and inclinations. Gustafson draws the conclusion that the "occasionalism" of Barth's divine command ethics, grounded in the imperative to be receptive to the overtures of grace arising in the existential moment or "occasion," is an inadequate and insufficient approach to the complexity that attends moral matters. Gustafson identifies a point of ecumenical convergence here between Protestant and Catholic moralists.

As Barth himself acknowledges, even in the fallen, "postlapsarian" state, the "orders of creation," such as marriage and family life, perdure despite the consequences of sin. The intelligibility of these social arrangements, even to a sin-darkened human intellect, continues to provide a pathway for moral discernment. A small concession, perhaps, to some form of residual, if imperfect, moral capacity, but nonetheless still significant for a more robust appraisal of and engagement with the natural law tradition.

In a telling riposte to Ramsey's indictment of a "wasteland of relativism," Charles McCoy, professor of ethics at the Pacific School of Religion in Berkeley, wryly noted that Ramsey, and his kindred spirits, the community of Catholic moralists and natural lawyers whose affinity for rules and principles Ramsey shared, inhabited a somewhat different desert, namely a "wasteland of rationalism."[9] McCoy's comment notes a shared commitment to the overarching principle of "right reason," anchored in the natural law tradition (and, also influenced by the Enlightenment ideal of universal reason) as the dominant, if not exclusive factor in moral deliberation.

Rationalism in ethics, according to McCoy, is a legacy shared by natural lawyers of varying stripes and like-minded moralists in the Protestant tradition such as Paul Ramsey, a legacy that affirms duties and obligations, an offshoot of the deontological model discussed in the previous chapter. Immanuel Kant's monograph *Religion within the Bounds of Reason Alone* captures this strain of Enlightenment rationalism. I will return to a deeper discussion of moral "rationality," but it suffices at this point to note that rationality is not a univocal concept. There is indeed a rationality appropriate to the intellectual faculty, however, there is also, *pace* Blaise Pascal, a certain intelligibility or "rationality of the heart," echoed in the famous observation from Pascal's *Pensées*: *Le cœur a ses raisons que l'raison n'est connaît pas* (The heart has its reasons that the mind does not know). A more textured understanding of moral knowledge attends to the cognitive power of dispositions, perceptions, and desires, the "conative" or affective dimension of the human grasp of what is morally and spiritually valued.[10] Fuchs's journey from an abstract and rather narrow construal of "right reason" in the natural law tradition to a more complex appraisal of "right reason" is noteworthy.

For one so steeped in the neo-Scholastic, Thomist tradition, Fuchs appeared to be an unlikely candidate for such an intellectual about-face, discarding his earlier natural law convictions (including its absolute and relative features) in which ethical deliberation resulted in indisputably clear and compelling moral norms, universally and invariantly applicable in all circumstances, historical epochs notwithstanding, in favor of a much more nuanced, contextually sensitive natural law discourse that privileges complexity over clarity and attends to the contingencies that influence knowledge and human experience. Mark Graham's monograph on Fuchs provides an insightful assessment tracing his odyssey from a "preconversion" natural law framework to his "postconversion" version of the tradition. What was the impetus for this somewhat surprising and dramatic reversal?

According to Graham's account, the catalyst was Fuchs's role as a theologian serving on the Pontifical Commission for Population and Family, also known as the Papal Birth Control Commission. In recounting this history, I want to make clear that I am not endorsing Fuchs's subsequent reversal of his original support for the moral tradition on birth control. Rather, I am exploring the epistemological significance of a more developed understanding of moral agency, a perspective that does not necessarily require agreement with Fuchs's opposition to Pope Paul VI's encyclical, *Humanae Vitae.* Established by Pope John XXIII during the first session of the Vatican Council, the original charge of the commission was to provide counsel for a Vatican response to a forthcoming international conference on family planning. When Pope John died, his successor, Pope Paul VI, decided to augment the number of commissioners and expand its remit to consider the feasibility of a change in Rome's firm teaching that each act of intercourse must be open to procreation, a position strongly reasserted by Pope Pius XI in his 1931 encyclical *Casti Connubii* (On Chaste Marriage).

The encyclical was prompted by the decision of the Anglican Church in its 1930 plenary gathering in Lambeth, England, to permit married couples to use methods of birth control in order to control the size of the family. This decision, the first by a major Christian denomination, was momentous. Several conferences on population growth in the late 1800s, fueled by the birth control movement spearheaded by Margaret Sanger, had set the stage for the reversal by the Anglican Communion. Pius XI saw this decision as a catastrophic departure with dire consequences for the stability of marriage and family life, the dignity of spouses, and the good of procreation as an essential and core commitment of the vocation of marriage. Listening to the voices of the laity who were added to the commission, specifically the founders of the Catholic Family Movement in Chicago, Pat and Patty Crowley, was extremely significant for Fuchs.

Along with his fellow commissioners, Fuchs learned from the surveys conducted by the Crowleys of the experience of married couples with the rhythm or temperature method of birth control (which enabled couples to determine the time of ovulation, so they could decide to refrain from intercourse) that the majority of couples were frustrated by the restrictions on the use of contraception. Fuchs would join the majority report of the Commission at the conclusion of its deliberations. The majority position advocated for modification of the strict insistence on the moral norm that each act intercourse must be open to the possibility of procreation. The minority, led by John Ford, SJ, argued strongly against any such modification due to the damage, in their view, that would be done to the authority of the Church's magisterium should the pope depart from the long-standing tradition and overturn the ban against artificial birth control.

In Fuchs's estimation, personal and distinctive circumstances confronting couples in their discernment could not be discounted or minimized by the majority. The choice of means to regulate family size had to be considered in a larger context, the "ensemble of married life conceived holistically," with the panoply of goods and practices essential for the couple to sustain their commitment to one another and to their family.[11] There is a substantial and powerful rebuttal to the rejection of papal teaching in the moral literature, which would require a much longer discussion that exceeds the focus of this essay. I am reporting, not endorsing, Fuchs's change of mind on the matter. For my purposes, what is of special significance is not so much Fuchs's embrace of a change in Church teaching, but the modification of his convictions about the presuppositions undergirding the neo-Thomist model of natural law. A key factor in this reappraisal was the influence of the theological anthropology and related epistemology of Karl Rahner, especially on the kind of certitude that is appropriate for the appraisal of concrete moral norms.

Rahner was in the forefront of a Catholic retrieval of Aquinas's thought focusing on the conditions of possibility for the knowing subject, the human person, to grasp reality. This retrieval of Aquinas was in response to the famous "turn to the subject" in the work of Immanuel Kant, discussed in the last chapter. Jesuit scholars such as Joseph Maréchal and Pierre Rousselot noted that Aquinas clearly affirmed that our ability to form concepts, ideas, is rooted in the ability of the intellect to grasp the intelligibility of empirical reality through our senses of sight, sound, smell, and touch. Without denying this "critical realism" of Aquinas (and Aristotle) that all explicit knowledge comes through the senses, these new Thomistic thinkers noted that there is also an implicit dimension to our knowing as human subjects that discloses an overarching, or in the words of Rahner and his colleagues, a "transcendental" set of conditions that ground our ability to grasp reality, hence the school known as "transcendental Thomism."[12]

The word *transcendental* means that in every distinctive act of knowing and acting, whether we are driving a car, solving a mathematical problem, doing a crossword puzzle, following a recipe, or caring for a loved one, are features or dimensions of our knowing that are not confined or restricted to explicit manifestations of our cognitive and volitional powers. The explicit, concrete knowledge that is displayed in my focused attention on what is presently at hand (e.g., I am driving to the supermarket), is, in the terminology of Rahner, "categorical" knowledge. There is also operating in our consciousness, perhaps subliminally, implicit awareness of a larger horizon of meaning in which our explicit, categorical, knowledge occurs. This sense of a horizon, of a taken-for-granted framework, that lies beneath the surface of our awareness, exceeds, goes beyond, or "transcends" the explicit act of knowing in which one is engaged. This horizon reveals itself when we step back and take a deeper dive into our acts of explicit knowledge, "taking a second look," as it were. This second look is like paying close attention to something that we are aware of through our peripheral vision, something that we notice while we are observing something else that is directly in our line of sight. What, then, are these "transcendental" features of our knowledge?

As we step back and reflect on our discrete acts of knowledge and choice, we discern the finitude of our grasp and knowledge of reality, that we are historical persons, mindful that we live in time and space, and that our present grasp of reality is located within a larger framework or horizon that lures us onward. These aspects haunt our awareness as we attend to the task at hand. They become available to our consciousness and are disclosed as we probe our experience of thinking and loving with further reflection. While we are engaged in a specific intellectual pursuit, or contemplating a moral choice, we are implicitly aware that there is something "more" for us to consider in our pursuit of the true, the good, and the beautiful. This horizon forms a "condition of possibility" for us, namely a framework whereby we can discern, or recognize specific moral claims upon us. There is a dynamic energy that animates our acts of cognition and choice. To invoke a metaphor, our minds do not simply record or capture reality like a still photograph, but rather incorporate them into an active, developing, schema or narrative that is more akin to cinematic flow and action.

The natural law tradition had always recognized that the concrete application of the fundamental precepts directing us to a specific action (e.g., self-preservation, seeking the good in its many forms such as procreation and health, avoiding evil or destructive impulses) allowed some degree of variability. Aquinas, as previously noted (*ST*, I–II, Q. 94, a. 2), observed that the further we probe the details of a particular item for action or choice, there is a greater likelihood that our knowledge and grasp of a precept or principle guiding our deliberations will encounter "defects" due to distinctive circumstances or conditions that influence or contextualize the applicability of the principle.

An analogy may be helpful. As you take your morning walk, a heavy fog covers the terrain. In the distance, you detect a shape that appears to be moving toward you. Due to the overcast, you lack sufficient detail to determine if it is your neighbor or one of the deer that inhabit the local woods. As the fog begins to lift with the onset of the morning light, it becomes clearer that the object is two-legged and walking purposefully. You quickly recognize your neighbor, share morning greetings, and pause to chat. Mystery solved. In summary, you have moved from a point of view where the barely discernible shape appearing in the mist could be any number of things, to the clarity of particularity, of concrete definition. The point of the analogy is that as we acquire more specificity, more precision in our perception of the concrete details and implications of our more general, more universal norms or principles, the more accurate our discernment of how the principle or norm applies to the presenting situation for decision. This process of careful interpretation and prudential judgment on the part of the moral agent does not override or erase the coequal and truthful claims of the existential, objective issue that presents itself for our judgment and subsequent action. Reclaiming the proper role of moral agency in this process of deliberation is not, in other words, code language for the assertion of purely subjective preference and self-interest. The Thomistic moral vision is holistic, holding subject and object together under the condition of truthfulness.

In the traditional approach to natural law, of which Fuchs was both a loyal heir and interpreter, these individuating circumstances were often deemed insufficient, or lacking invalidating force, to disqualify a moral norm from being applied to the concrete situation under consideration. Clarity was invested in the grasp of the "object," the external reality compelling deliberation and action. Less attention was devoted to the factors, no less objective, influencing the agency or capacities of the moral actor. These transcendental conditions of historicity, time, including the kind of implicit or "tacit" awareness of relationships and connections with previous knowledge as explored by the philosopher of science Michael Polanyi, deepen our grasp of what objectivity requires in moral deliberation.[13] With a much more robust understanding of the irreplaceable and essential agency of the human moral actor, incorporating into moral awareness these "transcendental" conditions of history, time, location, to name a few, emphasizes how irreducibly contextual our capacity for knowing the moral good to be sought and enacted is, as well as grasping how these factors influence the decision of the will to implement the good.

As Fuchs and the community of Catholic moral theologians wrestled with the implications of these newer anthropological insights and approaches, moral norms, while retaining their value as time-tested and generally reliable guides for ethical action, nonetheless required ongoing discernment and argument to assure their continued applicability to new and emerging questions.[14] Whereas the past tradition of natural law has stressed human nature as the source of moral imperatives, the newer interpretation of natural law, without abandoning the tradition, increasingly emphasized that the proximate norm of moral decision-making was not only the congruence of proposed action with the nature or essence of objectively distinct, external reality, but also whether the proposed action fulfilled the test of critical reason, the skill befitting a well-formed, virtuous, moral agent.

To be more precise, the measure now became whether the agent had exercised right reason in its capacity to interpret, analyze, and apply the rule or norm intelligently to a concrete situation requiring a decision. As greater complexity enters the picture, the clarity and security of earlier formulations can appear to be compromised or threatened.

This more nuanced appraisal of the role of right reason has implications for the role of the magisterium or teaching authority of the Church. As we have seen, the preconversion Fuchs affirmed, with the community of moral theologians, the role of the magisterium as the final arbiter when doubt or confusion arise concerning the compliance of a moral opinion with established doctrine and moral teaching. Chief Justice of the U.S. Supreme Court John Roberts famously described the Supreme Court as an umpire refereeing a baseball game, "calling balls and strikes." It is an apt analogy for the moral magisterium of the Church. The classic model of natural law recognized the central importance of divine guidance through the grace of the Holy Spirit animating episcopal leadership to proclaim, authoritatively, the authentic meaning of the natural law due to its role, insightfully claimed by Pope John Paul II, as the "expert in humanity."[15] In a newer construal of natural law that emphasizes the role of "right reason," this authoritative role of the magisterium is not denied but invites deeper collaboration among theologians and Church leadership.

Both are held to the canons of truthful encounter that inform careful discernment and wise deliberation. If the magisterium is to perform its essential function to "call balls and strikes," as it were, then the teaching Church (*ecclesia docens*), does so in response to its collateral responsibility to be a listening Church (*ecclesia discens*). Collaboration rather than polarization should characterize the relationship between the Church's ethical scholars and the irreplaceable role of the magisterium. The absence of such an authoritative voice to guide the Church is a source of lament and sadness in the Protestant world, most eloquently expressed by Paul Ramsey in his fine monograph *Who Speaks for the Church?*[16]

The odyssey of Josef Fuchs, ably and insightfully recounted by Mark Graham, has, thus far, provided me with an important introduction to developments in moral theology. Now I will enlarge our conversation to include additional voices and perspectives to round out the discussion of the landscape of moral theology. A critical bridge to the concluding section of this chapter, which stresses the need to integrate natural law reasoning with considerations of character and virtue, is a brief excursus on the vexatious question of the role of moral norms.

The question of the character and shape of moral norms, indeed, whether they are always binding absolutely in all circumstances, spawned an enormous debate about how the various factors influencing the crafting and shape of moral norms were to be understood. This debate generated an equally enormous literature over the theory of "moral proportionalism." Based on my review of the pertinent literature, I concur with critics of proportionalism, including Pope John Paul II, who find that it does not escape completely the problems associated with consequentialism, as discussed in chapter 2. I don't reach this conclusion lightly, and I hope to make clear in what follows, my reasons for this assessment.

A summary of this debate would take us far afield, but a few observations from this still regnant discussion are worth noting for my major claim in this chapter that an integrative model of an "imaginary of mercy," more cohesively linking the traditions of natural law and character/virtue, is a promising support for the pastoral vision of Pope Francis, a moral vision that is in continuity with the moral teaching of Pope John Paul II.

Proportionalism: A Brief Excursus and the Author's "Takeaway" for the Imaginary of Mercy[17]

A classic locus for the proportionalism debate is an essay by Joseph T. Mangan, SJ, "An Historical Analysis of the Principle of Double Effect,"[18] followed by two important essays by Peter Knauer, SJ, (1965) on the well-known principle of the double effect in classic Catholic moral theology, with special attention on one of the key features of the principle, the criterion of due "proportion" or measured judgment when confronting a situation of moral conflict.[19] These analyses lead Knauer to the conclusion that commensurate or proportionate reason is the governing element in the fourfold criteria of the principle of the double effect. This element of commensurate or proportional reason is operative in making moral decisions across the board, not just in situations of conflict. What then is proportionalism, and, more immediately, what is the principle of the double effect? Let us begin with the principle of the double effect.

A classic illustration of the principle of the double effect is its application to a 1957 request by Catholic anesthesiologists to Pope Pius XII to clarify whether it would be permissible to administer analgesics (pain medications) such as morphine in sufficiently high dosages to manage a patient's acute level of pain (the good effect of morphine), but with the concomitant result that the collateral, and inescapable, side effect of morphine, that the life of the patient is shortened (the bad effect of morphine).[20] In this case, there are two effects, one good, and one harmful. On the one hand, there is the good effect of palliative care provided by morphine. On the other hand, there is the harmful effect of shortening the life of the patient. Hence the dilemma. Can morphine be deployed in these circumstances?

The moral tradition developed four conditions to guide moral deliberations in the context of an action with two collateral, but ethically problematic, effects: (1) the contemplated action must be good or at least neutral; (2) the bad effect cannot be the vehicle or pathway for the realization of the good effect; (3) the good effect must be the object of the intention of the moral agent; (4) the contemplated action must be informed by a morally compelling or proportionate rationale to justify pursuit of an action with morally compromised features. Another way of understanding proportionality in the principle is that it provides a commensurate or justifying rationale to accept association, if not agreement, with the bad effect of the action considered in its totality.

With respect to the quandary posed by the Catholic physicians, the solution to the dilemma, employing the principle of the double effect, plays out in the following manner: (1) the analgesic, or palliative drug, in this case, morphine, has two effects as noted above, and its administration can be understood to be at least a defensible medical intervention, given its pain reduction qualities, and on this account, is morally neutral, until the intention guiding its use by the physicians is further specified; (2) the good effect of easing the patient's suffering and distress does not flow from or is caused by the bad effect (namely, premature death). If the medication had as its immediate and sole effect, ending the patient's life to alleviate suffering, that outcome would be an unacceptable acquiescence in euthanasia, namely the directly willed and unjust ending of a human life; (3) the physicians, complying with their Hippocratic Oath, adhere to the first principle of medical ethics, "first, do no harm," and thereby demonstrate their intention to do what is beneficial for the patient; (4) there is a proportionate or commensurate reason for recourse to morphine despite its unfortunate, although foreseen, negative impact of shortening the patient's life.

Knauer concludes that the most significant feature in the principle is proportionality or commensurate reason with the further observation that this notion is operative in all moral deliberations, not just conflict situations. To be more precise, proportionate reason refers to a rationale or argument that is sufficiently articulated and developed to serve as a warrant or justification for a moral conclusion. In this sense the terms *commensurate* and *proportionate*, in my estimation, are interchangeable. Clarifying and explicating the criteria that underwrite the ascription of commensurate reason to support a conclusion to a moral argument form the architecture of the prolonged debate throughout the latter half of the twentieth century by many Catholic theologians.

Moral choices invariably trade upon the notion of decision embraced by the moral agent. The word *decide* means to "cut away," a recognition that a choice necessarily entails that a selection from among various options that are on offer. Since there is an element of limitation involved, this limitation can be characterized in different ways, among them the idea of "disvalue." For example, in the process of selecting a marriage partner from among the range of possible candidates, only one can be chosen. Proportionalist thinkers frequently wrestle with the reality that in situations of conflict, some possible goods may have to be sacrificed or not realized to achieve a desired outcome. Terms such as *premoral good* or *premoral evil* are invoked to name the tentative status of factors influencing a moral decision, a determination that emerges from a comprehensive assessment of the object under consideration, the purpose or end of the action, and the pertinent circumstances that are essential to an adequate description of the action.

Commensurate or proportionate reason is invoked to evaluate as comprehensively as possible, the circumstances and foreseen consequences of a proposed action before reaching a final decision, whereby the premoral good or evil is appropriately accounted for in the intended outcome. Pursuant to this brief overview, I now turn to a more personal and critical assessment of proportionalist methodology.

Veritatis Splendor and Ethical Methodology

This sketch that I have provided concerning the proportionalism debate among Catholic moralists is, by no means, an exhaustive or detailed assessment. Moreover, I would be remiss not to address some implications of Pope John Paul II's powerful encyclical on moral theology, *Veritatis Splendor* (1993), that bear upon my assessment of proportionalism.[21] Permit me to highlight three implications that advance the case for continuity between the vision of Pope John Paul and an imaginary of mercy that undergirds the pastoral and moral vision of Pope Francis.

Discipleship. In the extensive literature of commentary on the encyclical, one theme that enjoys near unanimous approval is the biblical citation of the encounter between the rich young man and Jesus in the Gospel of Matthew (Matt 19). That the encyclical begins its profound reflection on the moral life with this invitation from the Savior for his youthful seeker to pursue a deeper relationship of discipleship is truly a significant contribution to the moral and pastoral mission of the Church, which constitutes a through line to the moral theology of Pope Francis. Echoing the recovery of biblical themes such as the primacy of charity (Fritz Tillman), the motif of divine call and human response to the divine initiative (Bernard Häring), Pope John Paul anchors moral theology in a new paradigm, namely a paradigm of personalism rooted in a theology of grace. (The lineaments of this personalist vision can be seen in the pope's early philosophical study *The Acting Person,* which uses the method of phenomenology to explore the search for transcendence in the actions and moral experience of humankind).[22] This motif forms the architecture for John

Paul's incisive critique of the moral anthropology of modern secular culture, namely the absolutization of autonomy that carries in its wake a corrosive notion of freedom tethered only to individual interests and desires rather than objective standards of goodness rooted in the virtue of truthfulness.

The Objectivity of Moral Norms. While the encyclical strongly supports the integrity and freedom of conscience, it also qualifies the meaning of moral freedom, not as a capacity to choose without restraint, but as the capacity to choose that is anchored in a truthful discernment of the moral good. The concern for moral truthfulness receives further expression as the encyclical directs its attention to the discussion in moral theology concerning the objective character of moral norms and the enduring validity of the notion of intrinsic evil. That is, the encyclical argues that the descriptions of certain moral actions as morally impermissible is a direct corollary of the determination of moral impermissibility based upon objective criteria of right or wrong, irrespective of the intentionality of the agent or the pertinent circumstances related to the execution of the act in question. At this juncture, the debate is joined with defenders of a proportionalist methodology, who claim that the ascription of "intrinsic evil" (an action that is always forbidden and never amenable to an exculpatory calculus) is not warranted until the action has been completely described through a process of reasoning that is inclusive of the objective features of the action, the agent's intention, and the context or circumstances associated with the performance of the action. Proponents of proportionalist methodology object that the encyclical misrepresents their approach and, accordingly, resist the portrayal of proportionalism as a form of consequentialism or utilitarianism that underwrites relativism in ethical analysis. From my perspective, the encyclical addresses a serious concern about how to address ambiguity or complexity in moral matters, especially when conflict arises among competing moral goods or values. The encyclical provides a wise criticism of the logic of moral theory. The key insight is to recognize the importance of the role of interpretation in moral theory. I find Jean Porter's careful distinctions and measured analysis of proportionalism to be quite compelling:

> In my view, many proportionalists have misunderstood the significance of the essential indeterminacy of moral

> judgment. That is, they have moved too quickly from the fact that we cannot always be certain how to apply our generic moral concepts, to the conclusion that these concepts can only be applied through an assessment of the proportion of good versus bad consequences that a given act did or would bring about. Thus, they have left themselves open to the interpretation that what they are proposing is a form of consequentialism, although clearly many do not wish to endorse the latter view.[23]

Instead, Porter argues that moral discernment is invariably an exercise in judgment, that is, an exercise in interpreting the scope of a moral principle and exercising prudence and wisdom in its application. She adds,

> There is a critical difference, however, between applying a moral rule in light of an interpretative judgment, based on some understanding of the point of the rule, and making a judgment on the basis of some overall assessment of good and bad consequences that the act would (or did) bring about. To borrow a famous example from Aquinas, someone who takes what is another's in order to sustain her own life in a case of necessity in not guilty of theft or robbery, because the point of the institution of property is precisely to guarantee that all persons receive the material means of life (see the *Summa Theologiae* (II–II, 66.7). It is important to note, as Aquinas insists, that the individual is not said to have committed a "justified" act of theft or robbery; rather, her act is not theft or robbery at all. Yet if I were to steal enough money from my rich, dissipated uncle to enable myself to go to medical school, that act would count as theft, even though the overall consequences of my successful completion of medical school would undoubtedly be far better (even for him) than the consequences of his ongoing pursuit of wine, women, and song.[24]

Porter, in turn, offers a modest criticism of the encyclical's correlative underestimation of the indeterminacy of moral concepts and the need for prudential judgment due to its central concern to affirm the universality and force of moral absolutes. Nonetheless, the task of theology, with respect to the nature of moral absolutes, is to help clarify them, not to explain them away. That we can recognize moral claims that are absolutely binding—consider some items mentioned by Pope John Paul such as torture, genocide, killing of the innocent, slavery, and sex trafficking—is not a matter of dispute. Our effort to understand, clarify, and explain matters requires interpretation as we address the concrete particularities of our lived experience. It is an exercise in sound moral epistemology. Moral theories are in service of a truthful account of our choices and actions. Moral realism is the ground and measure of good theory, not vice versa. Pope John Paul's stout defense of moral realism is a gift of the magisterium. It is a commitment shared by his successors, Pope Benedict and Pope Francis. While the proportionalism debate, to my mind, is largely unsuccessful in extricating proportionalism from criticisms of "creeping consequentialism," it has drawn attention to the challenge of complexity in applying rules and principles. However, complexity and ambiguity do not necessarily present insurmountable obstacles to the capacity of a wise, virtuously formed, intelligent moral agent, to interpret the scope and reach of a rule and to apply it, properly, to novel and challenging contexts for choice and action.

As Charles Pinches notes in *Theology and Action: After Theory in Christian Ethics*, for Aquinas, a human act, since it involves a deliberative exercise of intelligence and volition, is a moral act.[25] That is, morality, or the moral meaning of our actions, is not a feature imported from an external source, for example, a philosophical or theological theory, but is embedded in the language that we use to name and interpret our experience of the world. Rather than assigning moral value or creating moral meaning, Thomas argues that we discover or discern morality while naming and describing our actions. There is a "thickness" or richness of description already present in terms such as *adultery, murder, theft,* that resists efforts to redescribe such proscribed actions as justifiable, or potentially justifiable, human actions. The interplay of the intention of the agent, "why" she is performing the action, the object, namely the "what" that specifies the action to be what it is, and the pertinent circumstances, the sevenfold complex of features that further refine the action answerable by the following questions—who, what, when, where, how, and with what means—constitutes the holistic model of human action in Aquinas.

Ethical analysis that prescinds from this organic set of ordered relationships leads to infelicitous results. One problem with "situation ethics," among its many difficulties, is that it attempts to provide a justification of a moral dilemma by invoking a criterion such as "a loving intention," while neglecting consideration of the specific character and history of a distinctive, moral agent. Unless we know more concrete details about the character and dispositions of the agent, we are deprived of a larger narrative to make moral sense of what is going on, and more precisely how the components of intention, object, and circumstances are integrated. According to Aquinas, a good moral action must be good in all these aspects. If there is a defect, the goodness of the action fails, hence the formula *bonum ex integra causa, malum ex quocumque defectu.* The importance of this insight from Aquinas is that it helps us to "see," that is, to understand, the world as it truly is. Unless we have the right vision to understand the world, including its moral dimensions, we cannot act properly. That is why, recalling an early essay of Stanley Hauerwas on the importance of moral vision,[26] we cannot act in the world unless we have been trained to see it truthfully. As I argue, it is the integration of moral realism with virtuous agency, the holistic vision of the Catholic moral tradition, that provides the continuity for the ethics of mercy and discernment rooted in the teaching of Pope John Paul II and Pope Francis.

Formation of Conscience and Authentic Freedom. A central motif throughout the encyclical is the proper understanding of moral freedom and the exercise of conscience. The encyclical elaborates the Catholic commitment to the integrity and sanctity of the conscience of the individual, reflecting the sterling affirmation of conscience in paragraph 16 of the conciliar decree *Gaudium et Spes,* namely that "conscience is the inner most core and sanctuary of every human person, where the voice of God echoes in our depths." Conscience, however, is not to be confused with its counterfeit, namely, an assertion of moral autonomy unmoored from the truth of our human condition. Truth anchors the proper exercise of our conscience. Conscience is not the assertion of pure ego or will. It is the personal response to authentic goodness that we can discern and recognize as we encounter reality guided not only by our native intelligence, but also by our formation in virtues that shape us as faithful disciples of the Lord. Conscience is a call to love, and love cannot be coerced. Love flows from our authentic liberty in response to the gifts of creation and the Creator who has authored them. As Cardinal Newman beautifully writes in his famous *Letter to the Duke of Norfolk*, "conscience is the aboriginal Vicar of Christ."

Critics of proportionalism fault it for reducing decision-making to a form of utilitarian or consequentialist thinking, weighing the pros and cons to maximize as much good as possible. As we have seen in our map of ethical models, the deontologists reject the instrumentalizing of moral goods in favor of honoring some goods, such as truth and life, as irrefragable and intrinsic goods that are "incommensurable." The rather novel theory of basic goods, also known as the "new natural law" theory, proposed by Germain Grisez, John Boyle, and John Finnis (a scholarly trio described by philosopher Henry Veatch as "the GriffinBoyle"), departs from the teleological, or goal-directed, orientation of the classic Thomistic natural law tradition (i.e., the goal or *telos* of our basic inclinations, as they are subjected to reason for purposes of choice, is union with God), in favor of a set of basic goods (eight in number) that are deemed to be incommensurable and therefore inviolable.[27]

I would like to register my take on this quarrel that involves a critique of proportionalist methodology. To my mind, the disputants appear to concur that there are indeed actions that should always be forbidden, or characterized as "intrinsically evil," or, in the preferred framing of Richard McCormick, SJ, as "virtually exceptionless" actions. The issue is how to describe moral actions adequately, with John Paul II in *Veritatis Splendor* concerned to defend the capacity to make clear determinations about proscribed or forbidden actions, while defenders of proportionalism argue that arriving at this determination requires a more fulsome description that incorporates the nature of the action (the object), the intention of the agent, and the pertinent circumstances. My modest claim, in line with the argument of the encyclical, is to suggest that the contours of the debate require the recovery of the holistic vision of Aquinas that integrates the components of moral action (object, end, circumstances) in pursuit of the ultimate *telos* or goal of human life, ultimate beatitude with the Trinity of the divine persons. At stake in this debate is the issue of human action and the importance of attending to the careful insights of Aquinas.

Pinches challenges philosophical accounts of human action that "atomize" actions into discrete, individualized events for deliberation and choice.[28] Missing from this portrait of action sketched by analytic philosophers is the recognition that every human act (in line with the thought of Aquinas), because it is an exercise of intelligent deliberation and volition, is a moral act that occurs within a tradition of discourse that develops the language and practices to interpret our experience and to act in ways that are congruent with a distinctive way of life. For Pinches, that way of life is the Christian narrative of creation and redemption made manifest in Jesus of Nazareth. Absent this organic vision embedded in the narratives that we inhabit, "theories," including moral theories, can go astray by privileging certain aspects of moral deliberation while minimizing or discounting other features, for example the effort to evaluate sexual morality only from the standpoint of genital, physical, actuation. Such a perspective crucially misses the integral union of genital expression with the practice of marriage and family life that provides the proper moral warrants for its exercise according to the virtue and practice of chastity.

Provocatively, Pinches suggests a different framing to address the objections raised by the proportionalism debate. He claims that defenders of proportionalism share a flawed understanding of human action that views the human agent as somehow detached from the object or matter for moral deliberation, seeing such matter as inert or only provisionally valuable. In this perspective, an event or a "happening" in our experience must be viewed neutrally, or at best as "premorally good," or at a minimum, "premorally evil," as it awaits a final verdict by the agent concerning its rightness or wrongness. By Pinches's accounting, the proportionalist moral agent, exercising his or her intentionality, determines or awards moral goodness or badness based on an overall assessment of the ratio of premoral good to premoral evil. A common charge against traditional prohibitions of sexual morality by proportionalists is that these prohibitions are based on a narrow "physicalism" that arrives at a moral determination by inspecting the physical nature of the sexual faculties.

However, Pinches suggests, citing proportionalist critic Martin Rhonheimer, that proportionalists may be the "real physicalists" due to a moral anthropology that vests the moral agent with the power to establish or create value, subjecting the object or matter under consideration to a proportionalist calculus rather than recognizing the inherent meaning of the object.[29] This calculus, according to Rhonheimer, "to expand the meaning of the object," imports an unwarranted elasticity into the nature and scope of the moral object, the matter or "the what" that is under deliberation for choice and action. Moral descriptions, however, can be as varied and complex as necessary to describe the nature of the object that specifies a contemplated human action. This action, in turn, is always understood by Aquinas, since it involves the exercise of intelligence and volition, as a moral action. The moral anthropology of Aquinas is holistic and incarnational. It recognizes that as human actors we are embedded in a world of meaning. We are not mere external or angelic observers who oversee a vast sea of data of empirical or personal provenance and then assign or determine moral status of a choice or action based upon an assessment of whether the action maximizes good, or alternatively, minimizes evil outcomes.

I find these critiques persuasive but not essential to the argument that I am making, namely, that the pastoral and moral vision of Pope Francis and the moral vision of Pope John Paul II on the objective nature of moral discernment are in alignment. Pope Francis is not a proportionalist and makes clear that his recommendations for merciful accommodation support and do not change or undermine Church teaching in continuity with his predecessors in the Chair of Peter.

In a perceptive essay, Norbert Rigali, SJ, identifies a critical problem with the revisionist project of proportionalism, namely, its inadequate theology of sin.[30] The highly individualistic approach of the manuals of moral theology, designed to equip confessors with a checklist of sins and penances in the administration of the sacrament of reconciliation focused on "sins" (in the plural) as concrete violations of commandments or virtues, for example, not just "theft" in general, but plagiarism of another's intellectual property. This approach emphasized precision and clarity in assessing personal culpability and the freedom of the penitent to determine an appropriate remedy for moral and spiritual failure.

Absent from this calculus is a more encompassing, theological vision of the mystery of evil, the cosmic and existential dimensions of evil in the world. While registering appreciation for the revisionist project of proportionalism to modulate the rigidity and hard edges of the manualist tradition, Rigali argues for a more deeply grounded "relational" moral theology, a morality that also acknowledges the great scale of evil that still afflicts fallen humanity, a situation requiring the healing and ministrations of divine grace. Rigali shifts the fulcrum of moral and spiritual life to its deepest ground, namely relationship to the person of Christ and his redemptive love.

Moral theology must do more than assist human beings in managing or negotiating life in a world this side of heaven, which, notwithstanding the proleptic victory of Christ's redeeming death and resurrection, is still a contested site of good and evil. "Dis-grace," cosmic evil, still abides in a world suffused with grace. Arguing for a more holistic vision, Rigali challenges a temptation toward rationalism in the revisionist project that can appear to remain content with strategies for accommodation, if not compromise, in a world of conflicting values and visions of the moral life. Rigali worries that proportionalism may focus too heavily on conflict management. A serious theological appraisal of the dimensions and depths of iniquity widens our moral horizon to move beyond compromise. Ethical space emerges for deontological moral vetoes, understood as compelling, inviolable convictions firmly rooted in the Christ event to exercise their claims upon us. Rigali's verdict is helpful and provides support for a defense of moral absolutes, that is, moral values that may never be transgressed such as the dignity and life of the human person.

However, to amplify Rigali's comment, I think that the proportionalist project also suffers from an inadequate theology of grace. Grace expresses the gift of divine communion with human beings. As gift, it empowers disciples to adhere to God and to act with freedom and imagination. Aquinas states that charity is the form of all the virtues. It shapes and forms the character and conscience of disciples so that their agency is strengthened to act after the "mind of Christ Jesus." While navigating situations of conflict in a broken world requires perceptive judgment, it is also the case that a rich theology of grace can foster creativity and expansive thinking to reimagine other possibilities for moral deliberation, especially in times of crisis. In chapter 5, I will return to this theme of gift and its impact on the practice of moral discernment.

As I read proportionalist thinkers, pains are taken to resist the caricature of proportionalism as a more sophisticated version of instrumental, utilitarian theory, and they view their work as a constructive contribution to a more critically nuanced moral theory.[31] Rather than rejecting deontological claims outright, Curran, for example, describes his approach as "mixed teleology," an approach that attends to the role of consequences as well as principles in moral deliberation.[32] Nonetheless, I think that the challenge, according to my appraisal of consequentialism in chapter 2, to avoid instrumentalizing competing goods for choice and action, remains at least as a point of contention in this debate.

The proportionalism debate can be traced to a problem that emerged from the tradition of the morals manuals, largely preoccupied, as we have seen, with the nature of the moral act. Proportionalist thinkers have labored, with laudable intent, to dismantle an excessive focus on a narrow interpretation of the famous "three font principle" that has guided the theology of the manuals. The three fonts, or elements, that constitute a morally upright action are the object (the kind of action under consideration, e.g., a prospective surgery to remove a cancerous uterus), the intention of the agent (that is, the moral vector or freely chosen commitment of the agent, without which a moral act is not truly a human act), and the circumstances (Latin, *circum stantes*, literally elements that "stand around" the moral object), that is, the features that accompany the action (e.g., a certified, qualified medical practitioner to perform the prospective surgery).

From Proportionalism to Personalism in the Moral Imaginary

A major concern of revisionist thinkers is to recover a more holistic approach to these elements to overcome a reductionistic emphasis on the proposed action, the object, as a focus that invests the object with disproportionate, almost exclusive, power to determine or dictate the moral legitimacy of an action. Such a limitation can result in a form of physicalism, divorcing the object from its essential and coequal congruence with the intention of the agent and the pertinent circumstances. As Brian Johnstone astutely observes, whether revisionists have been successful in their efforts to repair this reductive form of "objectivism" in moral theology, what is of enduring merit is the awareness that more attention must be given to a more holistic appraisal of moral action that attends to the formation of the moral agent. In other words, a more personalistic approach is necessary that respects the nature of the moral agent as a person with intellect, will, and virtuously shaped capacities, who is also always socially and ecclesially situated. It is with this personalist outcome in mind that my imaginary of mercy is shaped.[33] In other words, personalism corrects the one-sided emphasis on moral action in proportionalism.

The details of these intense, complex debates involving the role of the manuals, the proportionalist/revisionist interpretations of moral action, and the meaning of the natural law tradition, much less declaring a victor among the disputants, need not detain us further. Rather, I wish to extract from this literature an observation that bears upon my essay, namely, a valuable insight that right reason does not easily come to secure and clear moral conclusions in the absence of formation in the virtues required to live a morally good life. As we have seen with the story of Fuchs and his appropriation of the theological anthropology of Rahner, given the contingencies inherent to the human condition, manifest in the historical, time-conditioned, limited, and partial grasp of reality by the human subject, there is always an element of the provisional in our ethical deliberations.

Reason is a critical tool, but it is a capacity or skill of a moral actor who confronts a moral choice within the context of a moral history. Will the moral choice or act at issue affirm the unfolding of this moral history in ways that strengthen the character that has been formed and shaped by the experiences of the past, or will it constitute a dramatic departure from this moral trajectory?

Ironically, it appears from our survey of the intellectual odyssey of Josef Fuchs that we have come full circle with respect to the situation ethics debate, from a perspective of outright disapproval of its flaws, to an acknowledgement that there is an important kernel of truth in its insistence that ethical analysis is always context laden. In a masterful and magisterial article in *The Harvard Theological Review* (1965), James Gustafson gets to the heart of the matter with the astute and perceptive title of his essay, "Context vs. Principles: A Misplaced Debate in Christian Ethics."[34] Contrary to proponents of a pure form of situation ethics, exemplified by Joseph Fletcher, while it is true that every situation is in some sense unique, Gustafson reminds us that we do not come to the situation bereft of the insight, wisdom, and experience from previous situations that can guide us in our thought and action. There is continuity as well as novelty in our moral lives. In other words, both context and principles are involved in our deliberations. They are twinned pairs, not binary opposites. Gustafson's approach mirrors the Catholic preference for "both/and" thinking, an approach that maintains the creative tension of context and rule while avoiding the perils of separating these critical dimensions.

Baptist scholar James Wm. McClendon Jr., in his insightful monograph *Biography as Theology*, and his magisterial three-volume *Systematic Theology*, shrewdly observes that lurking below the surface in this fight among situationists, proportionalists, deontologists, utilitarians, and principle-based natural lawyers is, strange as it may seem, a shared conviction. McClendon names this shared conviction "decisionism," that is, that ethics is chiefly, if not exclusively, about solving or deciding moral problems.[35]

The philosopher Edmund Pincoffs, in a seminal essay that appeared in the journal *Mind* (later expanded into an important book), describes this predilection for decisions as "quandary ethics." Escaping through the horns of seemingly insoluble dilemmas appears to be the central task of moral deliberation.[36] McClendon, building on this notion, sharpens his critique by observing that the dominance of ethical theories neglects what is and should be most distinctive about Christian ethics, namely Christ and the Church that continues his work throughout time.

McClendon has been a pioneer, along with his friend Stanley Hauerwas, in championing a different model of ethics, a model that focuses on the formation of persons of character, shaped by the compelling narratives or stories of the distinctive communities of Christian disciples. This trajectory in Christian ethics moves beyond the sterility of philosophical debates about rules and desirable outcomes to a more robust appraisal of the identity of the Church as the merciful presence of Christ in the task of moral deliberation. This story of Jesus the merciful has been elevated by Pope Francis to strengthen the pastoral duty of the Church to accompany the faithful in their struggles, including the difficult realities of divorce and remarriage. My contention is that a robust, moral theology requires schooling or formation into the mind of Christ. Certainly, we need rules, principles, clarity, keen thinking, and the philosophical acuity that moves us beyond our individualism and subjectivism. However, these skills are enlisted in service of a well-formed person of character whose moral vision is not confined to the forced limits of quandaries wherein solutions are dictated by the constraints of the prevailing culture and its presuppositions about what is morally desirable or feasible.

The famous "trolley" thought experiment (devised by British philosopher Philippa Foot) trades upon this penchant for action and dilemma-dominated decision strategies.[37] The trolley experiment takes many forms. To take one scenario, the trolley is out of control due to a brake failure putting the engineer squarely in a dilemma as he confronts a choice to steer the trolley onto one of two available tracks. On one track are two people stuck at a crossing unable to extricate themselves from a vehicle because the doors are jammed, and, on the other track are five people cruelly tied to the rails by a gang of robbers. What should the engineer do? Either choice leads to an unbearable tragedy. The point of the thought experiment is to force us to make a choice. That is the underlying and seductive appeal of the trolley experiment. Which track do you choose and why? Anguishing about the options invariably results in exhaustion and frustration. Perhaps, we tell ourselves, if we simply develop the right set of tools or rules, we can apply ethical algorithms to solve the problem. Herein lies the rub. The language of choice or decision seduces us into narrow, binary, "either/or" thinking. However, let's consider a more expansive notion of moral choice and decision-making, namely a choice to be faithful to deeply held convictions to which we adhere despite the tragedy and death that await the individuals trapped on the tracks. These convictions suggest a pathway beyond the narrow calculus of a risk/benefit assessment or a benefit/burden appraisal.

Due to the vagaries of human life, endless trolley problems can be identified and the goal of a perfect resolution of conflict with absolute certitude is also, frustratingly, unattainable. But there is a way out of our impasse if we allow ourselves to reframe our presuppositions. Quandaries, like the trolley experiment, tempt us with either/or choices such as the agonizing decision confronting the fictional mother in William Styron's novel *Sophie's Choice.*[38] She is ordered by the Nazi officer overseeing the transportation of families to the death camps to choose which of her two children she will take with her. No amount of casuistic "finetuning" can soften the edges of such an impossible dilemma. Yet, all is not lost, especially if our moral imaginations are stretched beyond the limits imposed by our own finitude.

The Moral Significance of the Doctrine of the Resurrection

Indeed, as scholars including the systematic theologian Gerald O'Collins, SJ, and moral theologians Brian Johnstone, CSSR, Anthony Kelly, CSSR, and Oliver O'Donovan, have noted, the doctrine of the resurrection requires more exploration and development by the Church's ethical thinkers.[39] Notions of generous altruism, transformation, and engagement with our ultimate destiny in eternal communion with God, move us beyond the constraints of self-preservation and self-interest.[40] O'Collins, as a systematic theologian, while noting the paucity of serious theological engagement with the doctrine of the resurrection among moral theologians, offers five constructive suggestions for ethical scholars. After listing these recommendations, I will suggest that my proposal for an imaginary of mercy is, at least, an initial response to his challenge:

> First of all, the resurrection of the crucified Jesus dramatically challenges any thinking that promotes "my" or "our" interests in a way that involves or may involve victimizing and sacrificing others (see John 11:50).
>
> Second, the resurrection embodies a *new solidarity* of all human beings. As "the firstborn from the dead," Christ has "reconciled" to God "all things, whether on earth or in heaven, by making peace through the blood of his cross" (Col 1:18, 20)....This cosmic vision of Colossians puts the question to ethicists: How do you

> understand and interpret human existence and behavior in a world reconciled to God by the events of the first Good Friday and Easter Sunday?
>
> Third, the common hope for resurrection from the dead (1 Cor 15:12–58) throws new light on questions of *sexual ethics* and *social justice*....How should we behave in the areas of sexuality and justice toward other people now that we know that in their bodily existence they are destined for resurrection and transformation?
>
> Fourth, what the hymn in Colossians (1:18, 20) says about the reconciliation to God of the whole cosmos ("whether on earth or in heaven") and, even more, what Paul teaches in Romans support human concern for the *well-being of the natural environment* (Rom 8:18–25).
>
> Fifth, Keenan [O'Collins's Jesuit confrere whose work we have cited earlier] summarizes and rightly praises the great contribution Bernard Haring made to moral theology—a contribution that recognizes Christ as "the principle, the norm, the center, and the goal" of this discipline. Yet, I can only wish that Haring would have more clearly presented the *risen and living* Christ as principle, norm, center, and goal of moral thinking, judging, and behavior.[41]

O'Collins also refers to the important work by Brian Johnstone: when sketching a resurrection-centered ethics, Johnstone has suggested that it could lead to a trinitarian morality of true peace and unity in relationship, not a peace created by violence.

Clearly, O'Collins has identified several promising directions for incorporating the theme of the resurrection into the work of moral theology. The imaginary of mercy that I am proposing is rooted in this doctrine of resurrection. The Eastern Church with its rich theology of Good Saturday, with Christ searching out the lost in the graves, captured in the "descent clause" in the Apostle's Creed, and then triumphantly raising them with him on Easter Sunday, as depicted in the great icon of the *Anastasis*, provides a crucial anchor for this vision.[42] The Johannine scholar Raymond Brown states that the message of the resurrection is that God desires "not annihilation, but transformation" of the creation he has made.[43]

The resurrection is God's unfathomable and astonishing gift of mercy and healing. As a gift, it radically displaces the imperial ego of modernity with a richer image of human solidarity and communion so that the manifold relationships with creation and our fellow travelers on life's sojourn can be seen in clearer relief. Pope Francis, by highlighting the grace of mercy, applies this resurrection charged doctrine with specific implications for the Christian life. Signature ideas from his allocutions and encyclicals, "No one can be lost forever"; "everything is connected"; "the Eucharist is a medicine for the weak and the needy, not a prize for the perfect," infuse moral theology with a profound pastoral aim to "reconcile all things in Christ."

O'Collins laments that, in the absence of a clearer focus on the resurrection, even the best efforts to renew moral theology in more christocentric terms, such as a greater focus on formation in the virtues and character, still lead back to "Aristotle and Socrates," rather than to the "risen Christ." The resurrection provides critical affirmation and an enduring challenge. On the one hand, it affirms the goodness of all that has been created, in its singularity and *haecceitas* ("thisness"—a concept of John Duns Scotus develops in chapter 5), and challenges our human propensity to restrict the reach of divine mercy to our finite linguistic and intellectual constructs. While invoking resurrection destiny is important to address specific moral issues that arise with respect to the embodied nexus of flesh and spirit in human being, ranging from complex psychosexual challenges such as gender dysphoria to the limits of scientific interventions into the human genome, I think that the most significant contribution of resurrection thinking for ethics lies in the arena of moral anthropology.

By grounding the anthropology that I am calling an imaginary of mercy, the resurrection expands the horizon of moral concern so that we are not constricted by narrow self-interest and the violence that follows in its wake. A new logic of gift, mutuality, and interdependence, echoing the relations within the divine Trinity, enlarges the circle of care so that there is room for everyone in a new economy of grace.

Brian Johnstone suggests that the language of gift, rooted in the doctrine of the resurrection, enriches the meaning of agency in moral deliberation. Rather than focusing on the philosophical arguments about the nature of the moral act, which has been the central preoccupation of the proportionalism debate, Johnstone contends that framing moral theology in terms of gift enables persons to be givers and receivers in response to life's challenges, and, in turn, to enable others to become givers and receivers. The logic of gift displaces self-centeredness, and its corollary, self-interest, with generosity and solidarity. Since our very existence, our own "being," depends upon the gracious gift of the Creator, all reality, all being, as Johnstone says, is "given being."[44] The imaginary of mercy is not a comprehensive response to O'Collins, but it is a promising beginning. Knowing that our ultimate destiny is secured by the cross and resurrection of Jesus frees us to face our mortality and finitude with hope and trust.

Johnstone and his Redemptorist confrere, moral theologian Anthony Kelly, have responded to the criticism of O'Collins with more expansive reflections on the implications of the resurrection for moral theology.[45] Johnstone argues that greater focus on the resurrection event frees moral theology from the domination of juridical concepts that have shaped the development of the penitential practices of the Church. Canon law emerged as the primary resource to equip confessors with the intellectual apparatus to interpret the experience of penitents and to provide appropriate counsel in the exercise of the sacrament of reconciliation.

In addition, Johnstone notes that the individual act of faith by a believer in the resurrection, "the first moral act," understood as a basic commitment or fundamental option, expands the deliberations of conscience from a narrow calculus of the boundaries between law and freedom to a more generous construal of possibilities for liberation and other-regarding care.[46] This expansive vision of conscience moves in the direction of communal discernment rather than restricting the deliberations of conscience to individualistic concerns. I will build upon these insights to describe a more developed notion of decision-making, or casuistry, expanding its reach to address not only the application of pertinent principles or rules to an analysis of specific moral actions, or paradigm "cases" (*casus*, in Latin), or moral dilemmas, but also to embrace the role of moral agency, in an approach that attends to the formation of character by sharpening core convictions, dispositions, and attitudes of the acting person. This more expansive use of casuistry will be discussed in chapter 5.

Anthony Kelly echoes and amplifies these themes signaled by Johnstone. He suggests a "Paschal Hermeneutics," a model of discernment that challenges the assumption that the historically conditioned settlements of the political and social order are immune to critique and revision. This model heightens our intellectual and spiritual resources to confront a world that awaits its fulfillment. As Paul testifies in the Letter to the Romans, "We know that the whole creation has been groaning as in the pains of childbirth right up to the present time" (Rom 8:22). Kelly states, "The enormous excess of evil, increasingly apparent in its global proportions, is met by another excess, that of love, stronger than any death we know."[47] Kelly highlights four dimensions of the resurrection: its *cognitive* power to illumine the full meaning of Christ's incarnation; its *constitutive* power to "inform and indwell the consciousness of faith, through the ultimate registers of faith, hope, and love"; its *communicative* effect that grounds a universal, "hope-filled solidarity with all victims of violence and injustice"; and finally, its capacity to fashion *effective* or "world-transforming praxis."[48]

These reflections of O'Collins, Johnstone, and Kelly provide a rich resource for appreciating the ethics of discernment in the work of Pope Francis. Confronted with the inescapably tragic dimensions of life, an ethics of "suffering presence," insightfully noted by Stanley Hauerwas, can sustain us with the virtue of hope, and further inspired by the promise of risen life, can help us resist the seductive appeal of the narrow binaries posed by quandary ethics.[49]

As we have seen, the trolley thought experiment ostensibly highlights the contrast between consequentialist/utilitarian logic and deontological/duty-based logic but does so at the risk of truncating the range of moral options available to us on the assumption that the condition of moral extremity is our normal, default, state of reality. This default position is the imperative to decide, even if the decision means choosing the lesser evil or doing evil to achieve as much good as we can. Metaphors and analogies, such as the trolley experiment, are useful to the extent that they illuminate a certain range of concerns, but they become tyrannical by confining us to a narrow rather than a wider lens of moral vision. Laid bare in the trolley strategy is the impoverishment of our moral imaginations reducing us to a limited, if not nugatory, set of ethical possibilities.

To invoke a computer metaphor, as human beings, and especially as Catholic Christian disciples, we have more moral bandwidth available to us in the form of the convictions that hold us and center us in our character and in our conscience. Moral life is not defined by fidelity to the requirements of various kinds of decision trees or ethical algorithms, but by fidelity to the imperatives that shape our characters and our deepest sense of self. For Catholic disciples, it is the person of Jesus Christ who ultimately shapes and forms our moral character.

Even in dire circumstances of moral extremity, one can still ask, "What kind of action, or indeed, nonaction, is appropriate?" Consider the suggestion of Hauerwas about "suffering presence," which opens the possibility of configuring oneself to the suffering of Christ. The seductive lure of decisions and quandaries can blind us to the larger questions of character and integrity that are always operative, subliminally, or "transcendentally" even in these situations of extremity. Some of our most critical moral actions cannot be addressed within the confines of a narrow construal of options, or can be reduced to a cold, cost-benefit calculus. Rather than abandoning or ignoring our disagreeable family relative or aggravating work colleague, we may find that responding with patience and forbearance involves us in a much more profound moral and spiritual assessment: "What kind of person do I become by this specific choice?"; "What kinds of dispositions, skills, or virtues, are essential for me to choose wisely and well?"

These questions challenge the unexamined presuppositions that undergird criteria for successful resolution of moral quandaries. Perhaps one may entertain the possibility of doing "nothing," namely not to pull the switch to change the tracks on which the careening trolley car is moving. Such a choice carries in its wake the inevitable collision with the mystery of tragedy, of suffering, of the confrontation with our finitude and limited ability to manage or control the world. There is an inescapable element of moral luck, of contingency and historical indeterminacy, that is involved.[50] We soon discover that we are not Shelley's *Prometheus Unbound,* but creatures in a world not of our own making. We must contend with the vicissitudes of moral luck and fate, realities that defy our transactional, managerial sensibilities, challenging the illusion, so brilliantly captured by Tom Wolfe in his satire of the financial titans of Wall Street, that we are "masters of the universe."[51]

Focusing exclusively on one's ability to make discrete choices is frequently an impoverishment of our moral imagination. When I reflect on the "choice" that I made to become a priest, I realize now, looking back over more than fifty years of ordained service, that in many ways, the choice of vocation had been shaped by elements antecedent to my adult decision. As the eldest son of a large Roman Catholic family of Irish heritage, blessed with devout, faith-filled parents and endowed with a sensitive, inquiring nature, when you add up these components, my decision was determinative, but not unimpeachably so. I could have "chosen" to pursue a career in miliary aviation, following the distinguished example of my father, but as I reflect more deeply on these matters, Caesar's remark upon crossing the Rubicon, *alea iacta est* (the die is cast), more accurately describes the mysterious promptings of the Holy Spirit in my eventual discernment of vocation.

The confluence of family, faith, spiritual awakening, and wonder generated dispositions, attitudes, and virtues that shaped my character in a manner congruent with the unfolding of a narrative of a vocation to ministry. Rather than a mere "choice," I think my vocation was the fruit of a discernment nurtured by a way of life that rendered it as an "emergent probability," steeped in my personal story of faith that, itself, was already rooted in the narrative of the high priest, Jesus of Nazareth. Perhaps, my vocation was a "fitting" response to the unique constellation of events, influences, and experiences in my life story that remains located within the larger narrative of the community of faith that anchors and holds all our stories within its capacious arms. Vocation, as Frederick Buechner beautifully reminds us, is the place "where your deep gladness and the world's deep hunger meet."[52]

Hauerwas makes a similar point with his story of a husband fantasizing about the prospect of a sexual proposition from a stranger. He is taken aback when the fantasy materializes in the form of an invitation from a flight attendant during a late-night flight with few passengers on board. Much to his surprise, the decision to be faithful to his spouse arises from the depths of his character, shaped by the covenant promise of marital fidelity.

Despite temptation, he refuses the offer. The thin language of "choice" seduces us with the idea that the deep scripts of our lives are revisable at a moment's notice. Issues of character are deep in the marrow of our bones; they are not reducible to surface conceits or the whims of the moment. Far more often than we realize, some choices or options are simply "off the table," when the crisis appears. Character is thicker than the thin reed of passing enticements or fancy.[53]

These elements of character and virtue are, to echo the language of Karl Rahner, "moral transcendentals," implicit in every choice and in every performative act.[54] As we have seen, the four models of ethical deliberation have value as heuristic devices clarifying what is at stake in a moral choice and providing insightful information about the relationships and configurations involved in our deliberations about outcomes, obligations, and responsibilities. Again, these models are helpful, and in many ways illuminating, but they are handmaids to the process of moral discernment. The character of the moral agent, how she or he is disposed to act by a lifetime of formation in the skills and virtues acquired by immersion into a community of moral wisdom, is ultimately determinative in the final analysis.

In his insightful appraisal of the proportionalism debate, Christopher Kaczor attributes the plausibility for its proponents to the neo-Scholastic presuppositions of the manualist tradition—a tradition that we have seen influenced the early career of Josef Fuchs, SJ. Among these features identified by Kaczor is "an emaciated theory of human action prevalent in many manualists and presupposed by proportionalism."[55] Lacking the nourishment of the moral virtues and a robust model of moral agency, theories of moral action in the manualist tradition suffer impoverishment due to the reductionism and narrow constraints of consequences, rules, and obligations. Rather than a separation of action from agency, a solid theory of moral action such as that of Aquinas, holds subject and object in a dynamic unity.[56]

Canadian theologian and philosopher Bernard Lonergan, SJ, emphasizes the dynamic interdependence of our intellectual and volitional capacities. Helpfully, he contrasts classical and modern approaches to the question of human cognition and choice. According to a classical understanding, the process of knowing proceeds in a "top down" fashion, deducing conclusions based on a priori assumptions and conceptual schemes. This model prizes the value of universalizability and searches for the essential core of reality, devoid as far as possible from the contingencies of history and the fluctuations of chance and probability. The modern approach is the regnant scientific method that proceeds inductively, from concrete manifestations of reality to plausible generalizable constructs. This model is at home with contingency and the phenomenon of chance.[57]

Cynthia Crysdale, an astute interpreter of Lonergan's work, highlights the notion of "emergent probability" as a critical qualifier in our grasp of reality.[58] Statistical, empirical variability and contingency are inescapable features of the empirical world in which we are immersed, disclosing novelties that elude predictability and emerge in surprising and diverse ways. The reality of probability, of chance occurrences, of unpredictability, in our experience, modulates the range and extent of our aspirations to realize universal understanding and standardize our expectations of the outcomes from our intellectual quests. Lonergan's assessment of natural law is, "Be Attentive, Be Intelligent, Be Reasonable, Be Responsible, and any other precepts you arrive at, you arrive at by observing these precepts."

These remarks of Lonergan align with the theme of "right reason" that we have seen in our discussion of the intellectual journey of Josef Fuchs. My purpose in this chapter is to trace an important shift in moral theology from a preoccupation with the contours of the moral act, the matter or object of moral deliberation, that is, the "what" we are called to address (e.g., adjudicating medical care for a dying patient, the just ordering of the economy) to a coequal concern for the "who," the moral agent, acting in accordance with her dispositions, inclinations, qualities, motives, and reasons. Formation in moral agency is a dynamic skill and requires the intentional integration of the mind and the heart. As Aristotle argues in *The Nicomachean Ethics*, the good, moral actor, is not someone who is merely "smart," who knows what is worthwhile to pursue, but who is "wise," capable of fine discernment not only with a perception of the good, but a "taste" for it, an experiential, felt inclination for it that moves her to actualize it. I ask my students in moral theology, preparing for ministry, to have "a hard head and a soft heart, not vice versa." In other words, critical thinking and a truthful appraisal of a moral issue is essential to ground a pastorally responsible interpretation and application of the Church's moral wisdom.

Reclaiming this integral, holistic understanding of moral theology is central to my argument for a more comprehensive account of moral rationality or right reason. Right reason includes not only an intellectual grasp of the meaning of moral rules and principles, but an important dimension that is often overlooked in our discernment of right and wrong. This dimension is what Fuchs describes as *cognitio aestimativa* or "estimative/evaluative knowledge." This form of knowing attends to the felt, appropriated, personal appreciation or ownership of a moral value. To know a value or a rule in this way is to claim it as one's own, as a commitment in which one invests wholehearted assent. To use the term preferred by Baptist scholar James Wm. McClendon Jr., moral notions are grasped as convictions not just ideas. They are firm beliefs that if changed, dramatically change us in the depths of our being.

Analogously, St. John Henry Newman famously distinguished between a "notional" assent to the act of faith and a "real" assent to faith.[59] A notional assent remains at the level of an abstract grasp of a doctrinal proposition, such as the statement in the Nicene Creed about the resurrection of Jesus from the dead. A real assent to this doctrine is self-involving, one commits one's whole being to its power and meaning. A commitment to one's participation in this resurrection destiny forms the ultimate horizon for moral deliberation and relativizes, in the process, short-term considerations in favor of deeper, more substantive moral claims. Convictions, as McClendon argues, are "gutsy" commitments to truths to which we cling for dear life.

Formation in these convictions invites us to a deeper conversation about the grammar of the moral life. Before we tease out the implications of the pastoral/moral vision of Pope Francis, a vision that moves us to reclaim the tradition of inductive casuistry, or, if you will, the morality of daily life, requires another step in our story of Catholic moral theology. That step requires consideration of the contributions of narratives and the stories of our moral communities to this process of formation.

In the next chapter, I will devote attention to the work of the leading proponent of communitarian or narrative ethics, Stanley Hauerwas. Despite his professed antipathy to the natural law tradition, I will argue that his understanding of moral character and the formation of the conscience of the moral self are firmly anchored in the deep waters of the moral virtues to which the tradition of natural law, as developed by Aquinas and exemplified in Fuchs's own intellectual journey, is a tributary. Hauerwas's concern for moral character and its careful formation is an authentically Catholic theological concern and echoed in the moral vision of Pope Francis.

4

The Ethics of Discernment

Formation of the Wise Moral Agent

THUS FAR, I HAVE PROVIDED sufficient support for a renewed focus on moral agency to complement the tradition's strong and essential attention to the careful appraisal of the structure of the moral act. Chapter 4 advances the focus on moral agency. I turn here to consider how a model of discernment as defined by Francis can be seen as key to the formation of a wise moral agent capable of good moral action. Discernment as attention to the particular and the distinctive elements in human experience is, in turn, related to a redefinition of the self away from an ethos of individualism and episodic action to one that considers moral actions within a communitarian or narrative trajectory. Inherent in the root meaning of the word *discern* is the capacity to "listen." Attending to the particularities of our experience, the details and shadings, the contours and contexts of the possibilities that emerge in our lives is at the heart of moral discernment.

This chapter also explores the work of the leading proponent of communitarian or narrative ethics, Stanley Hauerwas. Hauerwas's communitarian narrative approach contends that the image of the moral agent as a solitary rational actor, detached from a distinctive linguistic and cultural community, is a mistake. He claims that human beings are not free-floating, unmoored, independent moral entrepreneurs. Rather, they are inherently social; they are embedded in a specific community with a distinctive history whose ongoing story or narrative, including its relationship to God, self, and others, encodes the moral values by which it lives out its most important convictions and whereby they choose to live their lives with integrity. Moreover, their shared experience is expressed in the form of defining narratives or stories that ground and orient their experience of moral reality. I argue that Hauerwas's concern for the dynamic correlation between character and conscience is a helpful contribution to the important recovery of virtue ethics for both Catholic and Protestant ethics. I argue its relevance to the forming of wise moral agents is a quintessentially Catholic concern and outlines the skills or virtues that equip the moral actor to make wise choices and decisions. Acknowledging this narrative turn in ethics, I suggest that the natural law tradition itself is not "story neutral," indeed, the very fact that it constitutes a tradition of ethical discourse is a testament to its formative roots in historically informed philosophical and theological narratives.[1] In other words, the concept of the natural law is also rooted in a narrative tradition, for it too has a history of distinctive voices who have debated and disputed with one another in different contexts and epochs. In this sense, one can see that the natural law can be understood as fulfilling Alasdair MacIntyre's understanding of a tradition that is a sustained argument over time about significant matters.[2]

Hauerwas and Moral Anthropology

Charles Davis, in a short but insightful book, *Temptations of Religion*, observed that the first and perhaps most pernicious temptation of the religious instinct in humanity is the "lust for certitude."[3] The desire for secure knowledge, intellectually and morally, is a noble pursuit. However, such a pursuit, while a possibility for angelic, pure spirits, is both unrealistic and unattainable for finite, enfleshed human beings, whose spirits are wedded, inexorably and existentially, to the material conditions of finite, mortal bodies. For Christian disciples, the doctrine of the incarnation of the second person of the Trinity, divinely embodied in Jesus Christ, is a reminder that human life cannot escape the conditions of finitude, vulnerability, and dependence that are inherent in its very structure.[4] Such an admission, of course, is not a concession to, much less an endorsement of, moral relativism. Far from it.

Rather, as Aquinas makes clear, the certainty that accrues to moral deliberation and action is moral certainty, that is, the certainty appropriate to the ineluctable element of contingency that characterizes our lot as finite human beings subject to the vicissitudes of history, time, and mortality.

Inherent in the root meaning of the word *discernment* is the capacity to "listen." Attending to the particularities of our experience, the details and shadings, the contours and contexts of the possibilities that emerge in our lives is at the heart of moral discernment. It is an activity of skillful interpretation that involves evaluation, judgment, fine perception, and a capacity for objectivity, for seeing things as they truly are. Discernment is a critical tool of assessment to ascertain and then select, among an array of options for choice and action, which is the most fitting and desirable. Dennis Billy, CSSR, moral theologian and spiritual director, notes that "'discernment' comes from the Latin, *discernere*, which literally means 'to sever,' and which has been transferred metaphorically into 'to distinguish.'"[5] As a form of "wise discretion," according to the early Church father, the monk Cassian, discernment enabled the faithful to distinguish between good and evil. However, its significance expanded beyond a minimalistic determination of right and wrong to a much more supple tool to seek what is best in our striving for the good. Billy helpfully notes that discernment in the Catholic tradition attends "to three levels of meaning: a doctrinal dimension having to do with separating true from false teaching, a moral one having to do with telling good from evil, and an advanced spiritual sensitivity having to do with distinguishing between two goods in order to understand God's will for one's life and thus follow the more appropriate course of action."[6] I will focus my remarks on this moral aspect of the discernment process.

In an insightful, theologically rich, and practical guide to the process of discernment, moral theologian Richard Gula notes, "'Discernment' is the privileged name that we give to the decision-making process that reaches into the heart of one's fundamental commitment to God."[7] Moreover, he further comments that "in discernment, we ask not only, 'Is this action right?' but we also ask, 'Is acting this way consistent with my fundamental commitment to God? Does it fit who I am and who I want to become as a disciple of Jesus for today?'"[8]

The novelist and philosopher Iris Murdoch describes this

process as one of "un-selfing," that is, self-detachment that frees us from the tyranny of the "fat, relentless ego," and its imperial desires. The characters in Murdoch's fictional world traverse the journey to authentic discernment by adhering to the claims of a sovereign notion of goodness that delivers them from the illusory attractions of partial goods masquerading as ultimate values.[9]

To return to the "spoiler alert" that prefaced my discussion of ethical models, despite the heuristic value of these various approaches, the focus of these perspectives, especially those focused on outcomes or obligations, is on moral action with scant attention to agency and the character of the moral agent. Addressing these elements is crucial if we are to achieve a more coherent and integrated approach to the task of ethical deliberation. I am indebted to the labors of Stanley Hauerwas, who has been at the forefront of the effort to reclaim a different moral anthropology rooted in a recovery of crucial habits or virtues that require immersion and formation in communities of discourse shaped by traditions of argument and purpose that have developed over time. Recovering these skills is essential to wise deliberation and discernment of what is morally good for us.

Hauerwas reminds us that, as moral agents, we are never detached from the linguistic community whose narratives or stories provide the intellectual and moral architecture whereby we perceive, interpret, and respond to the world that we inhabit with life's fellow sojourners. One such story is the tale of Enlightenment rationalism that aspires to privilege reason as a "neutral" arbiter of meaning, detached from the entanglements of religion or other localized communities of discourse. Thomas Nagle describes this aspiration as the "view from nowhere."[10] Embedded in this claim to escape from the constraints of particularity, a story of "no-story" is quite a tale, nonetheless. In this account we are solitary decision-makers, occupying a perch on an intellectual Mt. Olympus, equipped with a panoramic view of reality, uniquely poised to apply our reason in search of pure, unsullied, universality.[11] The "narrative ethics" of Hauerwas, with its commitment to historical location and to the ineliminable particularity of morally freighted language, nursed and shaped by story-formed communities, is a bracing antidote to the flattening effects of the Enlightenment project of abstract rationalism that eviscerates differences in its pursuit of universalizable norms and concepts.

To frame my remarks on the contours of this contrast between the aspiration for a "common ground," or shared set of concepts and categories for ethical actions, and an alternative vision of ethics rooted in the assertion that we cannot escape the particularity of our distinctive cognitive communities, including our communities of faith, let me propose that when I refer to "narrative-dependent" moral notions, I am referring to "communitarian perspectives," that is, moral notions anchored in the lived experiences that fund the discourse and linguistic traditions of distinctive, historically vibrant communities of faith and wisdom. In this construal, moral notions and the practices they inspire cannot be separated from these stories encoded, in the case of the Christian Catholic tradition, in the canons of Sacred Scripture and its second-order reflections that constitute a rich, theological conversation with many interlocutors. On the other side of this debate, when I invoke the term *narrative independent,* I am referring to those who argue that moral notions, concepts, and patterns of ethical discernment are not exclusively or definitively confined to narrative accounts embedded in communities of faith. Hauerwas sharply disputes any such claims of narrative independent moral discourse. Mindful of a courtesy intrinsic to medieval Scholastic disputations, namely, not to contradict the major premise of one's opponent in an argument, I hope I will offer some helpful distinctions to bridge these divides in the spirit of *concedo, sed distinguo*... (I concede but distinguish...).

The explication of the narrative-independent characterization of moral principles, rules, and norms can also be described as a claim that there are open-source warrants for a fund of common ground or shared categories of moral knowledge. These arguably "narrative-neutral" notions are contrasted with closed-source concepts reflecting the imprimatur of a distinctive narrative community. Here is where the argument is joined. Communitarians contend that there are no "open-source" concepts, that each of them, in some fashion or other, owes its pedigree to the normative convictions encoded in a particular story or narrative.

Acknowledging this narrative turn in ethics, I suggest that the natural law tradition itself is not "story neutral," indeed, the very fact that it constitutes a tradition of ethical discourse is a testament to its formative roots in historically informed philosophical and theological narratives.[12] The location of the discussion of the natural law within the *Treatise on the Virtues* in the *Summa Theologiae* of Aquinas is a hermeneutical key to its theological significance, a point astutely noted by the Thomistic scholar Fergus Kerr, OP.[13] Nonetheless, I am disposed to argue that there are significant points of intersection rather than a sharp divide between formalistic, theoretical ethical constructs such as the Enlightenment project we have noted, a position Hauerwas characterizes as the "standard account of morality," and the narrative construal of moral discourse.

In his criticism of narrative ethics, James Gustafson raises the prospect of a sectarian temptation in communitarian ethical schemes, namely a retreat into privatized enclaves of moral language bereft of the capacity to engage, or achieve common ground, with alternative conceptions of the moral life.[14] Moreover, without careful discernment, proponents of the narrative turn are not immune from a form of the totalizing hubris that afflicts the standard account of morality, in this case, not the "view from nowhere," the fortress of the gods of reason declaiming from a purportedly objective and intellectually neutral Mt. Olympus, but a narrow fideism pontificating from the citadel of faith, Mt. Zion. However, as Hauerwas contends, successfully so in my opinion, the way to overcome this moral and intellectual cleavage is dialectical, critical engagement so that a sustained moral argument can clarify and purify distortions and misconceptions that creep into ethical deliberations.[15]

Hauerwas is rightly acknowledged as a champion of narrative ethics. The distinctive story-formed character of communities of faith enables these communities to develop a rigorous, internally coherent, and contextually sensitive logic that shapes our reasoning powers to discern choices and actions befitting disciples of a Savior, crucified and risen from the dead. This discernment occurs in the context of a world whose values are often alien to those of the gospel. There is much merit in this approach. The Christian "scandal of particularity" is maintained with vigor and sustains the mission of the Church to act as witness to a different world, a world seen in the light of the paschal mystery, the death and resurrection of Christ. Powerful as this vision of Christian ethics is, care is necessary to avoid a form of moral imperialism that can arise when underlying presuppositions and justifications for deeply held moral convictions are immunized from the annealing effects of critical debate, argument, and engagement with alternative and possibly contradictory philosophical, and theological viewpoints.

A critic of Hauerwas, albeit an appreciative one, Paul Nelson, challenges the Hauerwasian claim that narratability is the paramount lens through which the Christian moral agent assesses right and wrong. Nelson disputes that Hauerwas has adequately demonstrated that moral rules and principles are ineluctably narrative dependent, and that the liberty of the agent to make determinations about which narrative are true or false (and worthy of pursuit) is sufficiently addressed in terms of moral psychology. Is the individual free, in other words, to make these distinctions and judgments on grounds other than those provided by the warrants and commitments of a narrative community?[16]

Nelson is raising an important distinction that, in my view, is not destructive to the proponents of narrative ethics. That is, the capacity to make logical distinctions of inference, such as the principle of noncontradiction (a thing cannot be and not be at one and the same time), appears to me to be an example of a critical thinking skill that funds the capacity to discriminate among competing and conflicting moral claims, and is, in this sense, displayed by and not restricted to any narrative rendition. The content, of course, that funds the exercise of this skill is indeed narrative dependent. According to philosopher Stanley Cavell, "reason is nobody's property," an apt description of the innate capacity to exercise critical thinking that grounds the possibility of dialogue, and, perhaps, consensus among competing moral visions.

The Ugandan moral theologian Emmanuel Katongole has authored a masterful, critically acclaimed interpretation of Hauerwas's extensive body of work.[17] Hauerwas pens an approving introduction to the book, expressing appreciation for Katongole's skill in bringing order and clarity to the manifold intellectual trajectories in his eclectic and wide-ranging theological enterprise. Katongole provides a much-needed interpretive matrix to assess the kaleidoscope of themes, ideas, and arguments Hauerwas has elaborated in multiple formats—books, reviews, essays, and scholarly collaborations. Hauerwas refines and sharpens his insights in the parry and thrust of disputations with a diverse set of conversation partners. Among the key themes that Katongole has identified are the following (that we have also noted thus far): the flight from particularity in the standard account of ethics, the notions of historicity and contingency in moral matters, and the importance of character and moral agency that are formed and shaped through critical participation in distinctive communities of fellow travelers on life's journey.

Katongole helps us to appreciate that, absent substantive agreement or consensus about what is morally significant—the central indictment of Hauerwas and Alasdair MacIntyre of the Enlightenment project to secure universal reason—we are left with, at best, procedural rules to guide us in the contentious, fragmented culture of modernity. Kevin Wildes, SJ, in his insightful treatment of bioethical methodologies, *Moral Acquaintances*, makes a case for moral proceduralism as a defensible strategy to secure some form of consensus among contending and conflicting moral actors.[18] These actors, while they may not be friends with substantive agreement on how to approach life's dilemmas, may, however, as "acquaintances," that is, with a modicum of shared values (e.g., procedural justice in allocating medical resources), share sufficient overlapping commitments on contentious matters to provide a rough compact on how to navigate moral disagreement. The problem, of course, is that the consensus tends to be quite thin and breaks down under the weight of more complex and substantive matters. The question is, can we do better than the minimalism inherent in moral proceduralism? I believe that we can with a more robust model of moral discernment.

Notwithstanding the merits of Nelson's critique of Hauerwas (echoing similar criticisms from other scholars including Gene Outka and J. Wesley Robbins concerning the feasibility of non-narrative dependent moral notions), Nelson is, however, firmly in support of the claims of narrative ethics. He finds in Hauerwas a much-needed counterweight to the broken landscape of contemporary moral discourse that MacIntyre has described in *After Virtue*.[19]

That is, we are inheritors of discrete moral fragments, whether of Aristotelian, Scholastic, Kantian, or postmodern provenance, lacking coherence, and an integrating scheme of moral order. An example previously noted in chapter 1, the virtue of courage is illustrative. In the absence of attention to its distinctive shape within the social and moral architecture of the community in which it is housed, the meaning of courage is underdetermined.

For the Spartan warrior, courage is bravery under the auspices of an honor code that valorizes personal glory. For the Christian disciple, however, courage is bravery in the pursuit of the good of discipleship, even at the cost of one's life.

For purposes of the goal of this chapter, namely moral discernment, we need not be forced into an exclusive choice between a moral theology that draws insights from the ethical implications of the created order, accessible, at least inchoately, to critical intelligence (think natural law and Cavell's observation of the ability to reason), or an ethics grounded in the intellectual and moral vocabulary of revelation theology expressed in the biblical narratives that anchor Christian communities of faith.

The danger of relying on purely formal rules and principles to secure consensus among multiple stakeholders, theists and nontheists alike, is that these rules must necessarily be quite thin in terms of substantive content. The strength of narrative claims is that they provide a more robust or "thick" description of what is worthy of moral pursuit.[20] Another way to conceptualize this difference is to contrast an ethics for strangers with an ethics rooted in friendship.[21] Strangers share only minimal expectations, for example not to be killed or to abide by basic rules to govern the fair exchange of goods and services. An ethics of friendship, however, forms erstwhile strangers into a community sharing a vision, a goal that shapes opportunities for its members to flourish and thrive.

Discernment implies the ability to make discriminating assessments and judgments. As I will discuss in the next chapter, discernment is refined and developed in the practice of casuistry—the venerable tradition of comparing paradigm cases or examples of challenging ethical situations to extract criteria for evaluation that arise from the analogies and patterns observed in different, but similar contexts. Engagement with alternative portrayals of "the good life" invariably entails the virtues of honesty and a commitment to truthfulness. Though one may demur, as Hauerwas does, that the natural law tradition is, perforce, indebted to the richly textured narratives of distinctive moral communities to more fulsomely display the convictions that warrant our allegiance, nonetheless its importance as a valuable philosophical anchor that funds moral rationality should not be summarily discounted.

The narrative turn in ethics richly informs the insightful work of Thomistic scholar Pamela Hall. Her text *Narrative and the Natural Law* affirms the importance of historical discovery of moral claims to inform and shape the secondary precepts of the natural law, that is, the more explicit precepts or claims that emerge from the lived experience of human communities.[22] This attention to detail resists the crude reductionism of grand narratives, such as the Enlightenment aspiration to universal reason. This account of moral rationality views religion as a pernicious source of partisan conflict, pitting warring theological communities and their singular ethical convictions against one another, and contributing, in the process, to social discord and political violence. However, Enlightenment rationalism is not immune from the corrosive effects of intellectual imperialism, masking its own tyrannical aspiration to moral hegemony behind the cover of an allegedly neutral and benign technocratic logic to maintain cultural and political power.

In Hauerwas's telling criticism, the pretense that Enlightenment rationalism is "story neutral" hides the deeper truth that it is deeply entrenched in its own false narrative, "the story that it has no story." Narrative theological ethics requires, as mentioned previously, critical engagement with other voices lest the narrative approach fall victim to its own version of a false universalism. In weighing the arguments for narrative ethics and natural law, I opt for a complementary perspective that blends these approaches. The tradition of a basic human capacity to exercise critical intelligence, a capacity that funds the possibility of shared moral values, and communitarian, narrative ethical traditions, cohere in a relationship of critical correlation rather than binary isolation.

Tertullian's famous question, "What has Athens to do with Jerusalem?" is a perduring question for the Christian faith. Can or should the wisdom of the secular city, symbolized by Athens, the pinnacle of Greek culture and learning, influence Jerusalem, symbolizing the citadel of faith with its distinctive ethical grammar shaped by allegiance to the "elusive presence," or the wholly Other that is God?[23]

To be clear, I retain my Catholic bona fides of a "both/and" sensibility in support of natural law and narrative ethics. However, the main point that I want to extract from this critical correlation of narrative and natural law is the significance of the issue of character in shaping the practice of moral discernment. In this context, it is worthwhile to devote attention to an earlier work of

Hauerwas, especially the intellectual ecumenism displayed in his doctoral dissertation, *Character and the Christian Life: A Study in Theological Ethics.*[24]

In this study, Hauerwas finds language in Aquinas's retrieval of Aristotle to overcome the impasse in Protestant theology bifurcating, or perhaps more accurately, unduly privileging the singular moment of justification by faith from the ongoing process of growth in holiness and sanctification. For Hauerwas, the retrieval of the language of character and virtue serves as an acceptable scripturally informed narrative framework to account for the stability and structure of the moral life. This biblically friendly discourse serves as a counterpoint to natural law considerations of continuity and order rooted in the moral rationality that is a constitutive mark of human nature conceptualized according to Aristotelian and scholastic philosophical categories.

Character and virtue considerations provide Hauerwas with the tools to rescue Protestant ethics from the debilitating individualism and nominalism of the situation ethics debate we have previously explored. Absent these tools, Protestant ethics, and to be clear, the moral enterprise more broadly, is bereft of the resources to account for the reality of continuity and order in moral experience. Seduced by the lure of the *novum*, the novelty of contingent events, abetted by a theological attentiveness to distinctive moments or occasions of divine revelation, the path to the "wasteland of relativism," decried by Paul Ramsey, is all but assured.[25]

Hauerwas's definition of character as "the qualification of our self-agency by having distinctive qualities and dispositions" is an invitation to recover a thicker account of the moral life, that is, one not imprisoned by a narrow focus on what constitutes a "right" moral choice or action, but one that also attends to the "good" that attracts us and exerts a claim upon our ultimate allegiance to the purpose of our lives.[26]

In a truly fine appreciation of the work of Dame Iris Murdoch, Charles Taylor voices a similar lament about the narrow focus of modern moral philosophy:

> I have tried to sum this up by saying that Anglo-Saxon moral philosophy has tended to see morality as concerned with questions of what we ought to do and to occlude or exclude questions about what it is good to

> be or what it is good to love. The focus is on obligatory action, which means that it turns away from issues in which obligation is not really the issue, as well as those where not just actions but ways of life or ways of being are what we have to weigh.[27]

If moral theology is, at least at one level, helping people to become "whole people in a broken world," an ethics of character, shaped and formed by the cultivation of requisite virtues, is a necessary antidote to a narrow focus on right reason. The formation of a wise, discerning, moral agent is an essential, not a tangential or ancillary, dimension for a comprehensive moral theology. As the noted psychiatrist and devout Episcopalian Robert Coles observes, "Character is what you're like when no one else is looking."[28] Unless the moral good foregrounds our approach to ethics, what counts as a "right" moral action lacks the necessary context, breadth, and depth, to enable us to grasp how this distinctive choice fits with the direction, purpose, and ultimate *telos* of our lives.

A helpful contribution to this conversation about moral character, which concerns the relationship between the particularity of communitarian or narrative construals of the moral life and the universal aspirations of philosophical accounts such as the natural law, is provided by the African moral theologian Paulinus Odozor, CSSp, in his fine volume, *Morality: Truly Christian, Truly African.*[29]

Odozor invokes the novel by the acclaimed Nigerian writer Chinua Achebe, *Things Fall Apart,* to focus his argument.[30] Achebe's novel tells the story of the famed warrior, Okonkwo, and as his story unfolds, Achebe discloses the tension inherent in adhering to the narrow confines of a moral tradition, in this case, a tribal moral tradition, namely the propensity to overlook or dismiss potential distortions and limitations in its ethical architecture. As we have seen in the work of MacIntyre, rubbing shoulders with alternative ethical schemes, in a sustained argument over time, facilitates the potential for clarification, if not expansion, of the interpretive power of a moral tradition.[31]

The precipitating event of moral conflict in the novel is the murder of the wife of Okonkwo's clansman at the hands of a tribe from a neighboring village. To forestall an internecine war of revenge between the two tribes, the boy Ikemefuna is given to

Okonkwo as a ransom. Okonkwo dutifully raises the boy as his own son. However, the village elders, after a process of "palaver" or group discernment, determine that Ikemefuna should be killed to fulfill the demands for retribution by the tribal gods. Should this communal decision be carried out, and who should do so?

One of the elders, Okonkwo's friend Obierika, who dissented from the group decision, advises Okonkwo that he, as the boy's stepfather, should have nothing to do with the killing. Okonkwo refuses, preferring to uphold the traditions and corporate consensus of the tribe. However, as Odozor notes, there is room for Okonkwo to exercise liberty of conscience by refusing to participate in the execution. As Odozor notes,

> Obierika was persistent in his challenge to Okonkwo that he should not have done what he did. It is one thing for the gods to command evil, it is quite another for that command to be obeyed. In other words, human beings must exercise right judgment and act out of freedom and must never allow themselves to become instruments of evil, even if it is to please the divinity.... If there is doubt that human beings feel bound to their consciences in traditional African ethics, this story is proof that they do indeed. For despite possible pressure from the community or from some interest group in the community, Obierika's position makes it clear that, important as the community input is, the individual conscience is considered the ultimate guide and final arbiter in the choice an individual makes or in the position he or she takes on any given issue.[32]

Odozor's account underscores the importance of truthfulness as an essential criterion for the formation of an upright character responsive to the ethical imperatives that arise from the claims of conscience, a notion to which I will turn in short order. At this point, it is helpful to address a theological construct, developed in the work of Josef Fuchs and Karl Rahner, that parallels Hauerwas's depiction of character, namely, stable perseverance in pursuit of the good. This construct, the subject of significant debate among Catholic moralists, is the notion of the fundamental option.

The fundamental option is an exercise of a capacity within

the human person that Rahner calls "transcendental freedom." Transcendental freedom expresses an existential, perduring quality of moral and spiritual agency, an orientation or disposition toward ultimate goodness, that, in turn, is expressed in concrete, particular acts or choices, or, in Rahner's terminology, as moments of "categorical freedom."[33] There is a dynamic interplay between these two dimensions of moral agency. In an insightful review of the notion of the fundamental option, Thomistic scholar Jean Porter observes that the construct of the fundamental option, as developed by Fuchs and Rahner, is articulated at a high level of intellectual abstraction and suffers from the absence of examples of concrete instantiations of its significance for human moral agents. While the notion of the fundamental option is a philosophically useful device, I think the notion of character is a more robust and supple term. A person's character develops over time and requires formation in virtues if it is to be a truthful bearer of stability amid the vagaries and contingencies of life. Porter is sympathetic to the intention behind the notion, namely the effort to overcome a particular problem in moral theology that takes the form of a zero-sum game whereby the human subject, by virtue of a particular choice, is either in a state of grace or a state of alienation or sin.

However, mindful that by Aquinas's reckoning a singular departure from graced communion with the divine warrants the loss of *caritas* or loving union with the divine, Porter contends that Aquinas develops a robust notion of *caritas* that avoids a simplistic consignment of the sinner to perdition based on a singular lapse from grace.[34]

Porter's comments are well taken, and I prefer to expand upon them by appealing to the notion of character as an analogue to the notion of the fundamental option. In a similar vein, Charles Curran argues for the term *fundamental stance* as an alternative formulation of the fundamental option.[35] There are advantages in the terms *stance* and *character*. This linguistic reframing points to the key concept behind the fundamental option, namely a stable pattern of continuity in the moral life. The fundamental option, or character/stance, is the fruit of specific, determinative, moral choices and actions. It constitutes a *habitus*, or way of life that is cognizable and coherent. For example, my sister Mary Anne's actions on behalf of struggling students manifests her stance/option/character as a compassionate person.

However, while personal actions and choices contribute to this moral stability, there remains a certain level of indeterminacy about our actual status before the Creator. As finite human beings whose moral and spiritual history unfolds in time, we can never have perfect, complete, or to use Rahner's term *reflexive*, definitive knowledge about our actual relationship with God. The classic Latin adage *agere sequitur esse* (action flows from being) reminds us of the provisional character of the fundamental option, that it depends on and shaped by discrete choices and actions. It is a testament to the enduring quality of our moral history. This history is sturdy, but given the condition of finitude, not immutable, and can be gyroscopically disoriented if it is not carefully nurtured and tended by wise discernment.

To invoke a fine insight by the political scientist Sheldon Wolin, sociopolitical institutions and cultural arrangements that have emerged throughout human history coalesce into what he calls "tentative stabilities."[36] That is, they acquire normative status and are not easily destabilized. This notion of "tentative stability" can be aptly applied to the notion of the fundamental option or moral character.[37]

In its cautionary observations about the moral implications of the fundamental option debate, the Vatican declaration *Persona Humana* (1975) notes that to assert that one's ultimate disposition *avant de Dieu* (before God) can resist erosion from discrete, individual departures, from this basic orientation, would be a caricature of the moral life. Moreover, it would be no less of a caricature to claim that one's relationship with God is guaranteed despite individual transgressions. That would be to fall into the pernicious sin of presumption. An important takeaway from this debate is that the relationship between character (or fundamental option) and the choices and decisions we make is dynamic and interdependent.

The Interdependence of the Notions of Character and Conscience

Thus far, I have made a case for the significance of character and its formation as crucial to the process of moral discernment.

There is an intriguing overlap between the notion of character and the term *moral conscience,* more common in Catholic circles. What is the difference? After all, they often seem to be interchangeable, if not synonymous, concepts. Mohandas Gandhi, Thomas More, and Dr. Martin Luther King Jr. are often cited as paradigmatic instances of individuals who display ultimate allegiance to the claims of conscience, even at the cost of their lives. Whether it is Gandhi's *satyagraha* (nonviolent resistance), Dr. King's embrace of nonviolence in service of the "beloved community," Joan of Arc's fidelity to her guiding spiritual visions, or Thomas More's refusal to abandon obedience to papal authority, each of these commitments constitutes a sacrosanct boundary, a sacred core, that cannot be transgressed or violated.

Permit me to suggest a distinction.

Philippe Delhaye's deeply textured analysis of conscience traces the development of the notion of *synderesis* through Aristotle, Greco-Roman philosophy, and ultimately, its shape in the work of Aquinas. Synderesis is the basic disposition to recognize the claim of moral good wherever and whenever it appears. Delhaye highlights Aquinas's definition, namely conscience as "the habit of the first principles of the practical reason."[38] By this account, conscience or synderesis is not a discrete faculty, but an inclination, a disposition, an active orientation of the moral agent, or "habit," that responds to the lure of goodness and seeks its realization in our choices and actions. Popular images of conscience as a "light" or "voice" are helpful metaphors but should not be construed as though conscience somehow stands apart from the agent, holistically understood, as a kind of doppelganger or second self to guide moral deliberation. The beautiful description of conscience in the Vatican II document *Gaudium et Spes* (16) as "the inner most core and sanctuary of the human person where we are alone with God whose voice echoes in our depths," testifies to a divine presence within us that, like a tuning fork, resonates with our own spirit to awaken us to moral goodness. This harmonious synchronization of our deepest self with our divine destiny roots the practices that flow from the exercise of conscience as the "habitus" of our practical intellect, that aspect of our cognitive capacity directed to the contingent matters that constitute the moral life.

Conscience, as its Latin roots indicate, is *con-scire* (a "knowing with") a moral "north star" that links us to a truthful grasp of reality and solidarity with others in the human family. It is our most intimate sense of selfhood, the sanctuary that roots us and grounds our choices and actions. The great African American preacher and teacher Dr. Howard Thurman captures its essence beautifully, without mentioning the word *conscience*, in his 1980 commencement address at Spelman College, "The Sound of the Genuine":

> There is something in every one of you that waits, listens for the sound of the genuine in yourself and if you cannot hear it you will never find whatever it is for which you are searching and if you hear it and then do not follow it, it was better that you had never been born....
>
> You are the only you that has ever lived; your idiom is the only idiom of its kind in all of existence and if you cannot hear the sound of the genuine within you, you will all of your life spend your days on the ends of strings that somebody else pulls....
>
> There is in you something that waits and listens for the sound of the genuine in yourself and sometimes there is so much traffic going on through your minds, so many different kinds of signals, so many vast impulses floating through your organism that go back thousands of generations, long before you were even a thought in the mind of creation, and you are buffeted by these, and in the midst of all of this you have got to find out what your name is. Who are you? How does the sound of the genuine come through to you?
>
> ...The sound of the genuine is flowing through you. Don't be deceived and thrown off by all the noises that are a part even of your dreams, your ambitions, so that you don't hear the sound of the genuine in you, because that is the only true guide you will ever have, and if you don't have that you don't have a thing.[39]

These powerful words give depth to the equally poetic notion of *Gaudium et Spes* and its depiction of conscience as the "inner most core and sanctuary of every human person."[40] *Conscience* describes the sense of ultimate accountability that is critical to the formation of one's distinctive character or "way of being" in the world. It is a profound metaphor for our deepest sense of integrity, honor, and beauty. We catch glimpses of these values in our ordinary, daily round of choices and actions. This "sound of the genuine" accompanies us as a guardian angel, as it were, a reality perceived indirectly but no less truly in our lived experience. It is this call from our depth that persuades us to be faithful to our spouse when we are tempted to stray with another, or that enables us to resist a temptation to depart from our calling. Conversely, and more constructively, it is the summons to the "deep gladness," in the beautiful words of Frederick Buechner, that awakens us to meet the world's great need, a movement of the spirit whereby we find our life's vocation.[41]

Looming behind this compelling vision, is the towering figure of John Henry Newman, whose magisterial insights into the growth and development of Christian doctrine and the inviolable sanctity of conscience inform the theological architecture of the conciliar decrees of the Second Vatican Council.[42] This conscience is the moral center, captured by the biblical image of the "heart," of every person. It is an orientation, an inclination—to use Thomistic language—that responds to the claims of truth and goodness. We betray it to our peril. According to Newman, "conscience is the aboriginal Vicar of Christ."[43] Conscience in this conception awakens us and alerts us to values, to a basic notion of goodness, that invites our response.

As I reflect upon the relationship between conscience and character, conscience stands to character as a skill, a habitus or disposition that funds a set of practices or concrete actions, namely, habits or virtues that form, over time, a person of character, that is, someone with a stable moral identity. The relationship is one of dynamic interdependence—to strengthen or weaken one element of the dyad has a correlative impact on the other element. Discernment, accordingly, is the practice of disciplined attention to these components and nurturing their maturation.[44]

To balance an excessive focus on technical, abstract moral logic, formation of the wise moral actor requires skills and abilities that complement critical thinking skills. William Spohn devoted his scholarship to the pursuit of these attributes, expressed most cogently in his fine book *Go and Do Likewise: Jesus and Ethics*.[45] Influenced by the work of the Puritan divine Jonathan Edwards, especially *The Religious Affections*, Spohn describes these affections or dispositions as laden with cognitive power, not just the fruit of feeling and emotion. They are essential to the cultivation of a "reasoning heart." Spohn provides a pathway toward a different construal of the much-debated question about a "distinctively Christian ethics."

On one side of this question are those who dispute whether religious faith, expressed in the narrative forms of parables, images, stories, dispositions, and attitudes displayed in the Hebrew and Christian scriptures, contributes any substantive content to ethical deliberation. At best, by this accounting, such elements provide motivational support for ethical criteria arrived at on philosophical or secular grounds. Do faith-based narratives serve merely as a poetic accompaniment to ethical deliberation, or do these narratives provide substantive, distinctive, ethical content? Spohn takes the substantive side of the debate, contending that formation in Christian discipleship provides both content and motivation for action, and is constitutive and essential to the Christian moral life.

Spohn argues that a great deal of mischief about the relationship between scriptural narrative and ethics arises if we consider scripture exclusively as a book of rules filled with specific moral dictates.[46] To be sure, the narratives in Exodus and Deuteronomy about the gift of the law to Moses, the conferral of the commandments, as well as the proclamation of the Beatitudes in the Sermon on the Mount, provide evidence of morally charged teaching. However, scripture is a library of books forming a canon of literature that incorporates diverse literary genres—poetry (the Song of Songs), hymns, psalms, parables, prophecy—each of which requires skillful exegesis and interpretation. If, because of this complexity, scripture is construed quite differently, not as a rule book but as community-shaping discourse, forming disciples of character, a much richer and robust portrait of scripture as a moral resource emerges.[47]

Forming a community of disciples who discern their way in the world focuses on our identity as moral actors, as agents empowered with a counternarrative to the story of a world that knows not its Creator nor its final destiny. This more expansive view of scripture accentuates the cultivation of a moral imagination marked by root dispositions, virtues, attitudes, and skills. It develops, in other words, capacities beyond the faculty of critical reason, right reason.

Thus far, the case for discernment that I have been proposing rests on appeals to the cultivation of distinctive dispositions, virtues, and practices to orient the directive power of this key notion of right reason. Spohn's idea of the "reasoning heart" provides an entrée for a more fulsome description of a particular attribute for discernment that has been accentuated by Pope Francis, namely the notion of mercy. The Thomistic axiom that "mercy tempers justice" is well known, but Pope Francis has developed it as a guiding principle for moral discernment. A more expansive treatment of William Spohn's contributions to a holistic model of discernment to guide moral decisions is in order.

William Spohn, who died prematurely of cancer in 2005, left behind an impressive legacy of moral reflection with a special focus on the logic of moral discernment. As a doctoral student, he was strongly influenced by his teacher, James Gustafson, who noted that the relationship between Christian discipleship and the moral life involved more than adherence to publicly defensible, rationally articulated rules or principles specifying which desirable purposes, duties, or obligations, were worthy of pursuit. Spohn claims that the moral life moves beyond a response to the question "Is this action morally right?" to the more personal question of appropriateness, "Is this action consistent with who I am and want to become? What sort of person does this type of action?"[48]

The purpose of this contrast is not to undermine the necessity for establishing intellectually defensible reasons for one's actions, but to underscore the coequal necessity for "reasons of the heart" to complement "reasons of the head." As Spohn contends, human beings do not uniformly make moral decisions by a pure application of the "practical syllogism," that is, invoking a rule or principle, applying it to a concrete issue, and reaching a moral conclusion. For example, I offer this formulation of a principle: "Direct killing of a person to alleviate suffering (euthanasia) is wrong but administering a life-shortening pain medication to alleviate excruciating suffering for this patient is not a direct intention to kill the patient, therefore, the administration of the medication does not violate the rule and is permissible."

Just as one does not consciously advert to all the muscular movements involved in the act of walking as one decides to move from the living room to the dining room, so, Spohn argues, a similar pattern occurs with many, if not most, moral decisions. That is, the moral agent, who has cultivated well-formed habits, dispositions, and perceptions, "senses" what is most fitting and appropriate, justified by reasons of "affectivity" coordinated, of course, with criteria that pass the test of rational scrutiny. Reasons of affectivity are not irrational. Rather, they are subjected to publicly defensible criteria such as harmony, a sense of interior peace, order, beauty, due measure or proportion, and similar qualities. Moral judgments presuppose defensible, rational justifications, but, operationally, are exercised by the agent connaturally, or with ease, without requiring a formal application of discursive logic.

Moral discernment is the art of making discriminating judgements and requires both a reasoning head and a reasoning heart. Such judgments, as Spohn argues, involve a determination that the proposed action or choice is not only "right," but also "fitting," in that it satisfies a comprehensive process of evaluation. Criteria for rational judgment are global, that is they pass the test of consistency, fairness, and impartiality, in short, a capacity for applicability in a generalizable sense, beyond the limits of individual preference. These reasons are grounded in objectivity, the claim of reality upon all, which is the central claim of the natural moral law.

Reasons of affectivity and reasons of discursive intelligence, are, to invoke Romano Guardini's notion of polarity, interdependent, dynamic reference points, or poles of moral knowledge. They cannot be collapsed into one another. Judgements of affectivity, while they attend to matters that are particular and contingent, that are rooted in our immediate experience of the world, are not purely private assertions and are publicly defensible. The evidence can be examined, objectively, to test the fruitfulness of this coordinated wedding of mind and heart. Criteria of fruitfulness, peace, and joy in a decision are no less reasonable than recourse to the clarity of well-formed rules and principles expressed in propositional form. Reasons of the head and reasons of the heart form the ecology of moral knowledge.

Moral description is woven into the fabric of language, and is not reducible to a private, internal mental operation. Later, Wittgenstein moved away from his earlier position in the *Tractatus*, viewing language as communication that is reducible to its smallest "bits" of information, akin to reducing the atom to its fundamental particles. He shifted, in his *Philosophical Investigations,* to a more dynamic model of language that views human discourse as inextricably lodged in networks of communal, shared meaning, that it is inherently, and inescapably, woven into the social fabric of human life. Moral discernment is similarly rooted in communal networks of meaning that anchor shared values and perceptions of what is worthy of pursuit by moral agents. Discernment is the enterprise of connecting reasons of the head and reasons of the heart, viewing them as dialogical partners.

Our perceptions, our felt responses to multiple sources of information, attune us to the world around us. Aquinas, taking a cue from Aristotle, reminds us that "nothing is in the mind that is not first presented to us in the senses." Human knowledge is not angelic knowledge, a form of pure intellection, but a wedding of intellect with the information gleaned from our significance-laden senses that connect us to the world around us. Our perceptions and dispositions or inclinations are not mere registrations of our emotional response to the world around us. Our perceptions are, to put it more precisely, educable and amenable to further development by our immersion into the shared moral experience of the human family.

The feeling of compassion or mercy is, at one level, a "gut level" response to the suffering of a homeless person we encounter on a city street. In an intriguing typology of various models of Christian ethics, this strand of moral response has been described by James Wm. McClendon Jr. as the "splanchnic" strand of ethics, taken from the Greek word *splanchnein,* to be moved from one's "bowels" or depths. It is a word applied to the compassion of Jesus in the Gospel of Mark, as he is moved with pity for the hungry crowd on the shores of the Sea of Galilee (Mark 6:34–40).

McClendon notes that this first level, splanchnic response is further refined by experience with the shared sensibility of a moral community that expands and interprets this immediate, felt response of a "distressed heart" (the root meaning of the word *mercy,* from the Latin *miserum cors*—a distressed heart) at the suffering of another human person. McClendon describes this response rooted in the practices of a moral community, as the "somatic" strand, that is, not the "body" (the Greek word *soma*) of an individual, but the corporate body of a moral community and its correlative rule of life.

The third strand that McClendon develops is the "anastatic," from the Greek word *anastasis*, "against the static order," a term used in theology to describe the transcendent power of the resurrection of Christ from the dead. The anastatic strand in ethics is the prophetic, critical edge of a moral community that enlarges its moral horizons beyond even the contours of a specific community of faith. The key point is that together, these three strands contribute to the tensile strength of a moral community, which like a rope composed of individual strands of fibers, incorporates the strength of each moral dimension into a more comprehensive ethical vision.[49] It is this interdependence that informs the strength and contribution of the individual elements so that the whole is greater than the sum of the parts. An analogy from the world of aviation helps to underscore the constellation of skills required for discriminating moral discernment.

My father, a distinguished fighter pilot, with whom I flew as a private pilot in his Cessna 182 (love for flight was part of our family DNA), constantly stressed the critical importance of cultivating "relaxed awareness" when flying an aircraft. That is, the skill of flying is an artistic process, akin to the skills of a musician or a painter, involving multiple competencies, not just mastery of the technical principles of aerodynamics, but the ability to navigate and maintain the finely tuned attentiveness or "feel" for what the airplane is doing from moment to moment. These attributes contribute to the critical perspective known as "situational awareness." Good pilots make prompt, small adjustments to maintain a stable, smooth configuration in all parts of the flight envelope, from take-off to cruise control to landing. Situational awareness complements the equally necessary obligation to follow procedures, to "fly by the book," to operate an aircraft competently and safely. A good aviator combines finely honed habits or "stick and rudder" skills with intellectual mastery of the science of aviation to achieve proficiency in the craft of flight, just as a proficient moral actor combines knowledge of moral rules and principles with the practical skills of discernment to choose wisely and well.

Our repertoire of moral skills involves our rational and affective capabilities. Spohn explores the implications of this holistic appraisal of moral discernment in his excellent book *Go and Do Likewise: Jesus and Ethics.*[50] Spohn's study of the work of the nineteenth-century Puritan divine, Jonathan Edwards, especially

Edwards's acclaimed *Treatise on the Religious Affections*, enabled him to develop a more substantive, material content to the role of emotions and dispositions as an essential complement to discursive, propositionally formed, rules and principles. Spohn finds Edwards an important resource to refine and extend the model of personal moral and spiritual discernment developed by the founder of the Society of Jesus, Ignatius Loyola. The Ignatian exercises involve a tradition of progressive probing and testing of possible candidates for moral and spiritual action, to ascertain which of these offerings is authentic and genuinely worthy of pursuit. This intensive examination of these possible desiderata or "spirits" leads the individual to a distinctive, personal, appropriation of the human values and goals that undergird the global, moral experience of humankind.

In his astute essay on the implications of this "particularizing" refinement of Ignatian spirituality for moral theology, Karl Rahner contrasts two moments in this process that remain interdependent and connected. On the one hand, there is the "essential" component of ethics, or what can be described as the natural moral law, grounded in a confidence in the capacity of human reason to assess what are worthwhile and truthful goods to pursue and achieve. On the other hand, complementing this common ground morality of reasoned moral argument and discourse, is the more granular, fine-tuned, sensibility that attends to what is unique and distinctive to the individual person in his or her formation of conscience and interior life. This moment, or component, Rahner describes as "existential ethics."[51]

Matters such as determining one's calling or vocation in life, or one's personal encounter with divine grace in prayer, are examples of this heightened Ignatian process of discernment. Ultimately, however, Rahner relies upon a formal transcendental consciousness within the individual, albeit trained and schooled by the exercises of the Ignatian model, without developing more explicit descriptions of the elements that shape and form this level of heightened, existential, consciousness. It is at this point that Spohn's invocation of Edwards and H. Richard Niebuhr provides the tools to articulate a more substantive portrayal of the "reasoning heart."

The metaphor of a reasoning heart is not code for moral intuitionism or subjectivism. Rather, the inclinations or affections are educable and can be tutored and developed by critical reflection on experience. The similarities and patterns among the dispositions provide analogies that can be examined and tested for their applicability to novel situations and experiences. Spohn was fond of quoting the famous observation attributed to Mark Twain, that "history doesn't repeat itself, but it does rhyme."[52] In his very fine and astute appraisal of Spohn's ethics of discernment, Russell Connors notes that Spohn was directly influenced by William Wimsatt's important claim that Jesus is the "concrete universal" whose life and experience, attested to by the scriptures and subsequent experience of the Christian faithful, is the interpretive key to the moral and spiritual life.[53] Connors highlights Spohn's contention that "spotting the rhyme" among contingent, historically modulated events and opportunities operates by the "grace of indirection." This phrase means that the divine mystery is an "elusive presence," that defies the immediate grasp of the finite capacities of human beings.[54] However, there are traces and clues that provide invitations for the creative engagement and cultivation of the individual moral imagination in response to the challenges of the present moment. As Spohn makes clear in his fine book *Go and Do Likewise: Jesus and Ethics*, the phrase "go and do likewise," the famous conclusion to the Lucan parable of the Good Samaritan, does not mean to "go and do exactly the same," or to "do whatever you want," but to be faithful and creative in analogously applying the "concrete universal" of the example of Christ to the distinctive moments of our own moral experience. The parables, metaphors, and stories of the life of Jesus recounted in the scriptures provide a wellspring of imaginative resources that can be applied, analogously, to our contemporary moral challenges.

The notion of the "grace of indirection" permits me to connect Spohn's important work on the moral imagination to an important theme developed in the philosophy of phenomenology, namely the significance of disclosure or insight into the meaning of reality. According to the distinguished scholar of phenomenology Robert Sokolowski, "phenomenology is reason's self-discovery in the presence of intelligible objects."[55] This philosophical approach is the study of human experience, how things appear to us, that is as "phenomena," so that we can discern the truth of things.

Phenomenology is not our subjective experience alone, but on the contrary, is how our capacity to encounter the world through our senses and intellect enables us to reveal the truth of things. It is not the reduction of the world to the contours of the interior life of the mind, the philosophical legacy of Descartes and his successors, including Immanuel Kant, but the understanding of the complex relationships of the world beyond us, in its manifold dimensions, both by way of presence and absence, to us as human knowers. It is a return, albeit in a different key, to the classical understanding of Aristotle and Aquinas that there is a real correspondence between our grasp of the world and the world as it is as an objective reality. We can "intend" or direct our awareness, our consciousness, to the complexity of the world to understand its givenness and to discern the implications for our action and choice.

In a very fine phrase, Sokolowski describes human beings as "datives of manifestation" or "datives of disclosure."[56] In Latin grammar, the dative case is the analogue to what English speakers are familiar with as the indirect object, for example, "I pass the salt to my guest at the dinner table." The guest is the recipient of my direct action of passing the salt. The word *dative* means the "recipient" of the action. Possessed with language and intelligence, human knowers are the only beings who can be the "sites" for the disclosure of the truth of things.

To acknowledge that human beings are necessary to this process of disclosure is not to be confused with the assertion that human beings are the center of the universe. Rather, human beings are woven into the fabric of the world. The world, in its givenness and objectivity, is not an egocentric projection of human beings, but the site where the encounter with truth can occur. The Greek word for truth, *aletheia*, means "disclosure," "bringing to the light." These ideas of "gift" and "giving and receiving" will be further developed by theologian Brian Johnstone as key concepts in the Catholic understanding of moral anthropology, or the understanding of human moral agency. Johnstone's insights will be explored in chapter 5 of the book.

Sokolowski uses the example of our understanding of a cube to illustrate the ways in which we know it both directly and indirectly. We can perceive its sides as it appears in its immediate presence before us, but concurrently we also have an awareness of what is "absent" to our consciousness, the "behind and beyond" of the cube's other sides and contours. The complexity of this process of disclosure provides an analogy to Spohn's notion of the grace of indirection.

The art of moral discernment, then, is a necessary analogue to the skills of critical, analytical thinking that inform our moral deliberations. Spohn's citation of his teacher, James Gustafson, is worth mentioning in this context:

> "Discernment" seems to be appropriate for pointing to the ability to distinguish the important from the unimportant information and the insightful interpretations from the uninsightful. It refers to the ability to perceive relationships between aspects of the information that enables one to see how it all fits together, or how it cannot fit together. It refers to the ability to suggest inferences that can be drawn from the information and thus to an imaginative capacity.[57]

To summarize this discussion, the cultivation of our moral imagination involves an awareness of the subtle, robust, and supple ways we use our linguistic skills. John L. Austin, in an important book, *How to Do Things with Words,* reminds us of the adaptability and capaciousness of our language to describe the complexity of the world. Language can be used not only to name a situation or state of affairs, for example, "the cat is on the mat," but also to perform or enact more complex matters such as promise making, or declaring a new reality, for example, commissioning a new ship in the naval arsenal or issuing a command by someone in authority to issue such orders.[58] Communication via language is more akin to an event or an action, indeed, as described by philosopher, John Searle, it can be understood as a "speech-act," a performance or production of meaning that is not reducible to the elements of syntax or grammar.[59] Since communication is an action, a form of "doing" by the human speaker, Austin came to the realization that his distinction between constatives, or locutions involving statements or assertions (e.g., "the cat is on the mat") and performative statements such as commissioning the *USS McCarthy* (my preferred flagship needless to say), was not as hard and fast as he thought. Rather, all forms of speech can be understood as actions, or speech-acts. Successful communication involves not only a grasp of the basic syntax or structure of the words we use, the rules of the road as it were, but also a sense of "uptake," that is the context or conditions that frame and undergird our attempt to communicate. This sense of "uptake" in speech is a helpful analogue to the way the "uptake" of our perceptions, dispositions, and emotions complements the grammar of rules and principles in the process of moral discernment. Let me propose the following example.

A mother returns home from a trip to the grocery store. As she deposits the groceries on the kitchen table, she mentions to her daughter, who is doing her homework, that "the front door is open." Her daughter gets up and promptly closes the front door. The statement of fact, "the front door is open," is described by Austin as an example of a "constative" utterance. The grammatical elements of the statement constitute, in Austin's terminology, the "locutionary force" of the utterance. As a "locution," an intelligible sentence, its meaning is straightforward. There is, however, another force that is operating that changes the meaning from a straightforward physical observation to something quite different, namely a not-so-subtle command that the daughter should do something, namely, close the door. This more refined development, or "uptake," Austin describes as the "perlocutionary" force, the identifier, or effect, that changes the mother's utterance from a simple constative to a command. The speech-act is successfully completed, and the act of communication satisfactorily achieved (its perlocutionary effect), when the daughter closes the front door. This dimension of the speech-act constitutes the successful resolution of the mother's request that is embedded in her comment "the door is open." In Austin's terminology, the conditions for a successful enactment or performance of the speech event have been met, criteria that convey that the speech-act has been "happily" or "felicitously" achieved.

McClendon skillfully deploys the analytical tool of speech-act theory to argue for the reasonableness and truth conditions that justify the intelligibility and validity of "convictions," the self-involving commitments and obligations that characterize the doctrinal and moral discourse of communities of faith.[60] One of McClendon's enduring gifts to the study of ethics and moral theology is critical engagement with linguistic philosophy to defend the integrity and reasonableness of moral language. His labors rescue moral language from its dismissal by Alfred Ayer and the early analytic school of philosophy who reduce ethical discourse to emotive personal preference, or "Boo-Hurrah" expressions: "Boo" (I disapprove of "x" e.g., subsidized housing for the poor) or "Hurrah" (I approve of "x"). Moral language, or, indeed, theological discourse more broadly, in other words, need not be confined to the prison of empiricist assumptions and thereby dismissed as irrelevant by its "cultured despisers."[61]

Armed with this critical retrieval of moral language, the art of moral discernment is like our ability to engage in the art of communication and speech. We speak well and we act well when we attend to the multiple aspects involved in knowing how to interpret what is most "fitting" and appropriate in each of these spheres. Our perceptions, dispositions, and attitudes equip us with a basic level of "uptake" that attunes our sensibilities and operating in tandem with our discursive reasoning powers that develop principles and rules, and help us to become sophisticated, alert, moral agents. To return to a basic theme in this book, moral theology connects critical analysis of the elements of moral action with the well-formed habits or virtues that shape the character of the moral agent.

The tradition of casuistry is a tradition of exploring, with the aid of paradigm cases or situations, how basic rules of action can be discerned within the paradigm case and how the pertinent rule or rules may be appropriately applied, or, if necessary, modulated or adjusted considering the individuating circumstances. This casuistry of action operates by way of analogy, of noting similarities and differences, and generating an appropriate or fitting response. The art of discernment also considers the distinctive skills and experience of the moral agent whose deliberative engagement is essential for a successful moral act to be accomplished. At the risk of belaboring the point, may I suggest that a "casuistry of action" must be complemented by a similar "casuistry of agency." With his important work on the "reasoning heart," William Spohn has made an invaluable contribution that deeply informs the vision of the moral life discussed here.

Building upon this notion of discernment, I will devote the next chapter to a more detailed appraisal of Pope Francis's notion of mercy to shape his pastoral strategy for the care of divorced and remarried Catholics. Indeed, as I have forecast in the introductory chapter, an "imaginary of mercy" reframes the task of moral theology to encompass not only the adjudication of complex matters, focusing on discrete actions and behaviors, but also to accompany the faithful in deepening their discipleship-their allegiance to the Person of Jesus Christ. Pope Francis remarks that as a Church, "we have been called to form consciences, not to replace them."[62]

As we will see, Pope Francis invites us into an expansive and capacious horizon of mercy to address challenging moral and spiritual crises, especially the plight of those who are divorced and remarried and find themselves agonizingly bereft of the grace of the Eucharist to sustain them. With a careful look at *Amoris Laetitia,* I will attempt to bring together the threads of this essay into a concluding set of reflections.

Thus far, I think that I have provided sufficient support for a renewed focus on moral agency to complement the tradition's strong and essential attention to the careful appraisal of the structure of the moral act. In addition, I judge that the notion of discernment, especially the dynamic correlation between character and conscience, is a helpful contribution to the important recovery of virtue ethics for both Catholic and Protestant ethics. These chapters have attempted to lay the groundwork for a deeper dive into the moral theology of Pope Francis. In particular, the notions of polarity and analogy that were presented in chapter 1 will form an interpretive lens for the Pope's application of mercy to the pastoral ministry and moral theology of the Church. The notion or imaginary of mercy reminds us, perhaps in no more compelling way, of our utter dependence on the gift of grace. The idea of "gift," as it has been developed by the Catholic philosopher Jean-Luc Marion, and refined by the careful work of moral theologian Brian Johnstone, will provide a valuable resource to round out this discussion and suggests further trajectories for the development of moral theology to which I turn in the next chapter.

5

The Kenotic Moral Casuistry of Pope Francis and the Imaginary of Mercy

AS WE HAVE SEEN IN chapter 3, the theological doctrine of the resurrection of Christ provides a valuable interpretive framework for the imaginary of mercy. In this concluding chapter, the elements of the imaginary of mercy discussed in the preceding four chapters are folded into a reading of *Amoris Laetitia* by Pope Francis to illustrate a more integrated approach to moral agency, moral action, discernment, and casuistry. It begins with a close reading of the apostolic exhortation on marriage and family life, *Amoris Laetitia,* to argue that it returns us to the theme of "whole people in a broken world" in its call for a deeper grounding of moral theology in the central Christian doctrine of the resurrection of Christ from the dead. In this analysis of the encyclical, I draw upon the labors of two Australian Redemptorist moral theologians Brian V. Johnstone, CSSR, and Anthony Kelly, CSSR. These theologians, in turn, have mined a key insight from the work of the French Catholic philosopher Jean-Luc Marion, namely, the importance of the notions of gift and receptivity to specify the nature of human moral agency. The doctrine of resurrection emphasizes that the final destiny of creation, including human beings, is ultimate transformation and renewal. Mutual solidarity and relationships expand moral horizons beyond the narrow confines of self-interest and individual preference. This expansive moral anthropology is an alternative to the "corrosive individualism" of modernity, and has implications for grounding Catholic social teaching, a teaching that is concerned for the salvation and well-being of all creation, including the planet, "our common home" as Pope Francis states in his landmark environmental encyclical *Laudato Si'*.

The notion or imaginary of mercy reminds us, perhaps in no more compelling way, of our utter dependence on the gift of grace. The idea of gift will provide a valuable resource to round out this discussion and suggests further trajectories for the development of moral theology to which I turn in this chapter.

The descriptor *kenotic* that appears in the title for this chapter refers to a key theme in the Church's christological portrait of Jesus, namely his "self-emptying" or "kenosis" on behalf of others. Famously articulated in the great hymn of the Letter to the Philippians (2:1–11), the imaginary of mercy as discussed in previous chapters is refined by the notion of kenosis because it pulls us away from self-centeredness to Christ-like regard for our neighbor, especially the abandoned, the poor, the destitute, and the weakest among us. This generous, magnanimous concern is a distinguishing feature of Catholic anthropology and its social teaching. Echoing the other-regarding spirituality that informs the legacy of his papal predecessors who have contributed to a rich, robust, and developing body of social teaching, Pope Francis challenges the Church to move to the peripheries to risk encounter with a distressed humanity and planet. This kenotic vision of an imaginary of mercy can also be described as a "Samaritan turn," which reinforces a turn toward the needs and concerns of others from the beloved parable of the Good Samaritan in the Gospel of Luke. Thus, the kenotic imaginary of mercy provides a fruitful grounding for moral theology and for the social witness of the Church. This merciful sensibility is the connective tissue that links issues of sexuality and family life with the global concerns for social justice writ large. An examination of *Amoris Laetitia* will support this claim.[1] The papacy of Pope Francis has been characterized by breathtakingly beautiful and insightful reflections on this aspect of the mission and ministry of the Church. I will reflect on his signature apostolic exhortation *Amoris Laetitia* (The Joy of Love, hereafter abbreviated as *AL*) to draw together the threads of this proposed new model for an ethics of discernment especially by viewing his moral and pastoral outreach as an exercise in a new paradigm of moral theology, an imaginary of mercy. Picking up on the idea briefly sketched in the opening chapter, I propose here to tease out the lineaments of this imaginary, or worldview, by retrieving the notions of polarity and analogy that inform and shape the thinking of Pope Francis. As we have seen, two towering figures of Catholic theology who have informed the mind of Pope Francis are Romano Guardini for the notion of polarity, and Erich Przywara for the notion of analogy. For Pope Francis, following Guardini, polarity refers to the tensive unity that holds opposing ideas in dialogue, visually represented by the figure of the polyhedron. Similarly, following the thought of Przywara, analogy or the similarity in difference enables us to recognize patterns and convergences as well as distinctive differences amid the complexity of matters that present themselves to us for deliberation, choice, and action. I argue here that such notions blend in a holistic model of pastoral and moral theology that can be exemplified with a close reading of *AL*. I argue that the theme of mercy recovers the doctrine of the resurrection, which has been an overlooked and neglected resource for the development of moral theology.

Responding to *Amoris Laetitia*

Since its appearance in 2016, *AL* has been received with diverse responses. In a most helpful review of *AL* at its fifth anniversary, Emily Reimer-Barry addresses the reception of the document's key themes with a special focus on the famous chapter 8 of the exhortation concerned with the pastoral care of divorced and remarried persons.[2] Reimer-Barry notes, for instance, that readers' responses have tended to fall into three categories: one perspective, represented by objecting cardinals, sees the extension of mercy as corrupting the tradition; a second set of responses views the encyclical as restating traditional teaching; a third considers it a coherent development of marital theology.[3]

The post-synodal apostolic exhortation *AL* incorporates the insights and counsel of the two synods convened by the pope to address contemporary problems and difficulties of marriage and family life. The pope does not shy away from the complex and seemingly intractable dilemmas faced by couples who are not candidates for spiritual and pastoral relief via the "external forum" or arena of public resolution available through the ministrations of the Church's canon lawyers and marriage tribunals. Four cardinals registered significant concerns (*dubia*) challenging the pope's pastoral approach as a threat to established norms and regulations governing, and in many cases restricting, access to the sacraments due to the vagaries of irregular marital unions.[4]

With respect to the fears of corrupting the tradition, in my view the text is not a departure from the tradition, nor does it propose an approach to the pastoral care of the divorced and remarried that creates a new teaching.[5] Rather, Pope Francis, in concert with the synodal bishops, has proposed a pathway of accompaniment and discernment for the merciful application of the Church's moral teaching for those who find themselves in complex and troublesome marital situations. The moral casuistry of Pope Francis is in alignment with previous statements of the magisterium and is supported by an important commentary on chapter 8 of *AL* by Cardinal Francesco Coccopalmerio, president of the Pontifical Council for Legislative Texts.[6] As we will see, the principles of polarity and analogy inform and shape this casuistry of pastoral discernment. An important place to begin is with the 1981 apostolic exhortation *Familiaris Consortio,* written by Pope John Paul II pursuant to a previous synod on marriage and family life that he convened.[7]

Pope John Paul reinforces a key principle to guide pastoral and moral deliberations, the principle of "gradualness." Pope Francis builds on this principle in chapter 8 of *AL*. The pertinent texts from *Familiaris Consortio* (hereafter *FC*) are the following:

> Married people too are called upon to progress unceasingly in their moral life, with the support of a sincere and active desire to gain ever better knowledge of the values enshrined in and fostered by the law of God. They must also be supported by an upright and generous willingness to embody these values in their concrete decision. They cannot, however, look on the law as merely an ideal to be achieved in the future: they must consider it as a command of Christ the Lord to overcome difficulties with constancy. *And so, what is known*

> *as the "law of gradualness" or step-by-step advance cannot be identified with "gradualness of the law," as if there were different degrees or forms of precept in God's law for different individuals and situations.* (34, author's emphasis)

Pope John Paul notes that development in the moral/spiritual life proceeds in a dynamic fashion, "step-by-step" like the steps (from the Latin root *gradus*) of a staircase. Gradualness is not to be confused with its counterfeit, namely "gradualness of the law," which the pope understands as a relativistic, elastic, understanding of the moral law. Appropriating, internalizing, or "owning" moral and spiritual values is the challenge of Christian discipleship. Such acquisition of virtue takes time and requires commitment to moral growth and conversion. Another Vatican document, *The Vademecum for Confessors,* cites this principle in its counsel to priests as they administer the sacrament of reconciliation:

> The pastoral "law of gradualness," not to be confused with the "gradualness of the law" which would tend to diminish the demands it places on us, consists of requiring a *decisive break* with sin together with a *progressive path* towards a total union with the will of God and with his loving demands. (9)[8]

The skillful attention to the integration of challenging teaching with merciful accompaniment is a hallmark of much magisterial teaching, a feature that is not sufficiently appreciated. A good example is the following text from the declaration *Persona Humana* (1975),[9] advising pastors to be wise and circumspect in addressing the complexities and challenges of living the virtue of chastity:

> In the pastoral ministry, in order to form an adequate judgment in concrete cases, the habitual behavior of people will be considered in its totality, not only with regard to the individual's practice of charity and justice, but also with regard to the individual's care in observing the particular precepts of chastity. (9)

The document also cites the pastoral counsel of Pope Paul VI in his encyclical on responsible parenthood, *Humanae Vitae*:[10]

> To diminish in no way the saving teaching of Christ constitutes an eminent form of charity for souls. But this must ever be accompanied by patience and goodness, such as the Lord Himself gave example of in dealing with people. Having come not to condemn, but to save, He was indeed intransigent with evil, but merciful towards individuals. (26)

It is noteworthy that the moral and pastoral vision of Pope Francis stands in continuity with this recent tradition of the moral magisterium. Chapter 8 of *AL* embodies the signature themes of Pope Francis's imaginary of mercy: accompaniment, discernment, and the integration of weakness into a healing vision of moral theology. The pope takes an important cue from his predecessor, Pope John Paul II, by stressing recourse to the principle of gradualness. He admonishes pastors to be circumspect and not to hasten to judgment, since "no one can be condemned forever" (*AL* 297). The distinctive contexts and individuating circumstances of those who are caught in marital dilemmas are essential data for proper moral evaluation and resolution. Recognizing that since the degree of responsibility for marital failure is not equal in all cases, the consequences, or effects of a rule (or moral principle) require a proportionately measured response. Pope Francis makes a compelling case for incorporating the deliberations of individual conscience into the Church's praxis. Overly neat categorizations of those in irregular unions that foreclose further critical discernment of individuating circumstances must be resisted if a just and equitable resolution is to be attained.

Conscience, of course, must be enlightened. According to Pope Francis, as a Church, "we have been called to form consciences, not to replace them" (*AL* 31). The pope is not undermining doctrinal teaching concerning the indissolubility of the marital bond, but rather proposing a model of pastoral care with the goal of assisting those in troubled unions to proceed "step by step," according to the principle of gradualness to stronger discipleship and engagement with the faith community. Pope Francis is clearly steering a pathway that does not imply moral relativism or a form of "cheap" grace.[11]

A key pastoral insight that informs the thinking of Pope Francis is a citation from St. Thomas Aquinas, previously discussed in chapter 1:

> Although there is necessity in general principles, the more we descend to matters of detail, the more frequently we encounter defects....In matters of action, truth or practical rectitude is not the same for all, as to matters of detail, but only as to the general principles; and where there is the same rectitude in matters of detail, it is not known equally to all...the principle will be bound to fail, according as we descend further into detail.[12]

This important text from Aquinas supports the need for careful discernment and refinement in moral analysis. This sense of "fine-tuning," of attending to more granularity in our moral deliberations, is captured in the insightful work of bioethicist Carl Elliott.[13] Elliott, influenced by the work of Ludwig Wittgenstein, suggests that ethical issues that arise in the clinical setting in medicine require not only recourse to wise maxims and shrewd principles, often portrayed by various ethical theories (such as the models I sketched in chapter 2), but also the kind of contextual depth and situational sensitivity displayed by attention to the distinctive features of the patient's unique history and circumstances. These distinctives can be blurred by too keen a focus on the consistency and symmetry of moral principles and rules that are frequently invoked in ethically fraught medical situations, such as those involving matters of informed consent and proportionate medical care. However, moral theory, which contributes to the identification of patterns and similarities across a range of presenting issues, can also contribute to distortion if it is not prudentially informed and refined by careful attention to the particularity of the moral situation. This nuanced discernment, as exemplified in the careful work of Elliott, is an essential feature of the moral thought of Pope Francis.

I refer the reader to excellent monographs interpreting the teaching of *AL* by Louis Cameli and Gerald Bednar, both written with keen pastoral and ethical acuity, that do not warrant further comment from me other than strong praise and affirmation.[14] Since my concern is a focus on the moral casuistry of Pope Francis, an important text by Cardinal Francesco Coccopalmerio invites further scrutiny.[15] The cardinal offers a nuanced and careful commentary and interpretation of chapter 8 of *AL* that addresses the moral and pastoral approach to the plight of the divorced and remarried faithful of the Church. I will highlight two important observations in the commentary.

The first comment concerns the difficult question of how to understand an "objective" condition of moral disorder or sin that would disqualify those in a problematic marital union from reception of the Eucharist whose reception is conditioned upon an "objective" state of grace, manifested prima facie by a valid, sacramental union, in compliance with the canon law of the Church. The second comment pertains to the interesting discussion of the "ontology" of the human person, an insight identified by the cardinal as a hermeneutic key to the pastoral approach taken by Pope Francis. Let me address these comments in order.

With respect to couples who are in an objectively disordered union, but find themselves unable to leave for serious reasons (e.g., a secure relationship with a stable and mature partner, children from the second union, the severe risk of damage to the family if the second union were to be dissolved), Coccopalmerio rehearses the moral tradition on mitigating factors that qualify the severity of moral evaluation:

> The *Catechism of the Catholic Church* clearly mentions these factors: "imputability and responsibility for an action can be diminished or even nullified by ignorance, duress, fear, habit, inordinate attachments, and other psychological and social factors." In another paragraph, the *Catechism* refers once again to circumstances which mitigate moral responsibility, and mentions at length, "affective immaturity, force of acquired habit, conditions of anxiety or other psychological or social factors that lessen or even extenuate moral culpability." For this reason, a negative judgment about an objective situation does not imply a judgment about the imputability of culpability of the person involved. On the basis of these convictions, I consider very fitting what many Synod Fathers wanted to affirm: "Under certain circumstances people find it very difficult to act differently. Therefore, while upholding a general rule, it is necessary to recognize that responsibility with respect to certain actions or decisions is not the same in all cases."

> Pastoral discernment, while taking into account a person's properly formed conscience, must take responsibility for these situations. Even the consequences of actions taken are not necessarily the same in all cases. (*AL* 302)[16]

With respect to the idea of the "ontology" of the human person, that is, the philosophical understanding of the structure and meaning of human nature, Coccopalmerio identifies a "double aspect" in this ontology or anthropology of the human person:

> On the one hand, everyone has common elements that constitute the reality of the person, these are the ontology of the person considered in its generality, that is precisely, in the elements that are common to all people. On the other hand, each person, while he or she possesses the common elements referred to above, has at the same time individual elements, which constitute the reality of the person, these are also the ontology of the person, considered, however, in its individuality, in its singularity, in its concreteness.[17]

The reference by Coccopalmerio to the "double aspect" of the ontology of the human person, its general and singular dimensions that must be held in "tensive unity," is a formulation that is congruent with the notion of polarity in the thought of Romano Guardini. That is, these two dimensions stand in a relationship of mutual interdependence, such that neither element can be collapsed into the other, thereby obliterating the "unity in tension." In this instance, this is in line with the notion of analogy in the work of Przywara. This rich and complex insight of Coccopalmerio reflects not only the influence of Francis's intellectual mentors, but also, in my judgment, the influence of Karl Rahner and the legacy of the medieval Franciscan theologian John Duns Scotus. Some comments on Rahner and Scotus allow me to close the loop on the situation ethics debate previously discussed, and, in the process, hopefully, to minimize the fear of relativism that animates critics of Pope Francis. Closing the loop on this issue will set the stage for a deeper consideration of the kenotic moral casuistry of Pope Francis.

Coccopalmerio's reference to the "double aspect," the objective and individual elements of the human person, evokes and echoes an important distinction in Rahner's essay addressing the postwar debate on situation ethics, namely the distinction between a "formal existential ethics" and an "essential ethics."[18] "Essential ethics" refers to the morality of the natural law, the distinctive orientation to pursue the moral good, that applies to each person by virtue of a shared human nature. This morality pertains to the essence of a being blessed with the capacity for reason and choice, empowered to deliberate and to act accordingly.

Rahner questions whether this capacity to form universal rules and principles, which are then specified concretely in a distinctive action, exhausts the extent and depth of moral and spiritual aspiration in the human person. Mindful of our earlier description of "transcendental" attributes, namely those features of our intellectual, spiritual, and moral consciousness that beckon human beings toward an ultimate horizon of meaning, Rahner discerns within this essential, or normal, pattern of moral deliberation and choice an utterly personal, unique, and compelling set of moral imperatives that constitute the "existential" dimension of ethics for the individual human subject. Such imperatives are disclosed in the exercise of sovereign freedom, for example, to pursue a calling or to extend pardon and forgiveness to an offender despite the lure of anger and resentment tempting one to do otherwise. Such choices touch the intimate core of the self and activate the power of a free disposition of one's whole being, an action charged with eternal significance in Rahner's theological vision. In his astute commentary, Coccopalmerio suggests that Pope Francis's model of pastoral accompaniment of those in impossible marital dilemmas requires attention, not only to the objective features of the concrete situation of the couple, but also to the subjective conditions and capacities, indeed, the sanctuary of conscience of each partner in the relationship.

The payoff from this understanding of the ontology of the person is the deepening of our grasp of limiting or extenuating circumstances. Since ontology includes both common human attributes and distinctive, unique, individual capacities, it becomes clearer why pastoral practice prudently considers, without denying objective moral and doctrinal concerns, these mitigating factors to deal with human weakness in the Church's care for her divorced and remarried members.

In response to the *dubia* raised by four cardinals against chapter 8 of *AL*, despite claims that the pope has refused to answer their demands for further explanation, Pope Francis has chosen to respond by endorsing the consensus judgment of the Argentinian bishops. This statement claims that *AL* is not changing, revising, or undermining Church teaching concerning the indissolubility of marriage, nor is it departing from the Church's teaching on the meaning of intrinsic evil (most recently reaffirmed by Pope John Paul II in his encyclical on moral theology, *Veritatis Splendor*).[19] In the perceptive judgment of Gerald Bednar, Pope Francis applies the law mercifully for the faithful who are caught in dilemmas that cannot be easily fixed or remedied within the framework of the pastoral tools currently available to canon lawyers and marriage tribunals.[20] Bednar finds support for his argument that individuating circumstances are not just accidental features that influence the assessment of an action's moral status, but substantive co-determinants of the action's moral valence. Careful attention to these circumstances influences the assessment of culpability for moral failure.[21]

These interrelated elements of objectivity and subjectivity, or in the language of Guardini, correlative polarities held in dynamic, tensive unity, find an analogue in Rahner's dialectic between the existential and essential features of morality. Indeed, the ethics of Aquinas is a holistic, organic vision that holds the moral subject and the object for deliberation in a relationship of mutuality and interdependence.

Toward a More Holistic Approach: Reflections on the Problem and Limitations of "Nominalism" in Ethics

I will turn to the work of Redemptorist moral theologian Brian Johnstone toward the end of the chapter to explore ramifications of this important holistic vision of Thomistic moral theology for Pope Francis, but before doing so, it is important to return to a problem that has contributed to the fracturing of this organic unity of subject and object, exemplified in our earlier discussion of the situation ethics debate. That issue is the historical problem of nominalism. As I discuss its meaning and its various permutations, my purpose is not to burden the reader with an arcane retrieval of historical philosophical minutiae, but rather to see in the work of Aquinas, and an often unfairly maligned Scholastic peer (if not contemporary), John Duns Scotus, further support for the interrelationship of the subjective and objective features of moral discourse.

The reward from this excursus will be, I hope, a deeper appreciation for an important shift in moral philosophy and theology. This shift reverses the famous modern "turn to the subject" signaled by the emphasis on the individual knowing subject by René Descartes, whose legacy continues to pervade our contemporary social and moral consciousness. What I propose is a different "turn," not to the self, but to the "other," as captured by the imaginary of mercy in Pope Francis. He advocates for what I call a "Samaritan turn" signaled by the story of the Good Samaritan in the Gospel of Luke.[22] Disentangling moral theology from the tentacles of Cartesian imperial subjectivity and the distortion of situational morality requires disentangling it from the enduring scourge of nominalism, a concern that requires further explication.

Much overlooked as a resource for reimagining moral theology in the key of mercy, and for addressing the problem of nominalism, is the work of the medieval Franciscan theologian and philosopher John Duns Scotus. His most prominent contemporary interpreter is Daniel Horan, professor of theology at St. Mary's College, Notre Dame, Indiana.[23] Horan is concerned to rehabilitate the legacy of Scotus, who is portrayed as the villain in the rise of contemporary secularity with its attendant ills of subjectivism, relativism, and the collapse of an integrative philosophical and theological narrative to order work and life in contemporary culture. This secularity, captured by the term *postmodernity,* is subject to manifold interpretations.

For my purposes, I find the expression *centerless pluralism,* coined by the late Evangelical scholar Stanley Grenz, fruitful in that it conveys concisely the intellectual and cultural sensibility of the postmodern ethos.[24] The *post-* in *postmodernism* refers to the reaction to the modernity spawned by the Enlightenment project of "universal reason" with its confidence in the capacity of human intelligence to interpret, shape, and order the world. Reason or "logos" prizes order, clarity, and the capacity to harmonize differences in the interest of theoretical, or scientific coherence.[25] The criticism of the modern project is that it eviscerates differences in favor of universal explanations, that it overrides the contingencies, the particularity of history, and the experience of change in our lived experience in favor of order and uniformity of rational discourse.[26] I think the current conversation about postmodernity reflects the enduring debate in philosophy between two dialectical currents of thought represented by the ancient Greek thinkers Parmenides and Heraclitus. For Parmenides, being, or reality, is one and admits no imperfection, especially change and motion. For Heraclitus, being, or reality, is really "becoming," namely, constant change that ebbs and flows. Postmodernity can be described as a preference for a "Heraclitean" swing of the philosophical pendulum, a calibrated resistance to the preference for the attributes of order, uniformity, and stability that characterize the "Parmenidean" sensibility of Enlightenment rationality.

In other words, the postmodern suspicion of grand narratives or overarching explanations of reality, a suspicion abetted by the provisional nature of our knowledge claims due to the dynamics of change and contingency in our experience of the world, contributes to a sense of unease or anxiety about the validity of absolute claims to knowledge in either a philosophical or theological idiom.

In response to this climate of "centerless pluralism," John Milbank and like-minded intellectual colleagues (Catherine Pickstock, Gertrude Himmelfarb, and others) have fashioned a powerful movement known as "radical orthodoxy" that reclaims classic conceptions of philosophy and human nature ("radical" in the sense of a return to fundamental "roots") to countermand the anarchic subjectivity and epistemological relativism that fuels political, social, and religious arrangements untethered to normative (or "orthodox") conceptions of human good and well-being.[27] According to the narrative of radical orthodoxy, the one who is present at the creation of our contemporary malaise of rampant secularity is none other than the Franciscan friar John Duns Scotus. He is cast as the anti-Aquinas, denying the Thomistic analogy of being (see chapter 1) in favor of the univocity (that is, the sameness or equivalence) of being. According to the "Scotus story" of radical orthodoxy, as Horan recounts it, Scotus subsumes both the Creator and the creature under the general rubric or genus of the philosophical category of "being," and, in the process flattens or eviscerates the infinite, existential gap between Creator and creatures. This flattening contributes to the fashioning of an autonomous, independent, zone for creaturely action, thereby fostering the emergence of a secular realm alienated from its divine causality.

Inherent in this "carve out" of a secular realm is the seed of violence as both realms, the infinite and the finite, are viewed as competitors and rivals. Radical orthodoxy traces the ills of modernity and postmodernity (begging the reader's forbearance with the fluidity and fluctuating interpretations of the terms *modernity* and *postmodernity*) to this philosophical divide, and argues that only by retrieval of the participatory (and appropriately modulated) sharing in the gift of existence protected by the analogy of being, can the proper order and correct relationship between Creator and creature be restored, returning theology to its role as queen of the sciences.

Horan reassesses the analogy of being in Scotus and argues, against Milbank and others, that he is wrongly cast as the foe of Aquinas. Without taking a side in the ongoing debate concerning radical orthodoxy and the interpretation of the role of Scotus, or returning to yet another discussion of the analogy of being, which I have previously addressed in the earlier conversation about the work of Erich Przywara, SJ (chapter 1), I prefer to focus on a distinctive theme in the work of Scotus highlighted by Horan, namely the notion of "thisness," or in Latin, *haecceitas.*

"Thisness" merits attention and I hope the patience of the reader, as I explore the relevance and implications of what can appear to be an arcane medieval debate involving William of Ockham, nominalism, voluntarism, and the problem of "universals" in philosophy. I suggest that Scotus's notion of "thisness" provides an alternative to several philosophical cul-de-sacs (just mentioned) and provides a creative answer to the notorious problem of situation ethics. Presuming the reader's patience, this discussion, far from being an exercise in academic triviality, has real rewards in terms of the overarching theme of the book, a mercy-oriented,

Christ-formed, moral agent with a Samaritan heart. A discussion of nominalism is a helpful prelude to understanding what Scotus is up to with the notion of thisness.

What, then, is "nominalism" and why is it such a problematic notion? The contours of this story begin with a philosophical problem that occupied medieval thinkers, namely, the relationship between our knowledge of concrete individual "bits of reality," (e.g., trees, other human beings, the Getty Museum in Los Angeles) and our coequal capacity to ascertain commonalities among these individual units of reality. For example, we do not experience "humanity," or "human nature," in the abstract, but distinctive human individuals whom we recognize and identify by name: John, Mary, Penelope, Jeremiah. What is the epistemological status of our more generic descriptions of these individuals, who, each in her or his own way, incarnate or instantiate the attributes we assign to the term *humanity*, such as intelligence, volition, agency, language, to name a few?

Based on the evidence presented to our senses, we only know "individual" human beings. Our conceptual, abstract notion of humanity, appears, at best, to be nothing more than an intellectual construction, an artifact of our minds that lacks the specificity, the density, and the tangibility of our immediate sensory experience. Accordingly, it appears that we can genuinely know only the concrete individual that we can "name," hence the term *nominalism.* More general ideas that are applicable to individuals as a class or group are described as "universals." As mental constructs, these ideas are disparaged as "not real" or "nonexistent." The Franciscan friar William of Ockham, a medieval logician famous for "Ockham's razor"—that a simple solution is preferrable to a more complex explanation—maintained that only individual, singular beings really exist. Abstract concepts such as humanity or goodness possess a simulacrum of existence, an existence lodged purely in the mind. Ockham is the historical figure most associated with nominalism.[28]

The philosophical rebuttal to Ockham is critical realism, the view based on the realist epistemologies of Aristotle and Aquinas, which argue that ideas have an existential density or reality, since the formation of concepts is anchored in the information provided by the material senses. The intellect actively abstracts or excises from the material sensibility a truthful perception of the form or essence of the reality grasped by the mind. In other words, concepts, really but analogously, partake of the same existential reality as the universe of existing, real, things. Critical realism, by contrast with nominalism, makes distinctions without separation, yielding a more expansive conceptual modality of conjunctive or "both/and" thinking.[29] Critical realism maintains a unity between the mind and external reality. The Scholastic axiom "nothing is in the mind without first being in the senses" conveys this organic relationship between our minds and the external world. Nominalism, rather than distinguishing these elements, separates and divides these realities.

As such, nominalism gives rise to several philosophical puzzles or "aporias" emanating from the splitting of empirical reality from the intellect, which has the capacity to discern common threads or universal aspects shared by individuals. The earlier discussion in chapter 2 about the fact/value problem is, in my mind, one illustration. Similarly, the conundrum of the mind/body problem (can they be understood as distinct but congruent components of human nature, or must they be construed as utterly incommensurable dimensions of our humanity?), and the problem of situation ethics that denies universal principles or rules, forsaking them in favor of immediate, contextually driven, actions and choices by a moral agent, have a philosophical home in nominalism. At the root of these paradoxes is the bifurcation of these dimensions (mind from body, fact from value, situation from rule/principle) yielding a nominalist pattern of disjunctive or "either/or" thinking.

Nominalism promotes separation of these polarities rather than distinguishing their properties and holding them in tensive unity. The title of Jacques Maritain's treatise on epistemology, *Les Degrées du Savoir ou Distinguir pour l'Unir*, claims that making distinctions is in the service of unity and coherence in our exercise of reason.[30] Moreover, nominalism, by severely restricting the power of the intellect to establish commonalities and universals, overly accentuates the power of the will. Indeed, the faculty of the will becomes the dominant human attribute.[31] The ultimate ground for the reality of concrete things lies not the mind of the Creator but in the will of God.

Hence, nominalism gives birth to ethical paradigms that are rooted in the will or power of the divine lawgiver to shape and determine reality. Obedience to law becomes the dominant motif, and moralities of obligation and duty follow in its wake. These ethical models are voluntarist, emphasizing not the knowledge of the good, but the desire for the good and the power to enact it. The escape from the trap of voluntarism and its ethical corollary, situationism (affirming the power of the willing subject to choose a particular object, "here and now"), requires the conjunction, not the disjunction, of the intellect and the will. Here is where the concept of thisness in the work of Scotus is a helpful ally to an integral Catholic moral theology.

Scotus recognizes that there is a common nature inherent in things, but he also claims that to grasp the true reality of concrete, existing being, it is necessary to acknowledge a unique property that individuates it from all other beings. Scotus describes this principle as an *entitas individualis* (individual entity/characteristic), that constitutes its "thisness" (*haecceitas*). As Horan notes, the quality of thisness distinguishes *this* blade of grass from all others, distinguishes *this* human being from all others, and so on.[32] Lest the reader despair that I have wandered into a thicket of medieval philosophical minutiae, let me hasten to point out the reward from this excursus: an escape from the trap of moral situationism.

The problem of situationism is that it atomizes and isolates moments of decision and action. It is locked into the tyranny of the present moment. Only "this" moment, "this" context, "this" unique event exists. The thisness that is affirmed and valued is severed from the larger framework of relationships that weave these individual components into a structured pattern of meaning that integrates past, present, and future moments. For Scotus, thisness is a positive dimension of the unique mystery of every existing thing. The distinctive thisness inheres in, and is congruent with, the common nature that the existent shares with other similar beings. The lovely "Sonnet" by Edna St. Vincent Millay, addressing the fragmentation of the modern information age, is, I think, an apt metaphor for the disarray that lies at the heart of situational morality:

> Upon this gifted age, in its dark hour,
> Rains down from the sky a meteoric shower
> Of facts...they lie unquestioned, uncombined.
> Wisdom enough to leech us of our ill

Is daily spun; but there exists no loom
To weave it into fabric.[33]

Critical realism and an organic, holistic conception of the mutual relationships between subject and object, individual and community, of moral character formed over time, and the new event that presents itself for choice and action, provides an alternative to nominalist fragmentation, namely, a construal of these polarities as interrelated components of unified moral action. This organic sense of connection is the "loom" on which these elements are woven into "fabric," a cohesive moral unity. Consequently, the commonalities of human nature, broadly conceived, are inextricably paired with the individuating element, the thisness that pertains to the unique human subject.

In summary, both Aquinas and Scotus (if my interpretation of Scotus, *pace* Horan, passes muster), each in a different key, overcome the quagmire of nominalism. While there is an ineluctably distinctive feature of moral choice, its thisness is grasped by the discerning intelligence of the moral agent who interprets and integrates its significance with the wisdom gleaned from prior experience, with an eye to future choices and their bearing on the character of the individual.

Pope Francis, in his powerful encyclical on the environment, *Laudato Si'*, reminds us that "everything is connected." The analogy of being, central to the thought of Aquinas, and, as I think Horan has demonstrated convincingly with respect to Scotus, finds an ally in the Scotist notion of thisness. *Haecceitas* testifies to the connections that exist between and among concrete things. Reality is charged with multiple threads of relationships and associations. To coin a phrase, "monocausal reductionism" is a persistent temptation not only in philosophical and scientific discourse, but also in the realm of ethics.[34]

By this I mean that important elements of moral analysis, such as the nature of the moral act involving consideration of the agent's intention, the issue or object under consideration, and its attendant circumstances, do not stand alone but are connected to the moral actor, involving issues of character, dispositions, and virtues that shape this moral agency.

If there is merit to my critical reflections concerning moral situationism—on the one hand, it is indeed true that every moral issue is situationally positioned (we do live in the space/time continuum), but on the other hand, the moral appraisal of our actions includes more than the immediate context or situation (e.g., the significance of our moral history, our capacity to draw comparisons and note similarities and patterns in our moral experience)—then the case for a more holistic construal of moral action and its proper discernment comes into view.

Reclaiming the Tradition of Moral Casuistry in Service of the Moral and Pastoral Vision of Pope Francis

Such a holistic construal of moral action lies at the heart of what I am describing as an "imaginary of mercy," to capture the pastoral vision of Pope Francis. Discernment is an exercise in interpretation, a discriminating sense of judgment and proportion, whereby a moral actor, immersed in the practices and habits of a community of fellow sojourners in life, acquires the language and skills necessary to act wisely and well. Discernment is not a solitary enterprise. James Keenan notes the importance of social context and the learning it provides by reflection on previous history and experience.[35] This skill is cultivated and refined by reflection on accrued wisdom and insight that has been forged from experiences that have become models or "cases" for purposes of comparison and analysis.

Casuistry (from the Latin *casus*, or case) is the tradition of reflection on paradigmatic, morally charged events and, in the process, the development, by careful analysis of these exemplars, of strategies or principles for action that can be generalized and adapted to novel and emerging issues. The case study approach is widely practiced in medicine, law, and economics. The Harvard Business School, to cite one example, has popularized this methodology in its training of financial experts, business leaders, and entrepreneurs. My work with ethics committees in hospitals involves engagement with paradigmatic cases to apply insights and prior learning to the distinct medical problem at hand.

The history of moral casuistry has been brilliantly rehearsed and analyzed by two distinguished philosophers and ethicists, Albert Jonsen and Stephen Toulmin.[36] This elegant historical and ethical appraisal has also influenced James Keenan, SJ, in his efforts to revitalize and energize the tradition of casuistry.[37] For my purposes, this scholarship demonstrates that casuistry, far from being a clever strategy to justify the unthinkable, is an essential and necessary skill for wise moral deliberation.[38] Keenan cites the Anglican moralist Bishop Kenneth Kirk: "The abuse of casuistry is directed, properly, not against all casuistry, but against its abuse."[39] Jonsen and Toulmin carefully dismantle the excoriating critique of casuistry and its Jesuit practitioners by Blaise Pascal in his famous (or perhaps infamous) *Lettres Provinciales.* Casuistry must navigate between two extremes. On the one hand it must avoid the Scylla of laxism, and, on the other hand, the Charybdis of rigorism. Both tendencies, like the mythical dueling monsters and whirlpools that threatened sailors of old passing through the perilous straits of Messina, must be resisted.[40]

The approach to casuistry that I find most congruent with my sketch of an imaginary of mercy is that of Stanley Hauerwas, who describes casuistry as a "narrative art."[41] Critical engagement with paradigmatic cases is crucial to test the claims and warrants that sustain a distinctive community of faith, attentive to the narratives that sustain its existence in a world of conflicting and diverse accounts of human flourishing and welfare. Moral reasoning is an essential skill for a narrative construal of ethics, a skill that provides a critical check against false and misleading descriptions of moral *desiderata* and also forecloses the dismissal of narrative ethics as sectarian withdrawal into uncritical enclaves of ethical fideism.[42]

The great strength of casuistry is clearly the opportunity to clarify and delineate how accrued wisdom, crystallized into generalizable statements or principles of action, can be "fine-tuned" by attention to the granularity afforded by careful attention to the history and circumstances of an immediate issue with its distinctive context and challenges. Casuistry is a form of storytelling that permits a display of the convictions that anchor a moral community. From my experience in the clinical arena of medicine, the dynamics involved in this exercise of display and clarification move from a "casuistry of action," that is a focus on what is to be done, to a deeper "casuistry of agency," that is, what is required of all the stakeholders—patient, family members, medical professionals, chaplains, social workers—to choose and act wisely. A tale that unfolds in this exercise of deliberation is not just the correct application of an ethical algorithm, for example, "our past experience of a fetus with these conditions dictates early induction of labor," but rather a deeper engagement with the questions and considerations that shape the convictions central to the identity and vision of a moral community (in this instance, the Catholic community of health-care providers). These hard-won and tenaciously held convictions generate the imagination and skill required to assist "this" critically ill child and her suffering, worried parents.

The discussion moves beyond intervention options to deeper considerations: "How are we to accompany this dying child and her parents?" or "How is this impending death to be received, understood, and grieved?" Indeed, the very framing of this event in its tragic dimensions informs and shapes the kinds of options to be considered. Aristotle speaks of the example of the "wise" person as the source and inspiration for moral emulation. I suggest that the example of the *phronimos* (the wise one) invites us to consider how to cultivate, within our own experience, the wisdom or "phronetic imagination," an imagination that expands our horizons as we wrestle with difficult, complex, and often tragic choices. William Spohn in his masterful reflection on virtues and the moral life, reminds us of this phronetic dimension of moral deliberation:

> Rules are important in the moral life, but they are no substitute for wisdom. Discernment seeks not merely the right action but the appropriate one, that is, the one that fits the Christian way of life and the particular leanings of the Spirit.[43]

The casuistry of agency that I am suggesting, which amplifies the range of moral considerations beyond what is merely right to what is genuinely appropriate and fitting, is reflected in William F. May's profound meditation on the self-image and description of the role of the physician, *The Physician's Covenant.* How the physician understands her role, what kind of story shapes her imagination, is a crucial component of the physician's identity and the correlative deployment of medical skill in caring for a patient. Among the roles that May discusses, with insightful commentary on their implications for medical practice, are the following: parent, fighter, technician, teacher, and, finally, his preferred model, the physician as the "covenanter" who cultivates faithful relationships, not only with individual patients, but with the institutional structures and systems that make medical care possible.[44]

These case studies of how physicians see themselves form the vision that becomes operative in the way they exercise their skills on behalf of the patients they serve. Subscribing to one or more of these compelling narratives is revelatory in that a particular identity, or self-understanding, is an inescapable feature of the process of moral deliberation. Indeed, exactly what "counts" as a quandary or problem for clinical resolution depends upon the description, for example, of the physician as a "fighter."

For such a physician, confronted with a patient who has decided to forego further medical treatment in the face of end-stage cancer, his commitment to "fighting" for as long as possible to preserve life (as the physician sees it) may blind him to the genuine needs of the patient, and what is truly in the patient's best interest. There is indeed strength in the image of the doctor as warrior-defender, but it also requires the acknowledgement of its limitation in the face of inevitable tragedy—let's face it, medicine cannot conquer death. Testing these different stories or images is part of the "art" of casuistry, a skill that invites us to attend not only to action, but also to our agency.

Discernment, the focus of this chapter, is a holistic enterprise. It requires holding together action and agency, individual conscience and communal reflection, a skill that not only looks inward, but also outward to the claims of others. Spiritual conversion in the Christian life, which is also crucial for living a moral life, involves the ever-constant journey from self to the needs of the other. Walker Percy describes this penchant for self-preoccupation as sin, "the ceaseless suck of self."[45] As we have seen in an earlier chapter, Dame Iris Murdoch makes this process of conversion a central theme in her philosophically themed novels, which she names as "unselfing." The lure of goodness draws us from the labyrinthine preoccupation with self-interest, toward a world larger than "the fat, relentless, ego."[46]

The construal of this philosophical (and religious) moral journey from darkness to light, from self-centeredness to other-regarding care, supports Pope Francis's kenotic or "self-emptying" imaginary of mercy. The word *kenotic* signals the decentering of the moral self in ethical analysis. That is, Pope Francis's imaginary of mercy is an articulation of a profound anthropology that is a powerful rejoinder to the imaginary of modernity, which, among other attributes identified by Charles Taylor, accentuates the individualism and subjectivism that privilege the perspective and authority of the sovereign, autonomous moral self.

This imaginary/anthropology of modernity is a legacy of sixteenth-century philosopher René Descartes that continues to hold sway. Descartes, who famously separated the mind (*res cogitans*, the thinking thing) from external reality (*res extensa*, the materially extended universe of things), contributed to the rise of the anthropology of modernity, the famous "turn to the subject," that, for all its virtues affirming the dignity of the individual, insufficiently attends to the communal, social relationships that are no less crucial for authentic human identity.

Jean-Luc Marion and the Language of Gift and Receptivity: A Resource for the Imaginary of Mercy

A central claim that I wish to make in this reflection on the pastoral vision of Pope Francis is that reconnecting the traditional focus on moral action with the virtues and skills to be a wise moral agent is, at heart, a reclamation of the holistic vision of moral action by Aquinas. The Redemptorist moral theologian Brian Johnstone has sought to recover this more cohesive, Thomistic approach by incorporating a central insight from the French Catholic philosopher Jean-Luc Marion: the importance of a concept of "gift" and "receptivity" to counterbalance the "turn to the subject" in modern philosophy.[47] A brief excursus into this key theme in Marion will facilitate a deeper appreciation of Johnstone's important contribution to moral theology. My conclusion is that this holistic moral theology is the key to grasping the merciful imaginary or anthropology of Pope Francis.

Overcoming the tyranny of the imperial self, the dark side of the famous "turn to the subject" in modern moral philosophy, is a central concern for the prominent French Catholic philosopher Jean-Luc Marion. Marion's project is, at one level, an effort to wean the phenomenological tradition in modern philosophy away from the limitations of subjective consciousness or awareness as it "intuits" or grasps the "phenomenon," which is the dimension of reality as it presents itself to the knowing subject. The goal of phenomenology is to "return to the things themselves," the mantra of the founder of phenomenology, Edmund Husserl. The objective, the goal, is to discern the reality of things as they present themselves as phenomena or "appearances" to the knowing subject.

Marion argues that in every object that manifests itself to consciousness, there is a surplus of meaning, an excess, that surpasses the finite grasp of the individual knower. It is by acknowledging this givenness of the phenomenon that Marion provides a pathway for theology to emerge. The divine, as the ultimate expression of the surplus of meaning in our experience of reality as it appears to us in our consciousness, "bedazzles" the subject and cannot be fully or exhaustively grasped or understood by finite human categories such as the metaphysical concept of Being. The concept of Being (with a capital *B*) as explored by Martin Heidegger, Husserl's brilliant student, grounds and orients human understanding as the knowing subject seeks to grasp the multitude of finite beings (plural) in which the human subject is situated.

Marion's work in phenomenology is also an effort to confront the problem of "ontotheology," namely the mistaken conflation or flattening of the infinite distance between God, understood as the ultimate horizon of reality, and the plurality of finite beings. "Being" is intended to provide a common ground that applies uniformly to the infinite "Other" and finite existents. To defeat the problem of ontotheology, Marion accentuates the infinite distance that separates the horizon of divinity from finite human intellectual concepts, claiming that one cannot "speak *about* God, but only speak *to* God" via prayer and praise.[48]

Beginning with his landmark analyses of the work of René Descartes, and further developed in his most recent work on "givenness" and the importance of love to encounter the Infinite Other, Marion invokes the classical notion of analogy to overcome the reduction of the divine to human categories of knowledge whereby it becomes an object for analysis and comprehension by the finite human subject. Marion seeks to decenter this dominating gaze of human consciousness to prevent it from assuming unwarranted epistemological privilege to comprehend a reality that forever exceeds its grasp.

As we have seen with the work of Przywara, analogy steers a middle course between outright identity of meaning, that is, terms that are univocal or singular in sense and extension, and equivocal terms, which affirm total dissimilarity in meaning, to capture a dynamic interplay between these two senses (univocity and equivocity), namely, "similarity in difference," or as Przywara has framed it, "a unity in tension."[49] A univocal conception of the notion of Being subsumes both the Creator and the created, or the Infinite and the finite, to a flattened notion of "sameness" of being, and consequently collapses the existential gap between them. An equivocal understanding of being posits such a thin connection of meaning between Creator/created that the connection is, ultimately, tantamount to an unbridgeable chasm. Analogy steers a middle course between univocity and equivocity. Marion contends that only by way of love, an act that is open to receptivity of the utter gift of the divine, can God be approached and encountered. As such the divine is not controlled or dominated by human understanding and perception.

If God can only be encountered by a receptive openness to the gratuity of grace, then a decentered self is the only fit subject for such an encounter. Marion's philosophical/theological project in phenomenology provides a new vision for the moral life. The appropriate response to the utter excess and "saturated phenomenon" that is God is thanksgiving and praise. Another word for this magnanimous kindness and self-offer from God is mercy, a gift beyond all measure.

If the challenge of living a moral life is reoriented in a new direction, away from the imperial preoccupations of Descartes and Murdoch's "fat, relentless ego," we gain an important insight about how to envision or see moral possibilities. Implicit in this radical realignment of perspective is an imperative to redress obstacles to spiritual and moral receptivity by actions that move us beyond the self, actions to secure justice and reconciliation, perhaps captured by the Jewish mandate *tikkun 'olam,* "to heal the world." Actions and service on behalf of others deliver us from the constraints and demands of our selfish wills. They expand our hearts to embrace virtues of solidarity and communion. This profoundly Jewish sentiment also anchors our Catholic sensibility. Rabbi Jonathan Sacks, the distinguished chief rabbi of London, blessed us with his last book *Morality: Restoring the Common Good in Divided Times*, published posthumously.[50] The entire theme of this beautiful book can be summed up in one sentence: "the moral life is the journey from 'me' to 'we.'"

The connection with the vision of Pope Francis is clear. In this rabbinical teaching on the pursuit of the common good, we can discern the lineaments of Catholic Social Teaching in the work of Pope Francis and his predecessors in the papacy. Key themes—such as the common good; solidarity with others, especially the poor, the marginalized and the suffering; "integral ecology" (care for the created order, the planet, as well as human beings); the dignity of the human person; preferential option for the poor; just peacemaking and peacekeeping to complement the just war tradition—are all expressions of this displacement of the sovereign ego in favor of the moral self that gives and receives.

Brian Johnstone, CSSR, turned to Marion and his conception of the language of gift to recover the moral unity between the acting human subject and objective external reality. Johnstone argues that the subject/object divide, stemming from the project of modern philosophy ushered in by Descartes, continues to bedevil moral theology despite efforts to repair the breach by an amplified understanding of the personhood of the moral actor.

The bifurcation of the moral subject from the object for action and deliberation leads, in Johnstone's view, to two distorted patterns of moral theology. The location of moral obligation exclusively in the intentionality of the moral agent is a prescription for subjectivism and relativism, namely that one's intentions alone are sufficient to establish the moral contours of choice and action. Alternatively, to locate moral significance only in the object for consideration (for example, withholding or discontinuing a form of medical treatment) reduces moral theology to physicalism, namely, that moral meaning is exclusively vested in the material, physical descriptions of empirical reality.[51] To overcome this gulf, the move in contemporary work in moral theology toward an integral personalism is commendable. Johnstone, however, contends that personalism requires a more descriptive and substantive anthropological grounding. Marion's language of gift, receptivity, and giver, provides this more adequate framework.

According to Marion, all reality is understood within the horizon of "givenness." As Johnstone notes,

> Concretely, this means that everything has being as a gift from God. The destiny of all beings is to become receivers and givers to others to the fullest extent possible by their natures. In the case of human beings, the basic framework within which this destiny unfolds is provided by the structures of giver, gift, and receiver. A person is defined as one who is capable of receiving and giving to others, in freedom with knowledge. A person is "historical" in the sense that becoming a giver and receiver requires the gift of time.[52]

Johnstone's perceptive emphasis on the historical dimension of ourselves as moral agents, with its crucial reminder that temporality is a constitutive feature of our life journey, supports the narrative, tradition-shaped character of moral deliberation that we discussed earlier in the work of Stanley Hauerwas. Moreover, Marion's legacy for moral theologians is a resource for the cultivation of a "decentered" self to unseat the imperial Cartesian ego that dominates contemporary cultural discussions of controversial issues such as abortion, euthanasia, and assisted forms of reproduction.

O. Carter Snead, former director of the de Nicola Center for Ethics at the University of Notre Dame, argues that absolutizing the autonomous will of the individual erodes the bonds of solidarity and concern for others.[53] Snead, building on the insights of the distinguished sociologist of religion Robert Bellah, and the philosophers Charles Taylor and Alasdair McIntyre, defines this absolutization of autonomy as "expressive individualism." According to expressive individualism,

> persons are conceived merely as atomized individual wills whose highest flourishing consists in interrogating the interior depths of the self in order to express and freely follow the original truths discovered therein towards one's self-invented identity.[54]

The central implication of this expressive individualism is that the will of the individual to determine or express his or her own life project, with its values and concerns, emerging from within the preferences of the individual, cannot be restricted or impeded. Crucially missing from this narrative of the self is an observation from Alasdair MacIntyre that expressive individualism is "forgetful of the body." This forgetfulness loses sight of our embodied nature as human beings, that we are dependent upon others, that we are finite, and that we are vulnerable to the vicissitudes of mortality. As a result, such an attitude does not equip us with the skills to confront weakness and the inevitable diminution of our powers as we move through our life cycle on the planet. We all too easily forget that each of us is on a "continuum of disability" that manifests itself in the ageing process. There is no Ponce de León on the horizon who will find a magic elixir, a fountain of youth, to deliver us from the throes of death. Perhaps one of the clearest statements of the "expressive individualism" and absolutization of autonomy we have discussed is reflected in the concurring opinion of Justice Anthony Kennedy in the Supreme Court decision *Planned Parenthood v. Casey*:

> These matters, involving the most intimate and personal choices a person may make in a lifetime, choices central to personal dignity and autonomy, are central to the liberty protected by the Fourteenth Amendment. At the heart of liberty is the right to define one's own concept of existence, of meaning, of the universe, and of the mystery of human life. Beliefs about these matters could not define the attributes of personhood were they formed under the compulsion of the State.[55]

As Walker Percy whimsically notes (citing Alexis de Tocqueville's observation of Americans at the dawn of the new republic), "Americans are natural-born Cartesians without having read a word of Descartes."[56] In other words, the three-hundred-year-plus legacy of dualism, or the mind/body split that we have inherited from Descartes, is part and parcel of the cultural oxygen that we breathe as inhabitants of the imaginary of modernity so trenchantly analyzed by Charles Taylor.[57] This imperialism of the will is pernicious to any efforts to attend to the claims of others, especially the most vulnerable among us.

Fortunately, as I have endeavored to establish, there is an alternative to the transcendence-starved imaginary of modernity described by Charles Taylor, an imaginary that can entertain the heretofore unimaginable possibility of a God-absent universe. The imaginary of mercy that I am describing takes a cue from Taylor's astute assessment that questions of authenticity, meaning, and purpose persist and create space for renewed theological construals of these enduring yearnings. As one who lived for years on the famous San Andreas earthquake fault in Los Angeles as rector of St. John's Seminary in Camarillo, periodic tremors from below were stark reminders that the energy unleashed by shifting tectonic plates profoundly altered our perceptions of stability and order above ground. The imaginary of mercy that I discern in the work of Pope Francis is likewise attuned to the transformative energies of grace that move us beyond the self-enclosed immanentism of the Cartesian worldview. As Catholic Christians, we inhabit a world of grace, a gift that is not of our making, a gift, moreover, that has come in the form of an incarnate Savior.

A Catholic artist with a keen sensitivity to the perils of a culture ensnarled in the narcissism of a Cartesian disembodied anthropology, severing mind from body and body from soul, was the southern writer Flannery O'Connor. While the southern Georgia of her upbringing may not have been Christ-centered, it remained, nonetheless, Christ-haunted. Without the grace and witness of the Church, she claimed, "I would have been the stinkingest logical-positivist you ever saw right now."[58] O'Connor's astute insight is an apt segue to round out this chapter with remarks on the imaginary of mercy.

The hallmark of this imaginary is captured in the notion of mercy, literally to have "a distressed heart" aroused by the suffering and needs of others. The reflection of Pope Francis on the fortieth anniversary of the Vatican "Declaration on Euthanasia" (1980), *Samaritanus Bonus* (The Good Samaritan [2020]), serve as a vehicle for my concluding remarks. The beloved parable of the Good Samaritan in the Gospel of Luke tells us that the Samaritan did not leave the badly wounded victim, attacked by bandits and robbers, alone. He did not abandon him when others passed by who should have known better, pointedly religious leaders. He provided care and entrusted him to an innkeeper and continued to look after him when he returned from his journey. The Samaritan is the paradigm for a moral theology that, as James Keenan has noted, has shifted from a focus on avoiding wrongdoing to a fuller embrace of action on behalf of the gospel. It is a movement toward sanctification and a life of holiness, a holiness understood, not as an otherworldly sanctuary, but a holiness that is "wholeness" or integrity of life. Rather than the imaginary of secularity, with its conception of a "world without windows" that Taylor has so brilliantly analyzed, the imaginary of mercy breaks through the hardened carapace of modernity to remind us that grace, as it is proclaimed on the lips of the dying priest in Bernanos's novel *The Diary of a Country Priest*, "is everywhere."

Physicists describe two forces of motion. Centripetal force bends the arc toward the center of a physical object. Centrifugal force projects energy outward from the center. The "turn to the subject," famously signaled by the Cartesian and Kantian legacy in modern philosophy, is a centripetal force turning us ever inward. The imaginary of mercy, the "Samaritan turn," is, on the contrary, a centrifugal moral force moving us outward in search of others. It is the moral theology of Pope Francis that urges the Church not to be complacent and self-preoccupied, but instead to "go to the peripheries," to emulate the generosity of Christ in bringing the good news of healing and redemption to a broken, wounded world. The poet and musician Leonard Cohen, in a beautiful refrain from his song "Anthem," proclaims that "there is a crack, / a crack in everything, / That's how the light gets in." For Pope Francis, the brokenness of the world and the suffering of humanity are invitations to find ways for the "light" to get in.

Conclusion

As I indicate in chapter 1, the moral vision of Francis has been shaped by the insights of Przywara on the notion of analogy (that is, the paradoxical resemblance and nonresemblance of the creation and the Creator), and those of Romano Guardini on the notion of polarity (namely, that opposite viewpoints can be held simultaneously). Pope Francis invokes the image of the polyhedron as the symbol of his dialogical theology that embraces both analogy and polarity in a redefinition of encounter and mission. The polyhedron holds the opposing sides of the figure in unity, rather than collapsing them into a monochromatic unity or a circle. That is why, throughout this essay, I have endeavored to hold together action and agency, individual conscience and character, and the formative influence of a moral community. For similar reasons, as Johnstone has argued, subject and object must be held together in a "tensive unity."

The "samaritanism" of Pope Francis requires cultivation of distinctive virtues, in addition to the classic virtues of faith, hope, and charity. It requires attentiveness to the human condition, the capacity to be mindful of what lies before us, and in the classic formula of the Catholic Action Movement in the twentieth century, to "see, judge, and act." It also involves, as we have seen in *Amoris Laetitia*, the willingness to accompany those who are in distress, to be patient with the process of growth and conversion, and to hold together the gifts of pastoral compassion and prophetic challenge. This balancing is not easy, a point well noted by Bernard Häring, who titled his moral theology text *Free and Faithful in Christ*, not *Free and* Easy *in Christ*.[59] By delving into the dynamics of the art of discernment, I have attempted to describe a moral theology that does not merely assert moral claims or rest secure in the clarity of well-formulated principles, but moves to refine their application and reach sensitive to the modulations and contours that lie at the heart of the mystery of every human life.

I suppose that at some level an essay of this type is bound to be frustrating, perhaps, for those hungering for "clear and distinct" answers. I think that I have provided pathways to these kinds of answers, but I think the great gift of every theology, every moral theology worthy of the name, lies not so much in the answers that it can provide, but in its fidelity to the Great Mystery that defies all human constructs. *Si comprehendis, non est Deus*, says St. Augustine, "If you understand, it is not God."[60]

To bring this essay in moral theology to a close, I return to the opening story rooted in my encounter with another Francis, not Pope Francis, but Brother Francis Rees. He, like many of our holy mentors, whether beloved parents, friends, or relatives, do not enjoy the formal, canonical status of *Sanctus*, but each is assuredly an *Alter Christus* in our lives. Seeing the work of moral theology as forming "whole people in a broken world" is the framework for these reflections on the imaginary of mercy that I discern in the pastoral vision of Pope Francis. While the musings of the divine mind elude us, most especially its internal deliberations about the fate of our ever-erring humanity, the good news is that the final verdict is already decided in our favor, namely, in Jesus Christ. He is mercy incarnate, descended among the dead, who, as depicted in the great icon of the resurrection in the Eastern Church, the *Anastasis*, lifts us from the tomb with our ancestors Eve and Adam, rendering us "whole people" in a world no longer broken, but continuously healed and redeemed.

This book's contribution to moral theology is its proposal for a model of ethical discernment that integrates wise moral deliberation with the formation of a wise, moral agent. Confident that the world, despite the perduring struggle to overcome evil, is ultimately in the hands of a Savior, crucified by the "powers and principalities" of this world, but who has conquered these forces of darkness, who is risen, and sits at the right hand of the Father, Catholic disciples are empowered to engage and act in this world because the merciful love of God embraces them. They are "whole people in a broken world," who are destined not to dwell in the darkness of death, but to dwell with the One who has "descended among the dead" to rescue them.

Appendix

End of Life Health Care: A Catholic Perspective

AS EACH OF US CONFRONTS our mortality, we face inevitable questions about how we will die. The spiritual tradition of the Church always maintained a sober understanding of our finitude and counseled the practice of the *ars moriendi*, the art of dying well. Understandably, fear of dying, loss of control, fear of burdening loved ones, fear of pain—all these elements influence us. The comedian and filmmaker Woody Allen captures this ambivalence with his quip, "I'm not afraid of dying, I just don't want to be there when it happens."

Ethical issues concerning the practice of medicine, including challenging questions about the end of life, have long been a staple of Catholic moral theology. Hospitals emerged as an expression of the gospel mandate to care for the sick, one of the corporal works of mercy. Catholic theologians have been at the forefront of medical ethics since the Middle Ages. Questions about whether treatments could be foregone are not new. In ancient times, when anesthesia and the marvels of modern medicine were not yet conceived, the question about whether a patient could refuse amputation for gangrene and accept the inevitable death that would occur was resolved in favor of the patient's decision to determine whether the remedy was ordinary, appropriate, or standard care, or whether it now moved into the territory of extraordinary, optional, or heroic care.

The classic distinction between ordinary and extraordinary means of care is based on the dynamic, changing conditions facing a patient with a progressive series of ailments. It is not determined based on the state of the art of medicine or technology. Moreover, interventions once begun can be undone if it is in the best interests of the patient.

Modern practice is informed by this long history. *The Vatican Declaration on Euthanasia* (1980) specifies the kinds of factors that enter into the calculus of ordinary/extraordinary means:

> However, is it necessary in all circumstances to have recourse to all possible means? This reply, which as a principle still holds good, is perhaps less clear today, by reason of the imprecision of the term and the rapid progress made in the treatment of sickness. Thus, some people prefer to speak of "proportionate" and "disproportionate" means. In any case, it will be possible to make a correct judgment as to the means by studying the type of treatment to be used, its degree of complexity or risk, its cost and the possibilities of using it, and comparing these elements with the result that can be expected, taking into account the state of the sick person and his or her physical and moral resources.[1]

Determining cost versus benefit, or benefit versus burden is not a mathematical algorithm. It is a prudential, wise discernment by the medical professionals as well as the patient about what constitutes appropriate care in these circumstances. The medical adage is well known: "cure sometimes, relieve occasionally, but care always." When cure or restoration to optimal functioning is not possible, the goals of medicine shift to comfort care or palliative medicine.

In addition to the development of the venerable distinction between ordinary and extraordinary means, consideration of the notion of patient autonomy is a critical value. Patients must provide explicit, informed consent to be touched or cared for. For example, the consent forms we sign for dental treatments or eye care remind us that the law protects us from battery or unwanted touching or assault.

One important means for us to assert and exercise our autonomy and control is using advance directives that stipulate and clarify for our family members and health care providers what we want. While I am not an attorney and am not venturing a legal opinion, the durable power of attorney for health care (DPAH) has distinctive advantages. It empowers a living agent to speak on our behalf, to interpret our wishes and desires to a medical team when we become incompetent or unable to do so. Living wills are another instrument to indicate patient preferences, usually by specifying particular medical interventions that the patient wishes to forego or to withhold. Moreover, a benefit of a DPAH is that it does not prematurely foreclose access to specific medicines, interventions, or procedures. As we know, in life, things change. An empowered agent, acting in our best interests, protects us and provides us with the appropriate care that we need and deserve. Promoting advance directives is critical to promoting authentic patient autonomy and control over our medical care.

From my experience in working with parishioners and hospital ethics committees, I think we must support greater investment in palliative care. Palliative care is an important specialty and the medical advances to date ensure that virtually no patient should die in excruciating agony or pain. Again, this ethical challenge is nothing new. In 1957, in an address to Catholic anesthesiologists, Pope Pius XII responded in the affirmative to a question from these physicians concerning the administration of powerful pain sedatives, such as morphine, which carry with them the collateral side effect of shortening the physical life of the patient. Invoking the moral principle of the twofold effect, whereby an action can have two consequences, one good, one bad (e.g., pain relief—good; shortened life—bad), the pope correctly reasoned that the good intention—to relieve pain—permitted the shortening of life as an unintended, but collateral side effect. Proper pain management can help patients overcome the fear of an agonizing death.[2]

Palliative care must not be subtly redefined so that it encompasses means to end, directly, the life of a patient as part of an "integrated plan of medical care." The June 2020 statement by Pope Francis, "The Good Samaritan (*Samaritanus Bonus*): On the Care of Persons in the Critical and Terminal Phases of Life" is wise counsel:

> In some countries, national laws regulating palliative care (Palliative Care Act) as well as the laws on the "end of life" (End-of-Life Law) provide, along with palliative treatments, something called Medical Assistance to the Dying (MAID) that can include the possibility of requesting euthanasia and assisted suicide. Such legal provisions are a cause of grave cultural confusion: by including under palliative care the provision of integrated medical assistance for a voluntary death, they imply that it would be morally lawful to request euthanasia or assisted suicide. In addition, palliative interventions to reduce the suffering of gravely or terminally ill patients in these regulatory contexts can involve the administration of medications that intend to hasten death, as well as the suspension or interruption of hydration and nutrition even when death is not imminent. In fact, such practices are equivalent to a direct action or omission to bring about death and are therefore unlawful. [These practices constitute] a socially irresponsible threat to many people, including a growing number of vulnerable persons who needed only to be better cared for and comforted but are instead being led to choose euthanasia and suicide.[3]

It is morally permissible to say, "enough is enough." We are not obligated to use every medical intervention as we face our inevitable mortality. For Christians, while death is real and a fate that none of us can escape, it is, however, not ultimate given our belief in the divine intention that nothing in creation is to be lost. We believe in the resurrection of the dead and eternal life, not its annihilation.

Medical aid in dying (MAID), while well-intentioned, is, in the judgment of the Church and a great number of physicians, philosophers, ethicists, and public policy specialists, a misguided response to a real and important issue. Doctors are committed by oath to the proposition "first do no harm." Enlisting doctors in the direct activity of a patient to end his or her life is to undermine the ethos of the profession. Doctors are called to care not to kill.

A larger issue that warrants further debate is the absolutization in our culture of the value of autonomy. Autonomy is a guarantor of our intrinsic dignity and worth and must be maintained. However, it is a value that is part of a larger understanding of our humanity. We are indeed free actors, but we are also interdependent and sharers in a common humanity. We have bodies and they grow, they age, and they die. Death is inevitable. We cannot escape our finitude, nor, as a corollary, can we escape the imperfections of life that we all experience. To live our lives only on the condition that they be perfectly under our control is to dissolve the bonds that connect us to families, to loved ones, to those who will come after us. We can receive life gracefully and gratefully, and just as gracefully and gratefully accept its inevitable limits. Fortunately, for those of faith, at death, as our liturgical prayer proclaims, "life is changed, not ended."

O. Carter Snead, professor of law and former director of the de Nicola Center for Ethics at Notre Dame University, has written a powerful book about autonomy with the title *What It Means to Be Human: The Case for the Body in Public Bioethics.*[4] Professor Snead diagnoses a critical issue with the absolutization of autonomy, especially in the context of euthanasia and end of life ethics. Building on the insights of the distinguished sociologist of religion Robert Bellah and the philosophers Charles Taylor and Alasdair MacIntyre, Snead defines this absolutization of autonomy as "expressive individualism," which he explains as follows: "Persons are conceived merely as atomized individual wills whose highest flourishing consists in interrogating the interior depths of the self in order to express and freely follow the original truths discovered therein towards one's self-invented identity."[5]

Missing from this narrative of the self is Alasdair MacIntyre's observation that expressive individualism is "forgetful of the body." This forgetfulness loses sight of our dependency, our vulnerability, and our finitude. It does not equip us with the ability to confront weakness as we forget that each of us is on a "scale of disability" as we move through the life cycle. We privilege our solitary power and strength, forgetting that we are ineluctably dependent, vulnerable, and fragile as we navigate the dependencies of our birth and origin, and our dependency on others as we encounter the limits of our finite, earthly, lives. We can forget the critical need for solidarity.

Paradoxically, while aid in dying may seem to attend to the need to exercise our autonomy and power over our demise, it deprives us of the solidarity and connectedness to others that we also need to flourish and thrive.

If we see ourselves, in MacIntyre's words, as "dependent rational animals" we properly contextualize our autonomy. Surely, it invites us to reconsider what it means to be a "burden" on others.

When my mother was six weeks from the death that awaited her from end-stage colon/liver cancer, we had a tender moment in our family kitchen. I am the oldest of eleven. Mom and my father, an Air Force general and fighter pilot, raised the eleven of us, moving from one base to another. As a good Irish woman, she shared the belief that "with a good pot of tea and a chat, you can solve anything." So over that tea, she smiled at me and said, "Now, son, don't be sad. I have had a wonderful life with your faither and with all of you. So live as long as you can, and die when you can't." We had the blessing of hospice nurses to accompany her in her last days and hours. My two nurse sisters were relieved of the conflict they felt as her daughters. When we were distressed about her groaning, the nurses comforted us with the assurance that the body was shutting down and she was not in pain. We kept her comfortable with ice chips and lemon swabs rather than forcing hydration or any nutrition that she could not metabolize and that if ingested, would only further her discomfort. She knew and we knew when "enough was enough." We held her hand, said the Hail Mary, and prayed as she took her last breath. She bequeathed to us, in her dying, not a burden, but her ultimate gift. In the Catholic vision, life is a gift from the Creator. We are its stewards, not its owners. As the Protestant Reformer John Calvin proclaimed in his *Institutes of the Christian Religion*, "we are not our own."

So, the alternative to aid in dying is the following: accompaniment of the dying with palliative care, hospice care, advance directives, strategic investments in improving nursing facilities, skilled and long-term care facilities. Above all, acting in solidarity and love. Allowing death to take its course is normal, wise, and good. Taking it into our own hands is, I suppose, a form of autonomy, but it is not good enough because it deprives us of our human need to be present and to care for our loved ones to the very end. To quote from the *Declaration on Euthanasia*,

> Life is a gift of God, and on the other hand death is unavoidable; it is necessary, therefore, that we, without

in any way hastening the hour of death, should be able to accept it with full responsibility and dignity. It is true that death marks the end of our earthly existence, but at the same time it opens the door to immortal life. Therefore, all must prepare themselves for this event in the light of human values, and Christians, even more so in the light of faith.

Pain and suffering are endemic to the human condition. Christians are not masochists who choose pain because it strengthens the spirit. No, we accept suffering and see it in the light of faith, not as a cruel, meaningless affliction, but something that we endure and join to the sufferings of Christ the Savior.

Making decisions based on quality-of-life factors is certainly appropriate, but we must be careful to discern what we mean by "quality" of life. Robert Jay Lifton, in his magisterial psychological and historical study of the Nazi doctors, notes that the medical profession was co-opted into Hitler's euthanasia program by a gradual diminution of respect for life.[6] The disabled, those who were deemed misfits for religious or sexual reasons, or unable to work, were labeled *lebensunwertes Lebens*, "lives unworthy of life." It is far better to keep "equality" of life in mind when considering "quality" of life. At risk are those facing disabilities who suffer from the false ideology of perfectionism. None of us is perfect. We are all, as human, "on a scale of disability" as we move through the life cycle.

The issue of medical assistance in dying, or MAID, is the latest iteration of efforts to enlist the medical profession to exercise their expertise on behalf of individuals confronting terminal illness, who seek to end their lives with proactive measures rather than acquiesce to the natural biological rhythms of our mortality. The desire to assert control over the circumstances of one's demise appeals to the value of personal autonomy, a value that enjoys powerful support in the liberal culture of modern society. Despite that support, there are compelling reasons to resist the understandable lure of medical assistance in dying.

The recent op-ed in the pages of the *Arizona Republic* by an acclaimed oncologist, suffering from terminal illness himself, in support of MAID warrants further attention, especially since the physician in question, Dr. Tom Fitch, has an admirable record of providing supportive, palliative care to many individuals under his care. Dr. Fitch's essay is titled "I'm an Oncologist with Terminal Cancer, and I Support Medical Aid in Dying. Here's Why" (*Arizona Republic, May 30, 2020*). Dr. Fitch states, "As my cancers progress, I want to be in charge. I want the legal option to die, if need be, before it is too late to consent to my own death. I desperately want to avoid recruitment into that borderland where I would vegetate as neither here nor there."

By way of response to Dr. Fitch's article, I consulted with Fr. Peter Breslin, SJ, a PhD in the Department of Biology, which is a unit in the Department of Medicine at Loyola University, Chicago. Dr. Breslin's current research involves exploration of the "molecular pathology of acute myeloid leukemia in order to develop novel improved treatment approaches." Fr. Breslin notes the dangerous public policy implications of enshrining legal sanction for the practice of MAID. He offers a powerful rejoinder to Dr. Fitch:

> Everyone has the right to die well and to some extent on his/her own terms. But death comes to each person and does not admit of any consensual process. Fitch has reasoned that MAID involves a "challenge to the disease itself." But it is not a challenge, rather the opposite. It is a surrender to the disease. The notion that one can die on his/her own terms is philosophically hazy. This is not to say that end of life decision-making is easy. But I prefer to stress that medical science must be used to relieve persons of the burden of suffering as much as possible, not to eliminate the burden of life itself. The concept of caring for another should not extend to the intentional ending of life. We are human and as such we are not capable of giving life. Nor are we, therefore, morally empowered to take life away. (Personal correspondence with the author, 9/13/2020)

Bearing in mind Fr. Breslin's insights, from a Christian perspective, directly ending one's life by permitting aid in dying lacks limiting principles restricting access to these measures only to the terminally ill. Dr. O. Carter Snead, whose argument against the philosophy of "expressive individualism" we have previously noted, expands upon the fraught moral and legal implications of medical aid in dying:

> Because the law [that is, MAID legislation] fails to grasp the diminished agency of a human being whose body is dying, the framework it offers is rife with risks of fraud, abuse, duress, neglect, and coercion, especially for those populations who are already vulnerable because of old age, disability, poverty, or membership in a stigmatized class. The answer to this failure is not to seek additional processes and procedures that will allow for the autonomy of the solitary individual to annihilate himself, but rather to strengthen and support the networks of unarticulated giving and graceful receiving that cared for him when he was radically dependent as he entered the world and will do so again as he leaves it.

Dr. Snead argues for a more compassionate role for the law as it applies to the dying:

> The role of law is to encourage and reward the practice of just generosity, hospitality, and accompaniment in suffering (*misericordia*). It should support the opportunities for people to learn and practice gratitude, humility, openness to the unbidden, and tolerance of imperfection. The law should support the cultivation of the moral imagination to see our neighbor in the suffering other, and for those to see their own intrinsic and equal dignity despite suffering from a diminished and dependent condition. More concretely, the law must allow for the aggressive palliation of pain. And it must protect vulnerable populations by not creating legal regimes that teach that their lives are not worth living, and which they might even be pressured or coerced into ending them.[7]

A distinction here must be made. Aid in dying is an act of abandonment and not an act of care for the dying. Providing the severely depressed or the dying with a lethal cocktail that they can administer at the time and manner of their choosing is a form of abandonment. It says, "Your death has only the meaning you assign to it." It is a strange paradox is it not? On the one hand, we aggressively intervene to prevent our fellow humans from acts of self-destruction, and, on the other hand, turn around and endorse their self-induced demise with aid in dying. We leave them to the lonely solitude of a sterile choice, bereft of the care and love that we all deserve, especially at life's end. It takes courage to accept our inevitable fate, and when our spirits sag, and our knees are weak, when fear tries to paralyze us, we need the supporting, loving hands, of our loved ones to lift us and to help carry us over the threshold. That is the message of the parable of the Good Samaritan. He did not leave the badly wounded victim alone. He did not abandon him when others passed by who should have known better—pointedly, religious leaders. He provided palliative care and entrusted him to an innkeeper, a hospice of care, and looked after him when he returned from his journey. I am afraid that the spread of the ideology of aid in dying will develop, as it already has in too many countries in Europe, from a "right" to die to a "duty" to die. Some insurance companies, it is reported, have refused costly, long-term care, instead advising their beneficiaries to seek the cheap alternative of medical aid in dying.

In conclusion, in my opinion, aid in dying is a solution in search of a problem. We know how to confront our mortality with the medical, legal, moral, and spiritual resources already at our disposal. Two examples: we have in our parishes and congregations bereavement ministries who reach out to the dying and their families; some parishes create ministerial opportunities for teams of health care providers as a source of pro bono support beyond formal medical delivery systems. Palliative care, even aggressive palliative care, thoughtful advance directives, networks of social support, hospice care, nursing homes, solidarity, and above all, love and accompaniment are the means to equip us to face the ultimate mystery we all must face, death itself, but with gratitude for the gift of life, fragile though it is, which has been entrusted to us.

Notes

Chapter 1: Moral Theology in the Key of Mercy

1. In 1975, the Diocese of Tucson converted its high school seminary, Regina Cleri, to a pastoral center due to the loss of seminarian enrollment sufficient to keep it open and sustainable.

2. Hans Urs von Balthasar, *Presence and Thought: An Essay on the Religious Philosophy of Gregory of Nyssa* (San Francisco: Ignatius Press, 1995), 10–11.

3. St. Thomas Aquinas, *Summa Theologiae,* ST, I–II, Q. 94, a. 4.

4. Charles Pinches, *Theology and Action: After Theory in Christian Ethics* (Grand Rapids, MI: Eerdmans, 2002).

5. Massimo Borghesi, *The Mind of Pope Francis: Jorge Mario Bergoglio's Intellectual Journey* (Collegeville, MN: Liturgical Press, 2017).

6. Erich Przywara, Analogia Entis, *Metaphysics, Original Structure and Universal Rhythm,* trans. John R. Betz and David Bentley Hart (Grand Rapids, MI: Eerdmans, English translation, 2014, first published 1962). The introduction by John R. Betz is a superb analysis of Przywara's ideas. The citation from the Fourth Lateran Council can be found in Denzinger-Schonmetzer, *Enchiridion Symbolorum,* 43rd ed. (San Francisco: Ignatius Press, 2012), 289n806 (Denzinger-Schonmetzer paragraph notation). Pope John Paul II cites this text from the Fourth Lateran Council in his encyclical *Fides et Ratio* 84.

7. Romano Guardini, *Der Gegensatz: Versuche zu einer Philosophie des Lebendig-Konkreten* (Mainz: Matthias Grünewald, 1925) is the original text. The book has not been translated into English. The title of the book in the Italian edition, *L'opposizione polare:*

saggio per una filosofia del concreto vivente (Brescia: Morcelliana, 1997), expertly captures the trajectory of Guardini's thought. The Italian to English translation, *Polar Opposition: Towards a Philosophy of Concrete Living*, reflects the rhythm of unity in tension that is at the heart of polarity in Guardini's philosophy. Moreover, for Guardini, polarity is not an abstract intellectual construction, but rooted in the dynamism of everyday life, described as concrete living. This both/and sensibility is deeply attractive to Pope Francis as he weaves together systematic and moral theology in his papal teaching.

8. Bernard Häring, *Free and Faithful in Christ: Moral Theology for Clergy and Laity*, 3 vols. (New York: Seabury Press, 1978) and *The Law of Christ: Moral Theology for Priests and Laity*, 3 vols. (Westminster, MD: Newman Press, 1961–1967). Häring's book, *Shalom: Peace: The Sacrament of Reconciliation* (New York: Farrar, Strauss, and Giroux, 1968), with its reflections on the history and practice of the sacrament of reconciliation, echoes the christocentric focus of his major works.

9. Häring, *Free and Faithful in Christ*, 5–6.

10. Walter M. Abbott, SJ, and Msgr. Joseph Gallagher, "Decree on Priestly Formation" (*Optatam Totius*), *The Documents of Vatican II* (New York: America Press, 1966), 452.

11. Thomas Slater as cited in James Keenan, SJ, *A History of Catholic Moral Theology in the Twentieth Century: From Confessing Sins to Liberating Consciences* (New York: Continuum, 2010), 11. Slater's text is *A Manual of Moral Theology for English-Speaking Countries* (London: Benziger Brothers, 1906).

12. Pope Francis, Amoris Laetitia*: The Joy of Love, On Love and the Family* 37 (New York: Paulist Press, 2016), 23.

13. The literature on the virtues is, to put it mildly, extensive. For further reading, I recommend the bibliography cited by Fergus Kerr in *After Aquinas: Versions of Thomism* (Oxford: Blackwell, 2002). Chapter 7 of Kerr's fine book is an excellent summary of the ethics of Aquinas (114–34). Kerr's bibliography of significant monographs on the virtues is on 229–31. Two authors who also provide a solid overview and interpretation of virtue theory are Jean Porter, *The Recovery of Virtue: The Relevance of Aquinas for Christian Ethics* (London: SPCK, 1990) and Joseph J. Kotva Jr., *The Christian Case for Virtue Ethics* (Washington, DC: Georgetown University Press, 1996).

14. Flannery O'Connor, *The Letters of Flannery O'Connor: The Habit of Being*, ed. Sally Fitzgerald (New York: Farrar, Strauss, and Giroux, 1979), 354.

15. G. K. Chesterton, "On Paganism and Mr. Lowes-Dickinson," *The Collected Works of G. K. Chesterton*, vol. 1: *Heretics, Orthodoxy, The Blatchford Controversy* (San Francisco: Ignatius Press, 1986), 125.

16. Simone Weil, *The Iliad, or Poem of Force: A Critical Edition*, trans. and ed. James P. Holoka (New York: Peter Lang, 2006).

17. William Spohn, *Go and Do Likewise: Jesus and Ethics* (New York: Continuum, 1999).

18. The identity or character of the moral agent informs, shapes, and guides moral behavior and action. This relationship between identity and behavior has been a crucial element in the recovery of ethical trajectories in the Johannine corpus of writings in the New Testament. Traditionally, biblical scholars have noted more explicit references to the ethical implications of scripture in the Synoptic Gospels, for example, the frequent references to the law of Israel in the Gospel of Matthew. Johannine scholars increasingly note that the Johannine literature is also rich with ethical insight, specifically the notion of "mimesis" or imitation of the example and life of Jesus. Configuring one's life to Christ leads to performing Christlike actions of love and service. A fine example of this emerging literature is the essay by Cornelis Bennema, "Moral Transformation through Mimesis in the Johannine Tradition," *Tyndale Bulletin* 69 no. 2 (2018): 183–203.

19. Michael J. Buckley, SJ, *What Do You Seek? The Questions of Jesus as Challenge and Promise* (Grand Rapids, MI: Eerdmans, 2016), 55.

20. Norbert Rigali, SJ, "The Unity of Moral and Pastoral Truth," *Chicago Studies* 25 (1986): 224–32. Rigali's skillful interpretation of moral theology as a pastoral discipline is reflected in several essays: "Moral Theology and the Magisterium," *Horizons* 15, no. 1 (Spring 1988): 116–24; "Christian Models of Universal Morality," *Louvain Studies* 19 (1994): 18–33; and "The Moral Act," *Horizons* 10, no. 2 (1983): 252–66.

21. Charles Taylor, *Modern Social Imaginaries* (Durham, NC: Duke University Press, 2004), 2. Taylor's magisterial works, *Sources of the Self: The Making of the Modern Identity* (Cambridge, MA: Harvard University Press, 1989), and *A Secular Age* (Cambridge, MA: Harvard University Press, 2007) provide historical and

philosophical appraisals of the human subject facing the ethical and social implications of the modern technocratic state in post-Enlightenment Western culture.

22. James K. A. Smith, *How (Not) to Be Secular: Reading Charles Taylor* (Grand Rapids, MI: Eerdmans, 2014).

23. Ronald Rolheiser, OMI, *The Holy Longing: The Search for a Christian Spirituality* (New York: Doubleday, 1999); Peter Berger, *The Sacred Canopy: Elements for a Sociological Theory of Religion* (New York: Doubleday, 1967); *Rumors of Angels: Modern Society and the Rediscovery of the Supernatural* (New York: Doubleday, 1969).

24. Bernard Häring, *Shalom: Peace (The Sacrament of Reconciliation)* (New York: Farrar, Strauss, and Giroux, 1968).

25. Henry Fairlie, *The Seven Deadly Sins Today* (Notre Dame, IN: University of Notre Dame Press, 1979). Fairlie identifies "disordered love" as the tragic underpinning of humanity's propensity for moral and spiritual fault.

26. Walter Kasper, *Mercy: The Essence of the Gospel and the Key to Christian Life* (Mahwah, NJ: Paulist Press, 2013), 23 and 225n12.

27. Kasper, *Mercy*, 23, with additional notes, 225.

28. Catherine Ella Laufer, *Hell's Destruction: An Exploration of Christ's Descent* (Burlington, VT: Ashgate, 2013).

29. Michael Downey, *The Depth of God's Reach: A Spirituality of Christ's Descent* (Maryknoll, NY: Orbis, 2018).

30. Downey, *The Depth of God's Reach*, 66.

31. Pope John Paul II, *The Mercy of God:* Dives et Misericordia, *Rich in Mercy* (Boston: Pauline Books and Media, 1980), note 61. See also J. Sheila Galligan, "Mercy's Mystery: Womb-like Love," *Spiritual Life* (Spring 2019): 49–55.

32. Pope Francis, Amoris Laetitia*: The Joy of Love: On Love in the Family*.

33. Massimo Borghesi, *The Mind of Pope Francis: Jorge Mario Bergoglio's Intellectual Journey* (Collegeville, MN: Liturgical Press, 2017). Although I am focusing on the specific contributions of Guardini and Przywara to Francis's thinking, I encourage the reader to pursue Borghesi's excellent chapter 2 on other intellectual precursors to the notion of polarity, specifically the dialectical Thomism of the Uruguayan lay philosopher Alberto Methol Ferre, who had a substantial impact on Jorge Bergoglio, and, in addition to his Jesuit confreres Erich Przywara and Hans Urs von Balthasar, the French Jesuit Gaston Fessard. Borghesi also notes,

insightfully, the influence of the dialectical theology in the work of the nineteenth-century German theologian Johann Adam Mohler.

34. Pope Francis, "Video Message to Participants in an International Theological Congress Held at the Pontifical Catholic University of Argentina," Buenos Aires, September 1–2, 2015, cited in Borghesi, *The Mind of Pope Francis,* 134.

35. An excellent example is Ethna Regan, "The Bergoglian Principles: Pope Francis' Dialectical Approach to Political Theology," *Religions* (2019): 670 ff. from which my summary of these principles is drawn.

36. These characteristic themes occur in several papal addresses, especially, *Fratelli Tutti* (October 3, 2020); *Laudato Si'* (May 20, 2015); and the apostolic letter *Desiderio Desideravi* (June 29, 2022).

37. I refer the reader to n5 above, especially chap. 2, "A Philosophy of Polarity" in Borghesi, *The Mind of Pope Francis,* 57–101.

38. MacIntyre's books that are most significant, in my estimation, for the appraisal of the intellectual currents that have shaped the current malaise of modernity include *After Virtue,* 3rd ed. (Notre Dame, IN: University of Notre Dame Press, 2007); *Dependent Rational Animals: Why Human Beings Need the Virtues* (Chicago: Open Court Press, 2001); *Whose Justice, Which Rationality?* (Notre Dame, IN: University of Notre Dame Press, 1988); *Three Rival Versions of Moral Inquiry: Encyclopedia, Genealogy, and Tradition* (Notre Dame, IN: University of Notre Dame Press, 1999). A superb collection of essays by scholars applying MacIntyre's insights to contemporary debates in ethics is the following: Nancey Murphy, Brad J. Kallenberg, Mark Thiessen Nation, *Virtues and Practices in the Christian Tradition: Christian Ethics after MacIntyre* (Notre Dame, IN: University of Notre Dame Press, 2003). An earlier edition of the volume was published by Trinity Press International, Harrisburg, PA (1997).

39. O. Carter Snead, *What It Means to Be Human: The Case for the Body in Public Bioethics* (Cambridge, MA: Harvard University Press, 2020).

40. Mark Graham, *Josef Fuchs on Natural Law* (Washington, DC: Georgetown University Press, 2002).

41. John Mahoney, *The Making of Moral Theology: A Study of the Roman Catholic Tradition* (Oxford: Clarendon Press, 1987); Servais

Pinckaers, OP, *The Sources of Christian Ethics,* trans. Sr. Mary Thomas Noble, OP (Washington, DC: Catholic University of America Press, 1985); Charles Curran, *Catholic Moral Theology in the United States: A History* (Washington, DC: Georgetown University Press, 2008); Charles Curran, *The Development of Moral Theology* (Washington, DC: Georgetown University Press, 2013).

Chapter 2: Reviewing the Landscape of Moral Theology

1. *Optatam Totius* 16.

2. Gérard Gilleman, *The Primacy of Charity in Moral Theology* (Westminister, MD: Newman Press, 1959), Fritz Tillmann, *The Master Calls: A Handbook of Morals for the Layman,* trans. Gregory J. Roettger (Baltimore: Helicon Press, 1960).

3. Odon Lottin, *Psychologie et morale aux XIIe et XIIIe siécles* (Gembloux, Belgium: J. Duculot, 1942–1960), vol. I (1942), II (1948), III (1949), IV (1960).

4. The historical monographs by John Mahoney, Servais Pinckaers, and Charles Curran previously referenced provide critical context and background to the theological and ecclesial factors influencing the development of the tradition.

5. Avery Dulles, *Models of the Church,* expanded ed. (Garden City, NY: Image Books, 1987).

6. James Gustafson, *Protestant and Roman Catholic Ethics: Prospects for Rapprochement* (Chicago: University of Chicago Press, 1978), 33–35. See Ramsey, *Ethics at the Edges of Life* (New Haven, CT: Yale University Press, 1978) and *The Patient as Person: Explorations in Medical Ethics,* 2nd ed. (New Haven, CT: Yale University Press, 2002). Later in the essay, I will comment on a shrewd rebuttal to Ramsey's characterization of Protestant ethics by Charles McCoy, late professor of theology at the Pacific School of Religion, Berkeley, CA. McCoy counters Ramsey with the observation that Ramsey's deontologism has generated a "wasteland of rationalism," resulting in the exclusion of imagination from moral discourse. McCoy suggests that the work of the chemist/philosopher, Michael Polanyi, especially his notion of the "tacit dimension" in knowledge, namely, the importance of an imaginative construal of reality beyond the limits of what is clearly and conceptually

describable, has implications for the philosophy of science and the human sciences, including ethics. In other words, a deeper and richer construal of reason helps to rescue moral argument from an overly abstract and disembodied rationality. Charles Pinches, *Theology and Action: After Theory in Christian Ethics* (Grand Rapids, MI: Eerdmans, 2002), 42–54, observes that Ramsey shares an unlikely alliance with his erstwhile foe, the relativist and proponent of "situation ethics" Joseph Fletcher, in that both, in different ways, subscribe to a form of "principle monism," a phrase coined by Pinches to name the temptation to reduce ethics to a single, overarching, or "monistic" principle. Pinches suggests that a more robust understanding of the particularity and granularity of moral language enables us to fine-tune our arguments in response to moral complexity, and thereby avoid the seductive appeal of a "one size fits all" moral principle.

7. Ramsey, *Ethics at the Edges of Life*, 152.

8. Ramsey's position is reflected in his paper requested for the Ethics Advisory Board, convened to provide advice for the then-Department of Health and Human Services considering federal policy with respect to new reproductive technologies in 1978.

9. For example, Jean Porter, *Moral Action and Christian Ethics* (Cambridge: Cambridge University Press, 1995), and Roger Crisp and Michael Slote, *Virtue Ethics* (Oxford: Oxford University Press, 1997).

10. Robert Coles, *Harvard Diary: Reflections on the Sacred and Secular* (New York: Crossroad, 1989).

11. Albert Plé, *Duty or Pleasure? A New Appraisal of Christian Ethics*, trans. Matthew J. O'Connell (New York: Paragon House, 1987), 71. Plé edited for years the distinguished French spiritual and intellectual journal *La Vie Supplement.*

12. The term *affective maturity* is a key focus for priestly formation highlighted by Pope John Paul II in his 1992 apostolic exhortation on priestly training, *Pastores Dabo Vobis* (I Will Give You Shepherds). This notion has importance not only for assuring the church that candidates for the priesthood are well grounded in "human formation," that is, equipped with solid interpersonal gifts, such as emotional intelligence, and the psycho-sexual maturity to live a happy, celibate life, but also for ongoing formation in the life of discipleship for all the baptized faithful.

13. See Albert Plé, *Chastity and the Affective Life* (New York: Herder and Herder, 1966).

14. G. Simon Harak, SJ, *Virtuous Passions: The Formation of Christian Character* (Eugene OR: Wipf and Stock, 1993) provides a brilliant analysis of the role of the dynamic energies, known as the passions, in the work of Aquinas. He argues for the integration of the passions into a holistic moral psychology that overcomes the dualism that results when intellect and emotion, thought and feeling, are disconnected from one another in moral analysis.

15. Stanley Hauerwas, *Character and the Christian Life: A Study in Theological Ethics* (1975; repr.: Notre Dame, IN: University of Notre Dame Press, 1989), 11.

16. Stanley Hauerwas, *The Peaceable Kingdom: A Primer in Christian Ethics* (Notre Dame, IN: University of Notre Dame Press, 1978), 116. The Ugandan theologian Emmanuel Katongole is an astute interpreter of Hauerwas's eclectic oeuvre. He provides a careful catalog and appreciative critique of the major themes that are woven throughout Hauerwas's fertile and insightful writings. Emmanuel Katonogole, *Beyond Universal Reason: The Relation between Religion and Ethics in the Work of Stanley Hauerwas* (Notre Dame, IN: University of Notre Dame Press, 2000).

17. Neoliberalism can be characterized in many ways. For my purposes, it is a social and political configuration of the mechanisms of global trade that maximizes the free flow of capital with minimal constraints on corporations and other state actors. While purporting to be ethically neutral, rooting itself in an anthropology of liberalism that prizes the liberty and sovereignty of the individual actor, it often masks the structural, historically based, inequities of power that privilege the rich over the poor, or the "haves" from the "have nots."

18. John Neuhaus, *The Naked Public Square: Religion and Democracy in America* (Grand Rapids, MI: Eerdmans, 1984).

19. The insights developed in O. Carter Snead's excellent book, *What It Means to Be Human: The Case for the Body in Public Bioethics* (Cambridge, MA: Harvard University Press, 2020) will be addressed later in this essay.

20. Alasdair MacIntyre (see previous citation of his major works).

21. Stanley Cavell, *The Claim of Reason: Wittgenstein, Skepticism, Morality, and Tragedy* (Oxford: Oxford University Press, 1999).

22. Jonathan Edwards, *The Nature of True Virtue* (Ann Arbor: University of Michigan Press, 1960); *The Religious Affections* (Mineola, NY: Dover, 2013).

23. Fergus Kerr, *After Aquinas: Versions of Thomism* (Malden, MA: Blackwell, 2002).

24. Nicholas Austin, *Aquinas on Virtue: A Causal Reading* (Washington, DC: Georgetown University Press, 2017), 77–78. The phrase *ad imaginem Dei* in Aquinas suggests a dynamic, developmental model of ethics. The pertinent text from Aquinas is *Summa Theologiae,* 1.35 ad 2, "homo non solum dicitur imago, sed ad imaginem, per quod motus quidem tendentis in perfectionem designatur." According to Austin, this text is "about the motion of the rational creature into God." In other words, human beings are not a static "image" of the divine, but creatures fashioned with a dynamic capacity to grow into the "image of God" through virtuous action.

25. Heinrich A. Rommen, *The Natural Law: A Study in Legal and Social History and Philosophy,* trans. Thomas R. Hanley (St. Louis: Herder, 1947), 267. Cited by Stephen Pope in "Natural Law in Catholic Social Teachings," in *Modern Catholic Social Teaching: Commentaries and Interpretations,* 2nd ed., ed. Kenneth R. Himes, OFM, et al. (Washington, DC: Georgetown University Press, 2018), 73.

26. Charles Stevenson's book is the classic text for this trajectory in analytic philosophy, *Facts and Values: Studies in Ethical Analysis* (New Haven, CT: Yale University Press, 1963). Stevenson's essay, "The Emotive Meaning of Moral Terms" is reprinted in this collection, 10–31.

27. Julius Kovesi, *Moral Notions* (New York: Routledge & Kegan Paul, 1967), 119.

28. Anthony Lisska, *Aquinas's Theory of Natural Law: An Analytic Reconstruction* (Oxford: Clarendon Press, 1998); Henry Veatch, *Rational Man: A Modern Interpretation of Aristotelian Ethics* (Bloomington: Indiana University Press, 1962), and *Swimming against the Current in Contemporary Philosophy* (Washington, DC: Catholic University of America Press, 2018); Kerr, *After Aquinas.* I am, of course, wading into deep waters and an ongoing debate in the literature, but I will offer a modest conclusion from this conversation that will enhance appreciation, ultimately, of the moral theology of Pope Francis.

29. Recall here that the practical intellect is the human mind as directed toward the enactment of a desired good that is aligned with the *telos* or purpose of the human person.

30. Veatch, *Swimming against the Current,* 156.

31. Lisska, *Aquinas's Theory of Natural Law,* 177.

32. Henry Veatch and Joseph Rautenberg, "Does the Grisez-Finnis-Boyle Moral Philosophy Rest on a Mistake?," *The Review of Metaphysics* 44, no. 4 (June 1991): 807–30.

33. Germain G. Grisez, "First Principle of Practical Reason: A Commentary on the *Summa Theologiae,* 1–2, Question 94, Article 2," *Natural Law Forum* (1965): 168–201, http://scholarship.law.nd.edu/nd_naturallaw_forum/107. The literature detailing the critical reception of Grisez's proposal is considerable. Russell Hittinger, *A Critique of the New Natural Law Theory* (Notre Dame, IN: University of Notre Dame Press, 1987), Veatch, *Swimming against the Current,* and others have contributed significant rejoinders. A critically sympathetic and insightful appreciation of Grisez is available in the astute monograph by Rufus Black *Christian Moral Realism: Natural Law, Narrative, Virtue, and the Gospel* (Oxford: Clarendon Press, 2001). Black joins coauthor Nigel Biggar with a commentary on the new natural law theory of Grisez: *The Revival of Natural Law: Philosophical, Theological, and Ethical Responses to the Finnis-Grisez School* (New York: Routledge, 2010).

34. Walker Percy, *Signposts in a Strange Land: Collected Essays,* ed. Patrick Samway (New York: Farrar, Strauss, and Giroux, 1991), 369.

35. Pamela Hall, *Narrative and the Natural Law: An Interpretation of Thomistic Ethics* (Notre Dame, IN: University of Notre Dame Press, 1994); Jean Porter, *Nature and Reason: A Thomistic Theory of the Natural Law* (Grand Rapids, MI: Eerdmans, 2005); *The Recovery of Virtue: The Relevance of Aquinas in Christian Ethics* (Louisville, KY: Westminster/J. Knox Press, 1990); see especially Porter's essay, "Does the Natural Law Provide a Universally Valid Morality?" in *Intractable Disputes about the Natural Law: Alasdair MacIntyre and Critics,* ed. Lawrence S. Cunningham (Notre Dame, IN: University of Notre Dame Press, 1999), 53–97.

36. Henry Fairlie, *The Seven Deadly Sins Today* (Notre Dame, IN: University of Notre Dame Press, 1988).

37. James Gustafson, *Protestant and Roman Catholic Ethics: Prospects for Rapprochement* (Chicago: University of Chicago Press,

1978), 6–12. The entire volume is a masterful appraisal of both ethical traditions. The discussion of natural law, especially the effort to provide a more solid biblical warrant for its exposition, is especially keen on 101–8.

38. In addition to Gustafson, the work of Oliver O'Donovan, *Resurrection and Moral Order: An Outline for Evangelical Ethics* (Grand Rapids, MI: Eerdmans, 1986), and other Evangelical scholars on Calvin's approach to natural law should be noted. Josef Fuchs, SJ, *Natural Law: A Theological Investigation* (New York: Sheed and Ward, 1965) is a serious engagement with scriptural warrants for the tradition in response to Protestant criticisms. An important contribution addressing the deficit in Protestant reflection on the natural law is the study by J. Daryl Charles, *Retrieving the Natural Law: A Return to Moral First Things* (Grand Rapids, MI: Eerdmans, 2008).

39. John Berkman and William Mattison III, *Searching for a Universal Ethic: Multidisciplinary, Ecumenical, and Interfaith Responses to the Catholic Natural Law Tradition* (Grand Rapids, MI: Eerdmans, 2014) is an exemplary contribution to a multifaceted conversation about the natural law and its prospects in a contentious, postmodern cultural, political, and philosophical climate.

40. Albert Plé OP, "Moral Acts and the Pseudo-Morality of the Unconscious," *Cross Currents* 9, no. 1 (Winter 1959): 31–56 at 40. Speaking of the ordering of secondary ends, Plé notes, "In this way, every voluntary movement is magnetized by the act of the will towards the final end. The better known and loved this ultimate end is as such, the more active its attractive force in the willing of secondary ends and those *ea quae sunt ad finem* (things which are ordered to the end), the more these subordinate ends are loved by explicit and dynamic reference to the ultimate end, the more perfect is the human act, the greater its moral value, because it means a more rapid and definite return towards God of the human creature in so far as he is human."

41. Hall, *Narrative and the Natural Law.*

42. St. Thomas Aquinas, *Summa Theologiae,* I–II, Q. 94. a.4, response. Emphasis added.

43. Bernard Lonergan SJ, quoted by Cynthia Crysdale in her article, "Revising Natural Law: From the Classicist Paradigm to Emergent Probability," *Theological Studies* 56, no. 3 (1995): 464–84 at 483n55.

Chapter 3: Tracing the Shift to Moral Formation in the Landscape of Moral Theology

1. The 1958 essay of G. E. M. Anscombe, "Modern Moral Philosophy," *Philosophy* 33, no. 124 (1958): 1–16, is widely regarded as the precursor to the current revival in virtue ethics. She faulted the regnant models of utilitarianism (consequentialism) and deontology that ground notions of moral right or wrong in obligation, an assumption that makes no sense in the absence of consensus about "who" or "what" is the source of obligation. She sees a solution in a return to the classic notion of virtue in Plato and Aristotle that views moral blame or praise apart from considerations of duty or utility. However, she also argues that more philosophical work on notions such as "intention," "action," "wanting," or "pleasure" is needed to delineate the meaning of virtue. I am indebted to the work of Roger Crisp and Michael Slote, eds., *Virtue Ethics* (Oxford: Oxford University Press, 1997), 4, for this assessment of Anscombe's work.

2. Mark Graham, *Josef Fuchs on Natural Law* (Washington, DC: Georgetown University Press, 2002).

3. The meaning of "nature," of course is deeply influenced by the philosophical and scientific presuppositions that shape its significance for ethical discourse, especially the tradition of natural law that relies so heavily upon the concept of nature. Evolutionary science has radically altered the picture of "nature" by introducing notions such as historicity, contingency, adaptation, and emergent probability into the isomorphic, mathematically precise cosmologies of Aristotelian and pre-Baconian scientific worldviews. Moral theologians Stephen Pope and John Mahoney have carefully analyzed the implications for natural law ethics arising from engagement with the Darwinian paradigm of evolutionary development. Rather than posing a threat to moral stability and order, the authors argue that evolutionary perspectives deepen our grasp of the complexity of human nature and suggest opportunities to reground traditional conceptions such as altruism, cooperation, and interdependence, and to welcome emerging possibilities for human action. Again, the literature on this topic is vast, but I recommend Stephen Pope, *Human Evolu-*

tion and Christian Ethics (Cambridge: Cambridge University Press, 2007), and Jack Mahoney, *Christianity in Evolution: An Exploration* (Washington, DC: Georgetown University Press, 2011) for their provocative insights.

4. Josef Fuchs, *Natural Law: A Theological Introduction*, trans. Helmut Recter, SJ, and John Dowling (New York: Sheed and Ward, 1965).

5. As J. Daryl Charles has argued, the Reformers themselves, Luther and Calvin along with many of their coreligionists remained deeply committed to the natural law tradition even as they staked out critical theological positions on the relationship between law and gospel in the Christian life. Charles makes a compelling case that the bifurcation of the doctrines of creation and redemption in Protestant theology has contributed to the unfortunate dismissal of natural law as part of a fallen creation with no purchase in the redeemed order of salvation. See J. Daryl Charles, *Retrieving the Natural Law: A Return to Moral First Things* (Grand Rapids, MI: Eerdmans, 2008), 115–18.

6. Karl Barth, *Church Dogmatics* (Edinburgh: T&T Clark, 1958).

7. Joseph Fletcher, *Situation Ethics: The New Morality* (Philadelphia: Westminster Press, 1966).

8. James Gustafson, *Protestant and Roman Catholic Ethics: Prospects for Rapprochement* (Chicago: University of Chicago Press, 1978), 33–35 and 152–59.

9. Personal comment shared with me by Dr. McCoy during a graduate seminar at The Pacific School of Religion, Berkeley, ca. 1982. To recall an insight in an earlier note, McCoy affirms the more expansive notion of rationality developed by the chemist/philosopher of science Michael Polanyi, the "tacit" dimension of knowing that reclaims the critical importance of intuition and perceptive insight for the development of the formal, theoretical apparatus that characterizes scientific theories.

10. On this score, see William Spohn, *Go and Do Likewise: Jesus and Ethics* (New York: Continuum, 1999), and G. Simon Harak, SJ, *Virtuous Passions: The Formation of Christian Character* (Eugene OR: Wipf and Stock, 1993). Spohn's research draws upon the insights of Jonathan Edwards on the religious affections, as well as the work of American philosophers Josiah Royce and William James (exemplars of pragmatism in American philosophy) in

their explorations of notions such as loyalty and the nature of religious experience, to expand moral rationality beyond the rigid contours of formal propositions, or principles, and their logical entailments. Harak's treatment of the passions in Aquinas deepens our understanding of their role in the development of the virtues to shape wise deliberation and choice on the part of the moral agent.

11. The decision by Pope Paul VI, over which he anguished with a pastor's heart, to reaffirm the prohibition on birth control in the 1968 encyclical *Humanae Vitae*, spawned a huge debate and reaction that continues to roil the Church despite the passage of time. While I firmly support the teaching of the encyclical including the practice of natural fertility awareness and its clear affirmation of the intrinsic link between the unitive and procreative meanings of marital intimacy, there is a need to provide more education and resources to support couples in their discernment of this complex and challenging matter, a discernment informed and shaped by the moral and pastoral vision of Pope Francis on marriage and family life. Gerald Coleman, PSS, provides a most insightful reflection in his excellent essay, "Discerning the Meaning of *Humanae Vitae*," *Theological Studies* 79, no. 4 (2018): 864–78. Hopefully, this essay will contribute to a deeper appreciation of the moral vision of Pope Francis.

12. The critical dialogue between Aquinas and Kant, undertaken by Joseph Maréchal, SJ, in his magisterial work *Le point de départ de métaphysique: Leçons sur le développement historique et théoretique du problème de la connaisance*, 5 vols. (Bruges-Louvain, 1922–1947), is highlighted by Gerald McCool, *From Unity to Pluralism: The Internal Evolution of Thomism* (New York: Fordham University Press, 1989). McCool traces the development of Thomistic thought in the twentieth century, citing the contributions of four Thomistic scholars: Pierre Rousselot, Joseph Maréchal, Jacques Maritain, and Étienne Gilson. Moreover, the work of Canadian philosopher Bernard Lonergan, *Insight*, as well as that of fellow Jesuit, Karl Rahner, reflect a Thomistic response to the challenge of Kant's "turn to the subject," namely a recognition that the insights of Aquinas on human cognition and subjectivity, a subjectivity that remains anchored to the order of being broadly construed, are a critical rejoinder to the problem of Kantian subjectivity that underwrites the privatized, imperial ego of Enlight-

enment rationality. McCool's thesis is that the nineteenth-century neo-Thomist project spearheaded by Pope Leo XIII's encyclical *Aeterni Patris* suffered from a lack of critical historical scholarship, a lacuna corrected by the four scholars he cites, resulting in a much more thoughtfully nuanced reception of Aquinas in the twentieth century. More importantly, McCool also cites Erich Przywara, SJ (noted in chapter 1) and his explorations of the notions of analogy and polarity. These ideas attend to the contingency, finitude, and historicity endemic to the human condition that condition and limit the capacity of discursive thought, or ratio, to grasp, completely, or exhaustively, the intelligibility of empirical and moral realities.

13. Michael Polanyi, *The Tacit Dimension* (Chicago: University of Chicago Press, 1966).

14. An important essay by Fuchs, "The Absoluteness of Moral Terms" *Gregorianum* 52 (1971): 415–58, reflects this more critical appraisal of universalizability as the measure or distinctive test of the role of moral norms. Perhaps it is more accurate to see moral rules functioning as indicators of significant, roughly generalizable patterns and continuities among related moral events or choices rather than as monochromatic and invariant arbiters of morally charged issues. Christopher Jones, in his essay on the moral theology of Anglican bishop Kenneth Kirk, "The Historical and Ecumenical Value of Kenneth Kirk's Anglican Moral Theology," *Theological Studies* 79, no. 4 (2018): 801–17 at 813, reaches a similar verdict concerning Fuchs's understanding of absolute or universal moral notions.

15. Pope John Paul II, *Sollicitudo Rei Socialis* (On Social Concern), December 30, 1987. The encyclical is extensively reviewed by Charles Curran, Kenneth Himes, OFM, and Thomas Shannon in *Modern Catholic Social Teaching: Commentaries and Interpretations*, 2nd ed., ed. Kenneth R. Himes, OFM, et al. (Washington, DC: Georgetown University Press, 2018), 429–50.

16. Paul Ramsey, *Who Speaks for the Church?* (Nashville: Abingdon Press, 1967). An excellent essay by Ladislas Orsy, SJ, on the pluriform meanings inherent in the pregnant Latin phrase *obsequium religiosum* (religious assent/obedience), adopted in *Lumen Gentium* 25, stresses the importance of dialogue, debate, and nuance in ascertaining the binding character of ecclesial pronouncements.

Ladislas Orsy, SJ, "Magisterium: Assent and Dissent," *Theological Studies* 48 (1987): 473–97.

17. Bernard Hoose, *Proportionalism: The American Debate and Its European Roots* (Washington, DC: Georgetown University Press, 1987) is an excellent introduction to the American conversation and its many intellectual contours. Christopher Kaczor's book *Proportionalism and the Natural Law Tradition* (Washington, DC: Catholic University of America Press, 2002) is a careful and astute analysis of the history and significance of the debate on moral norms. The well-crafted summaries by Richard McCormick, SJ, of proportionalist arguments in "Notes on Moral Theology," a regular feature in the renowned Jesuit journal *Theological Studies*, provide an excellent historical record of the contributions from scholars across the theological spectrum. An early essay by McCormick adumbrates his later, mature thinking on moral norms: *Ambiguity in Moral Choice: The 1973 Père Marquette Theology Lecture* (Milwaukee, WI: Marquette University Press, 1973). More recently, the essay by Aline Kalbian, "Where Have All the Proportionalists Gone?," *Journal of Religious Ethics* 30, no. 1 (2002): 3–22, takes the form of a retrospective look at the debate. She draws several important conclusions, most notably, that moralists have moved on from a narrow preoccupation with the moral act and its philosophical contours to a deeper engagement with virtue theory and, correlatively, a greater emphasis on moral agency in ethical analysis. Brian Johnstone offers a constructive analysis of the proportionalist project, while also noting its problematic aspects, in an early essay, "The Revisionist Project in Roman Catholic Moral Theology," *Studies in Christian Ethics* 52 (August 1992): 18–31.

18. Joseph T. Mangan, SJ, "An Historical Analysis of the Principle of Double Effect," *Theological Studies* 10, no. 1 (March 1949): 41–61. An important essay by James Keenan, SJ, on the principle should be noted here: "The Function of the Principle of Double Effect," *Theological Studies* 54, no. 2 (1993): 294–315.

19. Peter Knauer, "The Hermeneutic Function of the Principle of Double Effect," in *Moral Norms and Catholic Tradition*, ed. Charles E. Curran and Richard McCormick, SJ (New York: Paulist Press, 1979). The debate about proportionalism is a significant point of concern in the encyclical on moral theology by Pope John Paul II, *Veritatis Splendor*, a debate that I will address further in this chapter. While the fires from this debate have somewhat subsided,

substantive issues remain, and my modest claim is to retrieve some insights, from the embers, that affirm the deeper thrust of the papal encyclical, namely formation in a virtuous moral life. The biblical opening of the encyclical, the story of the rich young man in Mark's Gospel, while insufficiently developed, is a most promising overture to the recovery of virtue and character, issues that are central to the imaginary of mercy that I am proposing.

20. Pius XII, "Address to Delegates to the Ninth National Congress of the Italian Society of the Science of Anesthetics," *Acta Apostolicae Sedis* 49 (February 24, 1957).

21. Pope John Paul II, *The Splendor of Truth Shines, Encyclical Letter* Veritatis Splendor (Vatican City: Libreria Editrice Vaticana, 1993).

22. Pope John Paul II, *The Acting Person: A Contribution to Phenomenological Anthropology*, Analecta Husserliana (New York: Springer, 1979).

23. Jean Porter, "Moral Reasoning, Authority, and Community in *Veritatis Splendor*," *Annual of the Society for Christian Ethics* 15 (1995): 201–19 at 207. Alasdair MacIntrye invokes the same passage from Aquinas to make a similar point concerning the application of a moral rule, "How Can We Learn What *Veritatis Splendor* Has to Teach?" *The Thomist* 58, no. 2 (1994): 171–95 at 180.

24. Porter, "Moral Reasoning, Authority, and Community in *Veritatis Splendor*," 208.

25. Charles Pinches, *Theology and Action: After Theory in Christian Ethics* (Grand Rapids, MI: Eerdmans, 2002), chapter 3: "*Veritatis Splendor* and Proportionalism: Contemporary Catholic Disagreement about Action," 59–87. For an insightful appraisal of the contours of the debate on moral norms, see the essay by Wilson Muoha Maina, "The Shaping of Moral Theology: *Veritatis Splendor* and the Debate on the Nature of Roman Catholic Moral Theology," *Journal for the Study of Religion and Ideologies* 12, no. 35 (Summer 2013): 178–221. An appreciative view of the encyclical after twenty-five years is the essay by Michael Dauphinais, "The Splendor and Gift of the Christian Moral Life: *Veritatis Splendor* at Twenty-Five," *Nova et Vetera* 15, no. 4 (Fall 2018): 1261–312. An important monograph on the ethics of Aquinas, although not directly addressing the issues raised by the encyclical, that should not be missed is the analysis of the virtues in Aquinas: Nicholas

Austin, *Aquinas on Virtue: A Causal Reading* (Washington, DC: Georgetown University Press, 2017).

26. Stanley Hauerwas, "The Significance of Vision: Toward an Aesthetic Ethic," in *Vision and Virtue: Essays in Christian Ethical Reflection* (Notre Dame, IN: Fides, 1974), 30–48. The significance of moral vision informs Hauerwas's powerful critique of situation ethics in an essay in the same collection, "Situation Ethics, Moral Notions, and Moral Theology," 11–30.

27. Henry Veatch, "Does the Grisez-Finnis-Boyle Moral Philosophy Rest on a Mistake?," *Review of Metaphysics* 44, no. 4 (June 1991): 807–30. Pope John Paul II's encyclical *Veritatis Splendor* (hereafter *VS*) is a stout defense of the traditional claim of moral absolutes over against the problems of relativism and consequentialism the encyclical discerns in the theory of proportionalism. There is a substantive and substantial response to *VS* in the literature. A good place to begin is with the essays available in Michael E. Allsopp and John F. O'Keefe, Veritatis Splendor: *American Responses* (Kansas City, MO: Sheed and Ward, 1995). A collection of essays favorable to the papal position is Augustine Di Noia and Romanus Cessario, eds., Veritatis Splendor *and the Renewal of Moral Theology* (Chicago: Midwest Theological Forum, 1999). A more critical reception of the encyclical (signaled by the title) is available in Joseph Selling and Jan Jans, eds., *The Splendor of Accuracy: An Examination of the Assertions Made by* Veritatis Splendor (Grand Rapids, MI: Eerdmans, 1994). Mindful of the tenacity of the debate, nonetheless, I prefer to escape "through the horns" of this dilemma by moving to a more holistic vision of moral formation that accentuates the character and agency of the moral actor as one who deliberates with wisdom, more so than as a moral logician. See the critiques of the new natural law theory by Russell Hittinger, *A Critique of The New Natural Law Theory* (Notre Dame, IN: University of Notre Dame Press, 1987), and Mark Massa, SJ, *The Structure of Theological Revolutions: How the Fight over Birth Control Transformed American Catholicism* (Oxford: Oxford University Press, 2018), chapter 5, "Germain Grisez and the 'New Natural Law,'" 106–28.

28. Pinches, *Theology and Action*, 59–87.

29. Martin Rhonheimer, "Intentional Actions and the Meaning of Object: A Reply to Richard McCormick," *Thomist* 59, no. 2

(April 1995): 279–313; "The Moral Viewpoint of *Veritatis Splendor*," *Thomist* 58/1 (January 1994): 1–44.

30. Norbert Rigali, SJ, "Moral Theology and the Magisterium," *Horizons* 15/1 (Spring 1988): 116–124. This pastoral sensitivity is reflected in Rigali's essay, "The Unity of Moral and Pastoral Truth," *Chicago Studies* 25 (1986): 224–232.

31. A helpful introduction to the complexities of the debate is available in Charles E. Curran and Richard A. McCormick SJ, *Readings in Moral Theology*, no. 1 (New York: Paulist Press, 1979).

32. Curran and McCormick, *Readings in Moral Theology* 1. Curran's essay in this volume, "Utilitarianism and Contemporary Moral Theology: Situating the Debates," 341–62, is representative of this claim that appears in many of his writings.

33. Brian Johnstone, "The Revisionist Project in Roman Catholic Moral Theology," *Studies in Christian Ethics* 5, no. 2 (August 1992): 18–31.

34. James Gustafson, "Context vs. Principles: A Misplaced Debate in Christian Ethics," *Harvard Theological Review* 58, no. 3 (April 1965): 171–202.

35. James Wm. McClendon Jr., *Biography as Theology: How Life Stories Can Re-make Today's Theology* (Nashville: Abingdon Press, 1974); *Systematic Theology*, vol. 1, *Ethics* (Nashville: Abingdon Press, 1986); *Understanding Religious Convictions* (with James M. Smith) (Notre Dame, IN: University of Notre Dame Press, 1975). Jim McClendon was friend, mentor, and one of my wonderful teachers at the Graduate Theological Union, Berkeley (1979–1982). His work on religious language with James Smith, building on the insights of John L. Austin, John Searle, and the later Wittgenstein in *Philosophical Investigations*, attacked the dismissal of religious language as "meaningless" by Oxford University philosophers such as Alfred Ayer (because adjudged "unverifiable" according to an empirical, quantitative standard of assessment), by establishing the inherent intelligibility and rationality of religious discourse to describe the world of evaluation. Jim was a friend of Stanley Hauerwas and helped Stanley develop the intellectual resources to address the issues of character and virtue that are Stanley's ongoing legacy to moral theology. Jim judged that the moral life, the lived stories, and actions of disciples, should be the primary starting point for theology, hence the first volume of his three-volume *Systematic Theology* begins with *Ethics*. Religious "convictions," therefore,

are to be understood as rationally defensible, holistic commitments, and not as arbitrary assertions of subjective preferences or feelings, or as pure "emotions" as claimed by Charles Stevenson and the "emotivist" school of moral philosophy. Overcoming the mischief caused by impoverished theories of language is one of McClendon's enduring gifts to the study of ethics. I hope my essay may lead others to Jim's outstanding contribution to theological ethics, lovingly crafted from his Baptist tradition, and with acute, ecumenical sensitivity to other perspectives. As Brad Kallenberg has also noted, careful philosophical work, following the example of Wittgenstein, is a therapeutic exercise to clear up muddles over language to facilitate theological work. See Kallenberg's fine book, *Ethics as Grammar: Changing the Postmodern Subject* (Notre Dame, IN: University of Notre Dame Press, 2001).

36. Edmund Pincoffs, "Quandary Ethics," *Mind* 80 (1971): 552–71, reprinted in Alasdair MacIntyre and Stanley Hauerwas, *Revisions: Changing Perspectives in Moral Philosophy* (Notre Dame, IN: University of Notre Dame Press, 1983), 92–113. Pincoffs expanded his thoughts in an important book, *Quandaries and Virtues: Against Reductivism in Ethics* (Lawrence: University Press of Kansas, 1986).

37. Philippa Foot, "The Problem of Abortion and the Doctrine of the Double Effect," in *Virtues and Vices* (Oxford: Blackwell, 1967). The essay originally appeared in *Oxford Review* 5 (1967).

38. William Styron, *Sophie's Choice: A Novel* (New York: Random House, 1979).

39. Gerald O'Collins's recent book on the resurrection devotes several pages to the moral implications of the resurrection in Catholic theology, *Believing in the Resurrection: The Meaning and Promise of the Risen Jesus* (Mahwah, NJ: Paulist, 2014), especially chapter 8, "Resurrection and Moral Theology: A Continuing Neglect," 116–21; Oliver O'Donovan, an Evangelical scholar, has written an important book, *Resurrection and Moral Order: An Outline for Evangelical Ethics* (Grand Rapids, MI: Eerdmans, 1986). Brian Johnstone, CSSR, an Australian Redemptorist moral theologian, has noted the importance of transformation as a critical implication of the ethical significance of Christ's resurrection from the dead. See the collection of essays, edited by Stephen T. Davis, Daniel Kendall, and Gerald O'Collins, *The Resurrection: An Interdisciplinary Symposium on the Resurrection of Jesus* (Oxford:

Oxford University Press, 1998). Johnstone's contribution to the collection is the essay "Transformation Ethics: The Moral Implications of the Resurrection," at page 361 and following. See Anthony Kelly, *The Resurrection Effect: Transforming Christian Life and Thought* (Maryknoll, NY: Orbis, 2008).

40. In his prolific scholarship Charles Curran develops a conceptual scheme for an adequate moral theology that includes "resurrection destiny" as a key theme. Although the notion of the resurrection is identified, it does not receive further extensive treatment in his writings.

41. O'Collins, *Believing in the Resurrection*, 116–21.

42. Biblical references undergirding the "descent clause" include Matt 27:51–53 and 1 Pet 3:8.

43. Raymond E. Brown, *A Risen Christ in Eastertime: Essays on the Gospel Narratives of the Resurrection of Jesus* (Collegeville, MN: Liturgical Press, 1991). His reflections echo his early book, *The Virginal Conception and Bodily Resurrection of Jesus* (New York: Paulist Press, 1973).

44. Brian Johnstone, "Intrinsically Evil Acts," *Studia Moralia* 43 (2005): 379–406, especially 402–6. Johnstone develops the idea of gift, incorporating insights from the Catholic philosopher Jean Luc-Marion, in several essays, including the following: "From Physicalism to Personalism," *Studia Moralia* 30 (1992): 71–96; "The Gift: Derrida, Marion and Moral Theology," *Studia Moralia* 42 (2004): 411–32; "'Objectivism,' 'Basic Human Goods,' and 'Proportionalism,' An Interpretation of the Contemporary History of Moral Theology," *Studia Moralia* 43 (2005): 97–126; "The Subject-Object Relation in Contemporary Catholic Moral Theology: A Reply to Joseph Selling," *Studia Moralia* 44 (2006): 41–62. The article by Joseph Selling, to which Johnstone is replying, is in the same issue: Joseph A. Selling, "Distinct but Not Separate: The Subject-Object Relation in Contemporary Moral Theology," *Studia Moralia* 44 (2006): 14–40. The exchange between Johnstone and Selling illuminates the polarizing tensions in the proportionalism debate, and importantly makes the case for a more robust and holistic conception of moral personalism.

45. Brian Johnstone, "Rising to New Life: A Moral Theology of Resurrection," *Studia Moralia* 55, no. 1 (2017): 141–68; Anthony Kelly, "The Resurrection and the Foundations of Moral Theology," *Studia Moralia* 48, no. 2 (2010): 349–69. Kelly's book-length

monograph discusses the transformative dimensions of the resurrection for every aspect of moral theology: *The Resurrection Effect: Transforming Christian Life and Thought* (Maryknoll, NY: Orbis, 2008).

46. Johnstone, "Rising to New Life," 165.

47. Kelly, "The Resurrection and the Foundations," 362.

48. Kelly, "The Resurrection and the Foundations," 367–68.

49. Stanley Hauerwas, *Suffering Presence: Theological Reflections on Medicine, the Mentally Handicapped, and the Church* (Notre Dame, IN: University of Notre Dame Press, 1986).

50. On this score, Bernard Williams, *Moral Luck: Philosophical Papers 1973–1980* (Cambridge: Cambridge University Press, 1981), and Martha Nussbaum, *The Fragility of Goodness: Luck and Ethics in Greek Tragedy and Philosophy* (Cambridge: Cambridge University Press, 1986) are invaluable conversation partners for a discussion of the contingencies and vagaries of human existence and the challenge they pose for ethical systems that discount the element of surprise and unpredictability in our moral experience.

51. Tom Wolfe, *Bonfire of the Vanities* (New York: Farrar, Strauss, Giroux, 1987).

52. Frederick Buechner, *Wishful Thinking* (see https://www.frederickbuechner.com/wishful-thinking-a-seekers-abc).

53. Stanley Hauerwas, "Casuistry as a Narrative Art," *Interpretation* 37, no. 4 (1983): 377–88.

54. An important essay by Rahner on the interdependence and reciprocity between humanity's shared, moral patrimony, (e.g., natural law), and the uniquely distinctive, nonreplicable, and personal destiny of the moral individual, will be further explored in support of the "polarity" that characterizes the pastoral vision of Pope Francis. Rahner's essay "On the Question of a Formal Existential Ethics" appears in the multivolume collection of his writings, *Theological Investigations*, vol. 2, *Man and the Church* (Baltimore, MD: Helicon Press, 1961), 217–35. I will argue that Rahner provides a constructive alternative to the narrow framing of the situation ethics debate as a binary contest between contexts/situations and moral rules.

55. Kaczor, *Proportionalism and the Natural Law Tradition*, 209.

56. Brian Johnstone, CSSR, has written extensively on this issue as we have seen in previous citations in many essays in *Studia Moralia.* Also see the following from Johnstone, "The Right to Pri-

vacy: The Ethical Perspective," *American Journal of Jurisprudence* 29, no. 1 (1984): 73–94, https://doi.org/10.1093/ajj/29.1.73; "The Moral Status of the Embryo," in *Test-Tube Babies: A Guide to Moral Questions, Present Techniques and Future Possibilities*, ed. William A. W. Walters and Peter Singer (Melbourne: Oxford University Press, 1982), 49–56; "The Human Embryo: Person and the Gift," in *Life and Learning. Proceedings of the Seventeenth University Faculty for Life Conference at Villanova University 2007*, ed. Joseph W. Koterski, SJ (Washington, DC: University Faculty for Life, 2007), 489–505.

57. Bernard Lonergan, *Insight: A Study of Human Understanding* (New York: Harper and Row, 1978).

58. Cynthia Crysdale, "Revising Natural Law: From the Classicist Paradigm to Emergent Probability," *Theological Studies* 56 (1995): 464–84 at 483n55.

59. John Henry Newman, *An Essay in Aid of a Grammar of Assent* (Notre Dame, IN: University of Notre Dame Press, 1979) with an introduction by Nicholas Lash and critical commentary by I. T. Ker.

Chapter 4: The Ethics of Discernment

1. The brilliant scholarship of Thomistic scholar Jean Porter is particularly compelling in its rendering of the social, political, and historical contexts that have shaped the development of the natural law tradition in Aquinas. See the following: *Nature as Reason: A Thomistic Theory of the Natural Law* (Grand Rapids, MI: Eerdmans, 2005); *The Recovery of Virtue: The Relevance of Aquinas for Christian Ethics* (Louisville, KY: Westminster/J. Knox Press, 1990); *Moral Action and Christian Ethics* (New York: Cambridge University Press, 1999). Pamela Hall, *Narrative and the Natural Law: An Interpretation of Thomistic Ethics* (Notre Dame, IN: University of Notre Dame Press,1994), establishes the critical importance of experiential knowledge, expressed and configured by the narratives of linguistic communities, to provide substance and depth to formal notions such as the secondary precepts of the natural law.

2. Alasdair MacIntyre, *After Virtue*, 3rd ed. (Notre Dame, IN: University of Notre Dame Press, 2007).

3. Charles Davis, *Temptations of Religion* (New York: Harper and Row, 1974).

4. This point is elegantly developed by O. Carter Snead in his fine book referenced in chapter 1.

5. Dennis Billy, "The Way of Discernment: Living the Gospel in the Present Moment," *Studia Moralia* 48, no. 1 (2010): 31–53 at 33.

6. Billy, "The Way of Discernment," 34–35.

7. Richard Gula, *Moral Discernment* (New York: Paulist Press, 1997), 47.

8. Gula, *Moral Discernment*, 48.

9. Iris Murdoch, *The Sovereignty of Good* (London: Routledge & Kegan Paul, 1970), 52. Her twenty-five novels explore the ramifications of the morally transformative effects of encounters with objective reality upon her various protagonists. Her early novel *The Bell* (1958) deals with the creative tensions and struggles with moral and spiritual conversion among the members of a quasi-monastic commune in the English countryside. The novel exemplifies her commitment to Platonic philosophy and the centrality of the Ideal Forms, especially the form of goodness and its claim on the moral allegiance of the human subject.

10. Thomas Nagle, *The View from Nowhere* (New York: Oxford University Press, 1989).

11. In a scintillating appraisal of Thomistic epistemology, Mortimer Adler's *The Angels and Us* (New York: Collier, 1988) finds in Aquinas's apparently esoteric discussion of the intellectual perspicacity of angels as pure spirits a cautionary tale for human beings whose knowledge is always mediated by the conditions of materiality and embodiment. That cautionary tale is the temptation of "angelism," the aspiration for pure "clear and distinct ideas," leading to false abstractions divorced from the reality of our embodied human condition. I think the Aryan ideal of *Die Volk* that spawned the horrors of the Holocaust is a reminder of the danger of such rarefied abstractions.

12. As cited in note 1, the work of Thomistic scholar Jean Porter is particularly compelling in its rendering of the social, political, and historical contexts that have shaped the development of the natural law tradition in Aquinas. Echoing the earlier observation in note 1, Pamela Hall's *Narrative and the Natural Law* establishes the critical importance of experiential knowledge, expressed and configured by the narratives of linguistic commu-

nities, to provide substance and depth to formal notions such as the secondary precepts of the natural law.

13. Fergus Kerr, *After Aquinas: Versions of Thomism* (Oxford: Blackwell Publishing, 2002), chapter 3: "Natural Law: Incommensurable Readings," 97–114.

14. Hauerwas has vigorously rebutted the charge of sectarianism lodged by Gustafson. See Stanley Hauerwas, "Why the 'Sectarian Temptation' Is a Misrepresentation: A Response to James Gustafson," reprinted in *The Hauerwas Reader: Stanley Hauerwas*, ed. John Berkman and Michael Cartwright (Durham, NC: Duke University Press, 2002), 90–111. Gustafson's essay, "The Sectarian Temptation: Reflections on Theology, the Church, and the University," appears in *The Proceedings of the Catholic Theological Society* 40 (1985): 83–94.

15. Hauerwas, as cited in note 14 above. Alasdair MacIntyre's philosophical oeuvre is masterful in navigating the fragmentation and disunity that characterizes much of contemporary ethical debate; see *After Virtue*, 3rd ed. (Notre Dame, IN: University of Notre Dame Press, 2007). Joseph Kotva has noted that the charge of sectarianism and/or withdrawal from broader philosophical debates is tendentious at best and is refuted by the inherent sociality of the virtue tradition that requires ongoing formation, discipline, and rigorous adherence to criteria of truthfulness and integrity. See Kotva, "Christian Virtue Ethics and the 'Sectarian Temptation,'" *Heythrop Journal* 35 (1994): 35–52.

16. Paul Nelson, *Narrative and Morality: A Theological Inquiry* (University Park: The Pennsylvania State University Press, 1987).

17. Emmanuel Katongole, *Beyond Universal Reason: The Relation between Religion and Ethics in the Work of Stanley Hauerwas* (Notre Dame, IN: University of Notre Dame Press, 2000). See MacIntyre, *After Virtue.*

18. Kevin Wilde, SJ, *Moral Acquaintances: Methodology in Bioethics* (Notre Dame, IN: University of Notre Dame Press, 2000).

19. MacIntyre, *After Virtue.*

20. This famous distinction between "thin" and "thick" accounts of the values and normative expectations of a particular culture is developed by the cultural anthropologist Clifford Geertz, *The Interpretation of Cultures* (New York: Basic Books, 1977).

21. For a fine discussion of the implications of friendship for the moral life, see Paul Waddell, *Friendship and the Moral Life* (Notre Dame, IN: University of Notre Dame Press, 1989).

22. Hall, *Narrative and the Natural Law.* The contributions of Catholic feminist scholars, among them Lisa Cahill and Cristina Traina, in their critical affirmations of the enduring value of the natural law tradition should be noted here. Traina's *Feminist Ethics and Natural Law: The End of the Anathemas* (Washington, DC: Georgetown University Press, 1999), in addition to its masterful review of feminist ethical scholarship, finds that the natural law tradition provides philosophical warrants for shared ethical discourse and moral consensus despite the challenges posed by postmodern suspicions of grand "metanarratives" such as the project of Enlightenment rationalism. The distinguished moral theologian Lisa Cahill has expounded a Catholic commitment to moral objectivity and critical realism to ground intercultural critique of injustice on a broad swath of issues ranging from gender to health care to economic well-being. From her extensive bibliography, see *Global Justice, Christology, and Christian Ethics* (Cambridge: Cambridge University Press, 2013); *Theological Bioethics: Participation, Justice, and Change* (Washington, DC: Georgetown University Press, 2005); *Love Your Enemies: Discipleship, Pacifism, Just War Theory* (Minneapolis: Fortress Press, 1994); *Sex, Gender, and Christian Ethics* (Cambridge: Cambridge University Press, 1996).

23. The marvelous phrase "the elusive presence" was coined by biblical scholar Samuel Terrien to capture the biblical notion of the *Deus absconditus,* the hidden God. See Terrien's book, *The Elusive Presence: Toward a New Biblical Theology* (New York: Harper and Row, 1978).

24. Stanley Hauerwas, *Character and the Christian Life: A Study in Theological Ethics* (1975; repr., Notre Dame, IN: University of Notre Dame Press, 1989).

25. Ramsey's characterization is noted in chapter 1.

26. Hauerwas, *Character and the Christian Life.*

27. Charles Taylor, "Iris Murdoch and Moral Philosophy," in *Dilemmas and Contradictions: Selected Essays* (Cambridge, MA: Belknap Press, 2011), 3–24 at 3–4.

28. Robert Coles, *Harvard Diary: Reflections on the Sacred and Secular* (New York: Crossroad, 1989).

29. Paulinus Odozor, CSSp, *Morality: Truly Christian, Truly African* (Notre Dame, IN: University of Notre Dame Press, 2014).

30. Chinua Achebe, *Things Fall Apart* (New York: Penguin, 1994).

31. This concern is a consistent theme in MacIntrye's writings that have been cited previously.

32. Odozor, *Morality*, 243.

33. James F. Bresnahan, "An Ethics of Faith," in a collection of essays on the work of Karl Rahner, ed. Leo J. O'Donovan, *A World of Grace: An Introduction to the Themes and Foundations of Karl Rahner's Theology* (New York: Crossroad, 1987). Bresnahan's essay is chapter 12, 169–85.

34. Jean Porter, "Moral Language and the Language of Grace: The Fundamental Option and the Virtue of Charity," *Philosophy and Theology* 10, no. 1 (1997): 169–98.

35. Charles Curran addresses this theme in various ways throughout his extensive reflections on moral theology. A good illustration of the significance of a basic "stance" or orientation is in his essay, "The Role and Function of the Scriptures in Moral Theology," an address that appeared in *The Proceedings of the Catholic Theological Society of America* (1971), reprinted in *Readings in Moral Theology*, no. 4, *The Use of Scripture in Moral Theology* (New York: Paulist Press, 1984), 178–213 at 199.

36. Sheldon Wolin, *The Politics of Vision: Continuity and Innovation in Western Political Thought* (Princeton, NJ: Princeton University Press, 2004), 60.

37. By extension, I think "tentative stability" can apply to the status of moral principles that partake of the quality of generalizability but lack the descriptive restrictions necessary to warrant the ascription of the category, "intrinsic evil," a category that rules out the possibility of what Paul Ramsey famously called "curious exceptions"; Paul Ramsey, "The Case of the Curious Exception," in *Norm and Context in Christian Ethics*, ed. Gene Outka and Paul Ramsey (New York: Scribner, 1968).

38. Philippe Delhaye, *The Christian Conscience*, trans. Charles Underhill Quinn (New York: Desclée, 1968), 26. Invoking a more psychological idiom, Sidney Callahan, *In Good Conscience: Reason and Emotion in Moral Decision-Making* (San Francisco: Harper San Francisco, 1991); Anne Patrick, *Liberating Conscience: Feminist Explorations in Catholic Moral Theology* (New York: Continuum, 1997);

and Walter Conn, *Conscience: Development and Self-Transcendence* (Birmingham, AL: Religious Education Press, 1981) expand the traditional philosophical and theological framework expounded by Delhaye by rooting the notion of conscience congruently in deeply personal and existential categories such as authenticity, integrity, and, in Conn's work, a rich portrayal of "self-transcending subjectivity."

39. Howard Thurman, "The Sound of the Genuine (Baccalaureate ceremony) (Spelman College), 1980 May 4," *The Howard Thurman Digital Archive*, accessed October 26, 2024, https://thurman.pitts.emory.edu/items/show/838.

40. *Gaudium et Spes* (The Pastoral Constitution on the Church in the Modern World) 16, in *The Documents of Vatican II*, ed. Walter M. Abbott, SJ (New York: America Press, 1966), 213.

41. Frederick Buechner, *Wishful Thinking: A Seeker's ABC* (New York: Harper One, 1993); see https://www.frederickbuechner.com/wishful-thinking-a-seekers-abc.

42. An excursus of the theological import of Newman's work for moral theology is a subject for another book, but his *Essay in Aid of a Grammar of Assent*, as well as his powerful "Letter to the Duke of Norfolk," V, in *Certain Difficulties Felt by Anglicans in Catholic Teaching II* (London: Longmans Green, 1885), 248, are eloquent testaments to his argument for a deeply existential, committed, and personal, "real assent" to faith, an assent rooted in the unassailable claims of truth that beckon from the depths of conscience.

43. Newman, "Letter to the Duke of Norfolk."

44. Matthew Levering, *The Abuse of Conscience: A Century of Catholic Moral Theology* (Grand Rapids, MI: Eerdmans, 2021), argues that the notion of a "conscience-centric" moral theology that he sees in the development of Catholic moral theology in the twentieth century burdens this important and vital concept with more weight than it should bear. In his accounting, conscience must be more fully integrated into a more theological account of the virtues and a Christocentric focus to strengthen Christian discipleship and the formation of character. I think that my characterization of the relationship between conscience and character is in line with his proposal for a "thicker" account of the role of conscience in the Christian life.

45. William Spohn, *Go and Do Likewise: Jesus and Ethics* (New York: Continuum/Crossroad, 1999).

46. William Spohn, *What Are They Saying about Scripture and Ethics?* (New York: Paulist Press, 1984). Spohn develops six different patterns to describe the construal of the relationship between scripture and ethics, ultimately preferring a creative integration of the various models.

47. The relationship between scripture and ethics has been a source of robust scholarship. From a vast literature, I single out the following: Richard B. Hays, *The Moral Vision of the New Testament: Community, Cross, New Creation, A Contemporary Introduction to New Testament Ethics* (San Francisco: Harper San Francisco, 1996); Thomas Ogletree, *The Use of the Bible in Christian Ethics* (Philadelphia: Fortress, 1983); Bruce Birch and Larry Rasmussen, *Bible and Ethics in the Christian Life* (Minneapolis: Augsburg, 1976); David Kelsey, *The Uses of Scripture in Recent Theology* (Philadelphia: Fortress, 1975).

48. Spohn, "The Reasoning Heart: An American Approach to Christian Discernment," *Theological Studies* 44 (1983): 30–52 at 30.

49. James Wm. McClendon Jr., "Three Strands of Christian Ethics," *Journal of Religious Ethics* 6, no. 1 (1978): 54–80. The image of a rope with multiple strands is drawn from Wittgenstein's *Philosophical Investigations.*

50. William Spohn, *Go and Do Likewise: Jesus and Ethics* (New York: Crossroad, 1999).

51. Karl Rahner, "On the Question of a Formal, Existential Ethics," *Theological Investigations*, vol. 2, *Man and the Church* (Baltimore: Helicon, 1961), 217–35.

52. Russell B. Connors Jr., "The Grace of Indirection and the Moral Imagination: Learning from William Spohn and Literature," *Theological Studies* 72 (2011): 345–69 at 351.

53. Connors, "The Grace of Indirection and the Moral Imagination," 351n19.

54. The phrase "elusive presence" to describe the divine mystery is taken from Samuel Terrien's fine book on the bible, *The Elusive Presence: Towards a New Biblical Theology.*

55. Robert Sokolowski, *Introduction to Phenomenology* (Cambridge: Cambridge University Press, 2000), 4.

56. This theme weaves its way throughout Sokolowski's account of phenomenology. Page 161 is a good illustration.

57. James Gustafson, *Theology and Christian Ethics* (Philadelphia: Pilgrim, 1974), 104, cited in Spohn, "The Reasoning Heart: An American Approach to Christian Discernment," *Theological Studies* 44 (1983): 30.

58. John L. Austin, *How to Do Things with Words* (Cambridge, MA: Harvard University Press, 1975).

59. John Searle, *Speech Acts: An Essay in the Philosophy of Language* (Cambridge: Cambridge University Press, 1969). An excellent commentary and critical interpretation of Searle's work is provided by Nick Fotion, *John Searle* (Princeton, NJ: Princeton University Press, 2000).

60. James Wm. McClendon Jr. and James M. Smith, *Understanding Religious Convictions* (Notre Dame, IN: University of Notre Dame Press, 1975), especially chapter three, "A Speech-Act Theory of Religious Language," 49–85.

61. Alfred Ayer, *Language, Truth, and Logic* (London: Victor Gollancz, 1936) is an historical locus for this dismissal of religious language. For a scintillating and engaging intellectual history of linguistic philosophy at Oxford, England, see the incisive work by Nikhil Krishnan, *A Terribly Serious Adventure: Philosophy and War at Oxford 1900–1960* (New York: Random House, 2023). The phrase "cultured despisers" is a nod to Friedrich Schleiermacher, *On Religion: Speeches to Its Cultured Despisers* (New York: Harper and Row, 1958).

62. Pope Francis, *Amoris Laetitia* 37.

Chapter 5: The Kenotic Moral Casuistry of Pope Francis and the Imaginary of Mercy

1. The perceived disparity between the sexual ethics of the Church and its social teaching, namely that the former partakes of a physicalist, static, conception of human nature, while the latter is shaped by a dynamic construal of moral reason responding to historical and social contingencies, is recast instead as a relationship of mutual correlation and interdependence in an insightful essay by John S. Grabowski and Michael J. Naughton, "Catholic

Social and Sexual Ethics: Inconsistent or Organic?" *The Thomist* 57, no. 4 (October 1993): 555–78.

2. Emily Reimer-Barry, "*Amoris Laetitia* at Five," *Theological Studies* 83, no. 1 (March 2022): 109–32.

3. Reimer-Barry, "*Amoris Laetitia* at Five," 115.

4. Reimer-Barry, "*Amoris Laetitia* at Five," 115.

5. James Bretzke provides an astute analysis of the five *dubia* raised by four cardinal objectors: Carlo Caffarra, Raymond Burke, Walter Brandmuller, and Joachim Meisner: Bretzke's essay appears as "*Responsum ad Dubia*: Harmonizing *Veritatis Splendor* and *Amoris Laetitia* through a Conscience-Informed Casuistry," *Journal of Catholic Social Thought* 15, no. 1 (Winter 2018) 2018: 211–22. The concerns of the cardinals are framed in an essay, "Seeking Clarity: A Plea to Untie the Knots in *Amoris Laetitia*," published by Edward Pentin, "Full Text and Explanatory Notes of Cardinals," *National Catholic Register*, November 14, 2016.

6. Cardinal Francesco Coccopalmerio, *A Commentary on Chapter Eight of* Amoris Laetitia (New York: Paulist Press, 2017).

7. See *Familiaris Consortio*. Papal documents are accessible via the Web site of the Holy. See https://www.vatican.va/content/john-paul-ii/en/apost_exhortations/documents/hf_jp-ii_exh_19811122_familiaris-consortio.html.

8. Cardinal Alfonso Lopez-Trujillo, President, Pontifical Council for the Family, "*Vademecum* for Confessors Concerning Some Aspects of the Morality of Conjugal Life," February 12, 1997, https://www.vatican.va/roman_curia/pontifical_councils/family/documents/rc_pc_family_doc_12021997_vademecum_en.html. Emphasis original. The Latin word *vademecum* literally means "walk with me." It is a term that is commonly applied to maps and navigation aids for travelers. In this context, it is a "guidebook" for confessors in responding to sensitive matters of sexual ethics that arise in the administration of the sacrament of reconciliation.

9. Sacred Congregation for the Doctrine of the Faith, *Personal Humana,* https://www.vatican.va/roman_curia/congregations/cfaith/documents/rc_con_cfaith_doc_19751229_persona-humana_en.html.

10. Paul VI, encyclical *Humanae Vitae,* https://www.vatican.va/content/paul-vi/en/encyclicals/documents/hf_p-vi_enc_25071968_humanae-vitae.html.

11. Gerald Bednar, *Mercy and the Rule of Law: A Theological Interpretation of* Amoris Laetitia (Collegeville, MN: Liturgical Press, 2021), in a masterful and careful appraisal of the tradition of canon law and moral theology on the sacrament of marriage, reaches a most judicious conclusion that deeply informs my own assessment: "Mercy is not an alternative to the law; it is a way of applying the law." I had the pleasure of reviewing the early manuscript of this fine book. Dietrich Bonhoeffer's famous contrast between the "cheap" grace that characterizes a superficial, lethargic, and lukewarm relationship with Christ, and the "costly" grace of mature discipleship expressed in self-sacrificial love for others, underlies this citation.

12. St. Thomas Aquinas, *Summa Theologiae* I–II, Q. 94 a. 4 responsum; cited in *AL* 304.

13. Carl Elliott, ed., *Slow Cures and Bad Philosophers: Essays on Wittgenstein, Medicine, and Bioethics* (Durham, NC: Duke University Press, 2001); and *Bioethics, Culture, and Identity: A Philosophical Disease* (New York: Routledge, 1999).

14. Louis Cameli, *A New Vision of Family Life: A Reflection on* Amoris Laetitia (Chicago: Liturgy Training Publications, 2018); Bednar, *Mercy, and the Rule of Law.*

15. Coccopalmerio (president of the Pontifical Council for Legislative Texts), *A Commentary on Chapter Eight of* Amoris Laetitia.

16. Coccopalmerio, *A Commentary on Chapter Eight*, 23–24, citing the pertinent paragraphs from *AL* 301–2.

17. Coccopalmerio, *A Commentary on Chapter Eight*, 35.

18. Karl Rahner, "On the Question of a Formal Existential Ethics," *Theological Investigations*, vol. 2, *Man in the Church* (Baltimore, MD: Helicon Press, 1966), 217–35.

19. See Bretzke, "*Responsum ad Dubia*," for his observations. The statement of the Argentinian bishops can be found in the journal *Crux*, "Guidelines of Buenos Aires Bishops on Divorced/Remarried," September 19, 2016. The response of the community of moral theologians to *Veritatis Splendor* (*VS*) is extensive and a commentary on it exceeds the scope of the present book. As mentioned in the earlier discussion of the encyclical in chapter 3, the following resources provide additional insight into the teaching of the encyclical. For instance, see Michael E. Allsopp and John F. O'Keefe, Veritatis Splendor*: American Responses* (Kansas City, MO: Sheed and Ward, 1995); Augustine Di Noia and Romanus Cessa-

rio, eds., Veritatis Splendor *and the Renewal of Moral Theology* (Chicago: Midwest Theological Forum, 1999); and Joseph Selling and Jan Jans, eds., *The Splendor of Accuracy: An Examination of the Assertions Made by* Veritatis Splendor (Grand Rapids, MI: Eerdmans, 1994). Points of affirmation, especially the appeal to the scriptural story of the rich young man in the Gospel narratives, can be found, as well as positive and negative assessments of the accuracy of the papal understanding of intrinsic evil and its rejection of proportionalist methodology. On this latter point, I think the observations of Charles Pinches, *Theology and Action: After Theory in Christian Ethics* (Grand Rapids, MI: Eerdmans, 2003), chapter 3, "*Veritatis Splendor* and Proportionalism," 59–87, are particularly cogent as a critique of proportionalist methodology.

20. Bednar, *Mercy and the Rule of Law.*

21. See Bednar, *Mercy and the Rule of Law*, 37.

22. Cardinal Luis Ladaria, Prefect, Congregation for the Doctrine of the Faith, "*Samaritanus Bonus* on the Care of Persons in the Critical and Terminal Phases of Life," September 22, 2020, available on https://www.vatican.va/roman_curia/congregations/cfaith/documents/rc_con_cfaith_doc_20200714_samaritanus-bonus_en.html. This elegant reflection on the issues of death and dying, with a special focus on the issue of euthanasia, celebrates the fortieth anniversary of the *Declaration on Euthanasia* (1980). Building on the themes of the 1980 statement, this instruction commissioned by Pope Francis highlights the biblical story of the Good Samaritan as the model for merciful accompaniment of the critically ill and the dying. This "Samaritan turn" is an apt metaphor for the imaginary of mercy I have been developing in this essay.

23. Daniel Horan, *Postmodernity and Univocity: A Critical Account of Radical Orthodoxy and John Duns Scotus* (Minneapolis: Fortress, 2014).

24. Stanley Grenz, *A Primer on Postmodernity* (Grand Rapids, MI: Eerdmans, 1996). The literature on postmodernity and its implications for theological reflection is a cottage industry of its own. I have found the work of Merold Westphal especially helpful in navigating the complexities involved in these critical conversations. See Merold Westphal, *Postmodern Philosophy and Christian Thought* (Bloomington: Indiana University Press, 1999).

25. Ugandan moral theologian Immanuel Katongole devotes considerable attention to the work of Stanley Hauerwas, who characterizes the Enlightenment flight from the particularity of narrative and communal moral discourse in favor of an overarching scheme of universal moral reason as the "standard account" of morality. Emmanuel Katonogole, *Beyond Universal Reason: The Relation between Religion and Ethics in the Work of Stanley Hauerwas* (Notre Dame, IN: University of Notre Dame Press, 2000).

26. Richard Bernstein, *Beyond Objectivism and Relativism: Science, Hermeneutics, and Praxis* (Philadelphia: University of Pennsylvania Press, 1983). Bernstein proposes a model of interpretation or hermeneutics, understood as the exercise of reason as it is applied, in the form of "praxis" or action, to the concrete practicalities of daily life, to adjudicate the polarization between two philosophical currents, namely, the perceived stability and rigor of "objectivism," that is, ahistorical scientific paradigms of knowledge as contrasted with the "relativism" of contingent, historically oriented intellectual schemes. Hermeneutics, as the "praxis" of practical wisdom, in other words, serves as a critical bridge between these perspectives, holding them together in a relationship of dynamic tension, rather than as polarized opposites.

27. Horan, *Postmodernity* (passim). Radical orthodoxy has generated a school of thought with a considerable body of scholarship. A good overview of this literature can be found in James K. A. Smith, *Introducing Radical Orthodoxy: Mapping a Post-secular Theology* (Grand Rapids, MI: Baker Academic, 2004).

28. A caveat to the reader. My overview of nominalism and Ockham's contributions to it does not begin to address the complexity of Ockham's thought. Marilyn McCord Adams has written a magisterial two-volume account of the philosophy and theology of Ockham that provides a constructive and revisionist portrait of the "Great Inceptor," including his moral theory. *William Ockham*, 2 vols. (Notre Dame, IN: University of Notre Dame Press, 1987). Adams painstakingly argues that a close reading of his works reveals an astute Franciscan Aristotelian thinker rather than the regnant portrait of him as an iconoclastic deconstructionist of medieval scholasticism and harbinger of subjectivism and moral relativism. McCord provides a concise overview of Ockham's moral theory in her essay, "The Structure of Ockham's Moral Theory," *Franciscan Studies* 46 (1968): 1–35, reprinted in James F. Keenan and

Thomas Shannon, eds., *The Context of Casuistry* (Washington, DC: Georgetown University Press, 1995), 25–53. My overview is admittedly a broad-stroke characterization, and not a comprehensive or detailed appraisal of nominalism and its many nuances, but I hope it is a reasonably fair appraisal (and not a caricature) since my real target is the problem of situation ethics in moral theory. Thomas Shannon's *The Ethical Theory of John Duns Scotus: A Dialogue with Medieval and Modern Thought* (St. Bonaventure, NY: Franciscan Institute Publications, 2013) has been an invaluable secondary source for my arguably limited perspective on these questions of nominalism and moral theory. In addition, Servais Pinckaers, OP, *The Sources of Christian Ethics,* trans. Sr. Mary Thomas Noble, OP (Washington, DC: Catholic University of America Press, 1995), provides an excellent appraisal of the issue of nominalism and its impact on Catholic moral theology.

29. I acknowledge the enormous philosophical debates on these matters and do not pretend to offer a solution to them. Rather, I am making the more modest claim that there is an alternative to the nominalist construal of these relationships and that a plausible case can be made, as the Aristotelian/Thomistic scholar Henry Veatch contends, for critical realism. See Henry Veatch, *Rational Man: A Modern Interpretation of Aristotelian Ethics* (Bloomington: Indiana University Press, 1962).

30. Jacques Maritain, *Les Degrés du Savoir ou Distinguir pour l'Unir* (The degrees of knowledge: Or to distinguish in order to unite) (Notre Dame, IN: University of Notre Dame Press, 1995).

31. Pinckaers, *The Sources of Christian Ethics,* 240–53. Pinckaers provides an excellent historical and critical appraisal of nominalism that I find to be compelling and persuasive.

32. Horan, *Postmodernity.*

33. Edna St. Vincent Millay, "Sonnet" in *Huntsman, What Quarry?* (New York: Harper, 1939).

34. Mary Midgley, the brilliant British philosopher of science, was a staunch critic of reductionism in her many intellectual labors to understand reality in all its complexity. Whether it was the question of how to treat animals, how to interpret evolutionary science, or the interface between mind and matter, she was unflinching in her sharp criticism of the practice of exclusively deferring to empiricist assumptions of knowledge at the expense of more complex and robust accounts available from

other sources of wisdom, including religion and philosophy. Two of her books, *Are You an Illusion?* (which skillfully deconstructs the reduction of our conception of a unitary, cohesive self to a mere congeries of its material substrate, hence an "illusion") and *Science and Poetry* (which argues for their mutual intellectual coherence) serve as exemplary illustrations of this central conviction. I am deeply indebted to her elegant, generous, and fair-minded criticism. She unfailingly grants her opponents, whether Richard Dawkins, Daniel Dennett, or G. E. Moore, the scholar's courtesy of on honest rehearsal of their views as she engages them with respectful disagreement.

35. James Keenan, SJ, "Moral Discernment in History," *Theological Studies* 79, no. 3 (2018): 668–79. Keenan highlights four examples of ecclesial, communal practices of discernment: the Council of Jerusalem in Acts 15, which addressed the new challenge of Gentile converts to the faith; the refined casuistry of the Irish penitential books for confessors, equipping them with nuanced responses in the exercise of the sacrament of reconciliation; the shipping magnates of Flanders in the sixteenth century who sought reinterpretation of the meaning of usury that had been used as a moral warrant to forbid maritime insurance; and the discernment of Fritz Tillman to move into the discipline of moral theology pursuant to a negative appraisal (now happily rescinded) by the Holy Office of his work on the New Testament Synoptic problem. These narratives expand the horizon of discernment beyond the narrow confines of an individualistic approach.

36. Albert R. Jonsen and Stephen Toulmin, *The Abuse of Casuistry: A History of Moral Reasoning* (Berkeley: University of California Press, 1988), 16.

37. James Keenan, SJ, *The Context of Casuistry*, and the astute reflections in his book, *A History of Catholic Moral Theology in the Twentieth Century: From Confessing Sins to Liberating Consciences* (New York: Continuum, 2010), 46–49 and 159–63. Keenan's brilliant scholarship and encyclopedic grasp of the global literature in Catholic moral theology deeply inform his excellent analyses and interpretations of issues in the discipline. It goes without saying that he has inherited the "mantle of Elijah" from his Jesuit confrere Richard McCormick, with the heartfelt and enduring gratitude of all teachers of moral theology. The essay by Christopher

Jones, "The Historical and Ecumenical Value of Kenneth Kirk's Anglican Moral Theology," *Theological Studies* 79, no. 4 (2018): 801–17 is a superb overview and appraisal of Kirk's contribution to ethics, and to his development of a pastorally sensitive, inductive approach to casuistry.

38. Pope Francis has made clear his distaste for the misuse of casuistry, echoing the famous attack on casuistry by Blaise Pascal. However, I am making an argument for a healthy model of casuistry that aligns with the pastoral vision of the pope. Cathleen Kaveny has written a careful essay rehabilitating casuistry that considers papal reservations, a view that comports with my reconstructive proposal: "A Companion, Not a Judge," *Commonweal* 150, no. 1 (January 2023): 26–30.

39. Keenan, *A History*, 46. The specific reference is to Kirk's book, *Conscience and Its Problems: An Introduction to Casuistry* (London: Longmans, 1948), 75.

40. The history of casuistry, as Toulmin and Jonsen brilliantly illustrate, is rife with examples of the laxist temptation to reduce morality to a form of corrosive rationalization. For good reason, the seventeenth-century Cistercian monk, bishop, and abbot Juan Caramuel y Lobkowitz is called "the prince of the laxists" (Toulmin and Jonsen, *The Abuse of Casuistry*, 156). The answer to bad casuistry is not to abandon casuistry, but to replace it with better casuistry.

41. Stanley Hauerwas, "Casuistry as a Narrative Art," *Interpretation* 37 (1993): 377–88.

42. Robert Aleksander Maryks, *Saint Cicero and the Jesuits: The Influence of Liberal Arts on the Adoption of Moral Probabilism* (New York: Routledge, 2016) provides an insightful appraisal of how the recovery of classic Roman rhetorical practices deeply influenced the new educational ministries undertaken by the fledgling community of Jesuits shortly after their founding by St. Ignatius of Loyola. A central insight of Ciceronian rhetorical strategies was the emphasis on persuasive arguments that relied on the convergence of multiple plausible and intellectually defensible rationales to support consensus on controversial social and political issues. Maryks sees "Saint Cicero" as the Jesuit model for resolving complex moral matters as well, resulting in agreements that "probable" certainty (hence the theory of moral "probabilism") was an adequately sufficient resolution of ethical dilemmas rather than

the apodictic certitude entailed by recourse to, arguably, exceptionless moral principles. These classical, rhetorical resources established a bridge from the early "tutiorism" (the "safer," stricter moral counsel recommended in the penitential manuals for Jesuit confessors) to more nuanced, plausible, "probable" opinions for spiritual and moral discernment.

43. William Spohn, *Go and Do Likewise* (New York: Continuum, 1999), 142.

44. William F. May, *The Physician's Covenant: Images of the Healer in Medical Ethics* (Philadelphia: Westminster Press, 1983).

45. Walker Percy, *The Second Coming* (London: Picador, 1999).

46. Iris Murdoch, *The Sovereignty of Good* (London: Routledge & Kegan Paul, 1970), 52.

47. I am indebted to the critical commentaries and interpretive essays of Cristina Gschwandtner and Robyn Horner for my appraisal of Marion's challenging and complex oeuvre: Cristina Gschwandtner, *Reading Jean-Luc Marion: Exceeding Metaphysics* (Bloomington: Indiana University Press, 2007); Robyn Horner, *Jean-Luc Marion: A Theo-logical Introduction* (Burlington, VT: Ashgate, 2005). Moral theologian Brian Johnstone continues to be an astute interpreter and critic of Marion and has brilliantly developed the notion of gift in Marion to overcome significant "aporias" or puzzles, especially the subject-object divide, that are problematic in the discipline of moral theology.

48. Quote from Gschwandtner, *Marion and Theology* (London: Bloomsbury, 2016); see 143, "Augustine does not speak about God but to God."

49. Recall the discussion earlier in chapter 1.

50. Jonathan Sacks, *Morality: Restoring the Common Good in Divided Times* (New York: Basic Books, 2020).

51. Echoing this theme, Charles Curran's impressive body of work has called attention to the problem of reductionism in moral theology typified by a narrow physicalism that can distort ecclesial teaching on sexual ethics. See Charles E. Curran and Richard A. McCormick, *Dialogue about Catholic Sexual Teaching: Readings in Moral Theology No. 8* (New York: Paulist Press, 1993). Efforts to deepen and enrich the teaching on sexuality is reflected in the work of Aline Kalbian in her book *Sexing the Church: Gender, Power, and Ethics in Contemporary Catholicism* (Bloomington: Indi-

ana University Press, 2005). Insightfully, Kalbian notes that the sexual ethics of the Church is rooted in a robust anthropology that views sexuality as a "set of ordered relationships." A fuller discussion of the complexities of sexual ethics is matter for another book and not for this one currently at hand.

52. Brian Johnstone, "The Subject-Object Relation in Contemporary Catholic Moral Theology: A Reply to Joseph Selling," *Studia Moralia* 44 (2006): 41–62 at 54–55.

53. O. Carter Snead, *What It Means to Be Human: The Case for the Body in Public Bioethics* (Cambridge, MA: Harvard University Press, 2020). The notion of expressive individualism as "forgetfulness of the body" also means forgetfulness of other creatures and requires a course correction to a renewed relationship with the rest of creation. This topic warrants further conversation; see Christopher Steck, SJ, *All God's Animals: A Catholic Theological Framework for Animal Ethics* (Washington, DC: Georgetown University Press, 2019).

54. Snead, *What It Means to Be Human*, 5. Snead draws upon the work of Taylor, *Sources of the Self: The Making of the Modern Identity* (Cambridge, MA: Harvard University Press, 1989); Alasdair MacIntyre, *Dependent Rational Animals: Why Human Beings Need the Virtues* (Chicago: Open Court, 2001); and Robert Bellah, Richard Madsen, William M. Sullivan, Ann Swidler, and Steven M. Tipton, *Habits of the Heart: Individualism and Commitment in American Life* (Oakland: University of California Press, 1985).

55. *Planned Parenthood of Southeastern PA v. Casey*, 505 U.S. 833 (1992).

56. Walker Percy, "The Fateful Rift: The San Andreas Fault in the Modern Mind," in *Signposts in a Strange Land* (New York: Farrar, Struss, and Giroux, 1991), 274.

57. Charles Taylor, *A Secular Age*. See the comments on Taylor's idea of a "social imaginary" in chapter 1.

58. Flannery O'Connor, "Letter to 'A,'" August 28, 1958, in *Collected Works*, ed. Sally Fitzgerald (New York: Library of America, 1988), 949. O'Connor's fiction is a sustained meditation on the contest between the devil, which she described as an "Evil Intelligence," and the power of grace. Evil is a malevolent force in O'Connor's fiction with its tentacles reaching into every fiber of human life, but despite its cunning and sway, it is no match for the redemptive grace of Christ at the heart of all things. Her incarnational vision of

grace and its workings, as she puts it, "behind enemy lines largely occupied by the devil," is an argument against the Gnosticism and dualism (expressions of the mind/body split we have inherited from Descartes) endemic to modern philosophy. Logical positivism is an expression of these philosophical currents that essentially reduces reality to its empirical, material dimensions, and, correlatively, sees the world confined to what the finite human being can logically "posit" or comprehend, grasp, or construct. There is no room for the spirit or the transcendent in logical positivism, hence her solace in the tough-minded, critical realism of the Catholic intellectual and moral vision. The full quote is powerful: "If you live today, you breathe in nihilism. In or out of the Church, it's the gas you breathe. If I hadn't the Church to fight it with or tell me the necessity of fighting it, I would be the stinkingest logical-positivist you ever saw right now."

59. Bernard Häring, *Free and Faithful in Christ*, 3 vols. (New York: Crossroad, 1979).

60. St. Augustine, *Sermon* 52:16.

Appendix

1. Sacred Congregation for the Doctrine of the Faith, "Declaration on Euthanasia" (1980), https://www.vatican.va/roman_curia/congregations/cfaith/documents/rc_con_cfaith_doc_19800505_eutanasia_en.html.

2. Pius XII, "Address to Delegates to the Ninth National Congress of the Italian Society of the Science of Anesthetics," *Acta Apostolicae Sedis* 49 (February 24, 1957).

3. Congregation for the Doctrine of the Faith, *Samaritanus Bonus* (On the Care of Persons in the Critical and Terminal Phases of Life), September 22, 2020, https://www.vatican.va/roman_curia/congregations/cfaith/documents/rc_con_cfaith_doc_20200714_samaritanus-bonus_en.html. This elegant reflection on the issues of death and dying, with a special focus on the issue of euthanasia, celebrates the fortieth anniversary of the *Declaration on Euthanasia* (1980). Building on the themes of the 1980 statement, this instruction commissioned by Pope Francis highlights the biblical story of the Good Samaritan as the model for merciful accompaniment of the critically ill and the dying.

4. O. Carter Snead, *What It Means to Be Human: The Case for the Body in Public Bioethics* (Cambridge, MA: Harvard University Press, 2020).

5. Snead, *What It Means to Be Human*, 5. Snead draws upon the work of Taylor, *Sources of the Self: The Making of the Modern Identity* (Cambridge, MA: Harvard University Press, 1989); Alasdair MacIntyre, *Dependent Rational Animals: Why Human Beings Need the Virtues* (Chicago: Open Court, 2001); and Robert Bellah, Richard Madsen, William M. Sullivan, Ann Swidler, and Steven M. Tipton, *Habits of the Heart: Individualism and Commitment in American Life* (Oakland: University of California Press, 1985).

6. Robert Jay Lifton, *The Nazi Doctors: Medical Killing and the Psychology of Genocide* (New York: Basic Books, 1986).

7. Snead, *What It Means to Be Human*, 267–68.

Index